att least among the Courtiers & statesmen. ——

I have seriously considerd one thinge, That of the three Buisnisses of this Age, Woemen, Pollitticks & drinking, the Last is the only exercise att w.ch you & I have nott prouv'd our selves Errant fumblers if you have the vanity to thinke otherwise, When wee meete next lett us appeale to freinds of both sexes & as they shall determine, live & dye sheere Drunkards, or intire Lovers; for as wee ministe the matter, it is hard to & say w.ch is the most tiresome Creature, the Loving Drunkard or the Drunken Lover.

If you ventur'd y.r fatt Buttocks a gallopp to Portsmouth, I Donbt not but through extreame gatting you now lye bedridd of the piles or fistula in Ano, & have the Leasure towrite to y.r Country aquaintance, w.ch if you omitt, I shall take the liberty to conclude you very prownde: such a Letter should bee directed to mee att Adderbury heare Banbury, where I intend to bee within these three dayes —

                    Bathe the 22 of June from

                    Y.r obedient humble

THE LETTERS OF
John Wilmot

❧

EARL OF
ROCHESTER

THE LETTERS OF
John Wilmot
EARL OF ROCHESTER

EDITED AND ANNOTATED
WITH AN INTRODUCTION BY
Jeremy Treglown

The University of Chicago Press

The University of Chicago Press, Chicago 60637
Basil Blackwell, Oxford

Published 1980

Library of Congress Catalog Card Number 80-20592

ISBN 0-226-81181-6

Printed in Great Britain

K7

Contents

1673–75: IMMINENT PERIL OF SOBRIETY

1675: DEAR MADAM

1675–76: RUN DOWN BY A COMPANY OF ROGUES

1676–77: MUCH BUSINESS

1677: PISSING OF BLOOD

Contents

1678: ANGER, SPLEEN, REVENGE AND SHAME

1678–79: UNDIGESTED HEAP OF THOUGHTS

1679–80: WISE ABOUT FOLLIES

Contents

Appendixes

Acknowledgements

In any attempt to annotate historical letters the biggest debt is to the thousands of previous researchers, many of them anonymous, whose work has gone into the reports of the Historical Manuscripts Commission, the Calendars of State Papers and Treasury Books, and all the other indispensable works of reference, from the *Dictionary of National Biography* to the card-indexes of manuscript holdings in individual libraries. I have particular obligations to earlier editors of Rochester—in the modern period, especially John Harold Wilson and David Vieth. I owe a lot to the former, not only for his annotation of the Rochester–Savile correspondence but for his numerous other publications about the Restoration Court, on which he is the leading authority. Many reservations are expressed in these pages about points of detail in *The Rochester–Savile Letters*, but I have rarely spent a day on Rochester's correspondence without at least one of Wilson's books on my desk. David Vieth's edition of the poems has also always been there, and I am glad to be able to acknowledge my personal gratitude to him for many kindnesses, including his invitation to me to read a paper on Rochester and his group at the annual conference of the American Society of Eighteenth Century Studies at Victoria, B.C., in 1977.

I have also been helped at various stages by many colleagues and friends. My former tutor, Francis Warner, introduced me to Rochester's poems, and John Wilders supervised my Oxford B.Litt. thesis on them. Anne Barton (Anne Righter), J. W. Johnson, Paul Langford, Harry Levin, Redmond O'Hanlon, Kenneth Palmer, Joan Ruddle, Eric Sidebottom, James Tierney, David Trotter, Donald Whitton, Nigel Wilson and Sarah

Wintle have helped answer questions of various kinds. My parents, Beryl and Geoffrey Treglown, have been an unfailing source of information on biblical and liturgical matters. Shortly before he died, my friend Charles Taylor generously devoted some of his busy time in Barbados to examining a portrait supposedly of Rochester, attributed to Lely, in a collection there. I am grateful to David Piper, of the Ashmolean Museum, Oxford, and Sir Oliver Millar, Surveyor of the Queen's Pictures, for further advice about the painting: the sitter, who seems to be neither Rochester nor Lawrence Hyde (who took the title when it became extinct), remains unknown.

I have had invaluable help from many librarians and archivists, particularly Miss B. M. Austin, Librarian and Archivist to the Marquess of Bath and her assistant Miss Fowles; W. H. Kelliher, Assistant Keeper in the Department of Manuscripts at the British Library, and his colleagues; Miss M. A. Welch, Keeper of Manuscripts at the University of Nottingham, and her assistant A. Cameron; S. J. Barnes and H. A. Henley, County Archivists of Oxfordshire and Buckinghamshire respectively; Barbara Bowen, Editor of the Journal of the Ditchley Foundation; C. S. L. Davies, Keeper of the Archives at Wadham College, Oxford; P. F. D. Duffie, Administrator of Blenheim Palace; P. A. L. Pepys, Librarian of Warwick Castle; H. R. H. Cox, Librarian of Claydon House; G. M. Griffiths, Keeper of Manuscripts and Records at the National Library of Wales; and the librarians and staff of the Public Record Office and the Bodleian Library. I must also thank the Rector of Goathurst, Somerset, for checking the Enmore registers for me; the Vicar of Adderbury, Oxfordshire, for letting me search the parish registers there; the Vicar of Spelsbury and the Warden of Adderbury House for answering various questions; and the Earl of Lisburne, a descendant of Rochester, for answering an enquiry about his family manuscripts. The Marquess of Bath has kindly given permission for a number of letters to Rochester to be printed from manuscripts in his possession.

xii   Acknowledgements

Drafts of the whole edition were read by Basil Greenslade,
Harold Brooks and Howard Erskine-Hill, all of whom made
helpful suggestions and saved me from some mistakes. Karl
Miller also commented usefully on the introduction.

I am grateful to Helen Backhouse and Jane Havell, who
spent many hours helping me check references; to University
College, London, for a term's leave of absence in which the
edition was completed; to two of the college's secretaries, Jan
Cheney and Jacquie Brown, for typing it; and to Anna Pavord,
who prepared the index.

It would not be right to add my own dedication to someone
else's letters, but the editor's share in this book is for my wife,
Rona.

Introduction

In the letters that pass between friends, Thomas Sprat wrote, 'the souls of men should appear undressed; and in that negligent habit they may be fit to be seen by one or two in a chamber, but not to go abroad into the streets.'[1] Sprat's aristocratic Restoration contemporaries did not all share his inhibitions, and because even their negligence was calculated, their private life ostentatious, the correspondence of the 'Court wits'—the clever, self-destructive group that surrounded Charles II—was quickly treated as public property. *Familiar Letters: Written by the Right Honourable John late Earl of Rochester, And several other Persons of Honour and Quality* first appeared in 1697. It was followed by a second volume including more of Rochester's letters and a number by Buckingham, Henry Savile, Etherege, and others, and the whole collection ran to four or possibly five editions within eight years.[2] Whether or not the story is true that Rochester's mother burned a trunkful of his correspondence after his death in 1680,[3] the rumour suggests something of the extent to which open season had been declared on writers' lives, as well as their work.

Of course, the interest was partly prompted by the very close interconnection between the two. Samuel Johnson was to write that Rochester 'blazed out his youth and his health in lavish

---

[1] *An Account of the Life and Writings of Mr. Abraham Cowley*, 1668, in *Critical Essays of the Seventeenth Century*, ed. J. E. Spingarn, 1908, ii, p. 137. Here and throughout the introduction, quotations in the main text have been modernized for the sake of consistency. [Throughout these footnotes, place of publication is London except where otherwise stated.]

[2] See Prinz, pp. 401–4.

[3] See Horace Walpole, *Letters*, ed. Mrs Paget Toynbee, 1903–5, ix, p. 308.

voluptuousness.'[4] The blaze is compelling in a straightforwardly
human way, but it would be less impressive if it did not involve
such a good poet, and if it were not seen and felt in his work
itself. It would be hard to name a writer who has contemplated
his own moral and physical ruin with a more satisfied kind of
horror:

> *Rochester:* Son of a whore, God damn you! can you tell
> A peerless peer the readiest way to Hell?
> I've outswilled Bacchus, sworn of my own make
> Oaths would fright Furies, and make Pluto quake;
> I've swived more whores more ways than Sodom's walls
> E'er knew, or the College of Rome's Cardinals.
> Witness heroic scars—Look here, ne'er go!—
> Cerecloths and ulcers from the top to toe!
> Frighted at my own mischiefs, I have fled
> And bravely left my life's defender dead;
> Broke houses to break chastity, and dyed
> That floor with murder which my lust denied.
> Pox on 't, why do I speak of these poor things?
> I have blasphemed my God, and libelled Kings!
> The readiest way to Hell—Come, quick!
> *Boy:*   Ne'er stir:
> The readiest way, my Lord, 's by Rochester.[5]

If this stance and tone, a real-life adoption of the role of
a villainous Renaissance stage malcontent, are peculiar to
Rochester, he is remarkable too for his range of style. Although
in quantity his output was that of a dilettante (and a dilettante
who died at the age of 33), in other respects he needs comparison with a number of major Renaissance and Augustan
English poets. The emotional complexity of some of his lyrics is
reminiscent of Shakespeare's sonnets, or of Donne, though in

---

[4] Samuel Johnson, *Lives of the English Poets*, ed. G. Birkbeck Hill, 1905, i,
p. 221.
[5] *Complete Poems*, p. 130.

their ironic simplicity of surface they are closer to his near-contemporary, Marvell. And if he is the last important Metaphysical poet, his satires give him a good claim as one of the first of the Augustans. Marvell admired the satires; Dryden, Swift and Pope were all influenced by them. While such comparisons point up deficiencies in Rochester's work, they also draw attention to its individual memorableness: above all, perhaps, to its humour. He is the funniest poet of his time—indeed, arguably the most irresponsibly hilarious in the language. His poems break every kind of taboo, not only by being obscene, malicious, untrue (in a literal sense), or any combination of these, but through an imaginative recklessness that disregards any rule of moderation or common sense. In a letter to his mistress Elizabeth Barry he called himself 'the wildest and most fantastical odd man alive', and it is this enjoyment of the fantastic that gives the satires some of their distinctiveness. He imagines the trees in St James's Park, for example, as having been seeded by an incestuous relationship between sexually frustrated Picts and their mother earth; and in *A Satyr against Reason and Mankind*, in a passage admired by Goethe and Tennyson,[6] he ridicules scholastic philosophy by embodying it in the person of an exhausted explorer drowning in 'doubt's boundless sea', helplessly trying to keep himself afloat with books and intellectual bladders.

The humour and metaphorical energy of Rochester's imagination charge his letters, as well as his poems. The poet-critic who attacks Dryden so pointedly and so amusingly in *An Allusion to Horace* ('Five hundred verses every morning writ/Proves you no more a poet than a wit') is the correspondent who tells his friend Savile that he is fond of the laureate 'as of a hog that could fiddle, or a singing owl'.[7] (The passage anticipates some of Byron's letters, with their similarly aristocratic mockery of Wordsworth.) Much of the interest of the letters comes from

[6] See *Rochester: the Critical Heritage*, ed. D. Farley-Hills, 1972, pp. 213–14, 244.
[7] See p. 120.

this kind of iconoclastic private freedom with public reputations. But there is more to them. Rochester's hilarity is related to his seriousness, and particularly to the intensity with which he questioned traditional, metaphysically-based notions of goodness and tried to find workable empirical alternatives to them. This search, most fully articulated in the last part of *A Satyr against Reason and Mankind*, is carried on in the letters, too, most movingly in a few of those he wrote to his wife. There is a poignant intersection between the life and the poems in a fragment addressed to her in which he complains that human existence involves 'so great a disproportion 'twixt our desires and what it has ordained to content them.'[8] Almost all his poems relate to this disappointment, in one way or another: either in their wry, elusive comments on the pleasures which 'lessen still as they draw near'[9] and which disappear into the past as soon as they have entered the present;[10] or in their fierce attacks on the inadequacies of individuals and types generally held up for admiration (the King, politicians, churchmen, literary notables, people of fashion); or in those poems which transform a dull, unsatisfying world into a fantastic sexual baroque of the imagination. He is, after all, the author of the best poem ever written about premature ejaculation.[11]

It was suggested earlier that the correspondence of Rochester and his friends immediately lent itself to publication because of the ambivalence of the relationship between the men's private lives and their pleasure in notoriety. In Rochester, this duality is almost pathological, and one of the fascinations of his letters lies in the conflict between his relish of the scandalous, exposed life of the Court and his love of domestic privacy. The letters to his wife, which escaped contemporary publication but have survived in manuscript, are intensely intimate—not least when they are irritable, brow-beating and guilt-laden, or merely trivial. Partly

[8] p. 241.   [9] 'The Fall', *Complete Poems*, p. 86.
[10] 'Love and Life', ed. cit., p. 90.
[11] *The Imperfect Enjoyment*, ed. cit., p. 37.

because of this intimacy, they cannot easily be read without some knowledge of the poet's life and background. What follows is a brief, straightforward biographical note, with some comments, where they seem to fit in, on the development of his ideas, and on the points of connection between them, his main personal relationships, and the correspondence itself.

Rochester was born on April 1, 1647, in the old house at Ditchley, Oxfordshire, left to his mother Anne by her first husband.[12] Her second husband, Rochester's father, was probably away at the time. Certainly he was in France that October and fought a duel there (a situation that was to be duplicated twenty-two years later, when Rochester's own first child was born while he was on a similarly pugnacious visit to Paris).[13] Henry, Lord Wilmot was a career soldier, the son of a former commander-in-chief of the army in Ireland, from whom he had inherited some plundered Irish estates, mortgaged lands in Hertfordshire and Buckinghamshire[14] and the leases on a town house in Charing Cross and a country house at Adderbury, near Banbury, Oxfordshire.

Around the time that Anne's first husband, Sir Henry Lee, died in 1639, Wilmot was fighting for Charles I in the Bishops' Wars. In September 1642 he was quartered on Lee's mother, Lady Sussex, at St Albans:[15] perhaps it was here that he and Anne met. They married around 1644, and between then and his death in 1658 lived the hectic, fugitive life of everyone close

12 Except when other sources are mentioned, information about Rochester's ancestors is taken from *GEC* and *DNB*. These and other standard reference works have normally only been checked against primary sources when they bear directly on Rochester's own life. In this case both works follow Bliss's annotation of Wood in mistakenly giving the date of his birth as April 10, a misreading of '1°' in the source, the April entry in John Gadbury's almanac *Ephemeris, or, a Diary*, 1695.

13 See Thomas Carte, *A Collection of Original Letters and Papers*, 1739, pp. 148f.

14 *The Ancestor*, xi, 1904, p. 20.   15 *Verney Memoirs*, i, pp. 263–4.

2

to the Court. For Wilmot this was a relatively simple matter. Clarendon says he was haughty and impatient, but drank hard and had a 'companionable wit' which made him popular and influential.[16] His job was to follow the King and to fight battles, which he did courageously and effectively. A cavalry commander at Edgehill, he was made Lieutenant General of Horse in April 1643 and Baron Wilmot of Adderbury that June. He distinguished himself at Roundway Down the following year and again in June 1644 at Cropredy Bridge, where he was captured twice and rescued twice, the second time by Robert Howard, who was knighted for bringing him back and later proved helpful to his son.[17] Never securely in favour in high quarters, Wilmot made himself unpopular by trying to reconcile the King with parliament that year, and was imprisoned and then in exile for a time.[18] But in 1650 he accompanied Charles on his ill-fated Scottish expedition, helping him to escape from the battle of Worcester. In December 1652 he was created Earl of Rochester, and in March 1655 took part in the Marston Moor rising, only just escaping in disguise.

During all this, his wife was leading a less glamorous and more complicated existence. Her personal allegiances, like those of many of her contemporaries, were hard to reconcile. She came from a family of distinguished parliamentarians, the St Johns, and her first husband had been of the same party. He had left her with two sons, Henry and Francis—the elder about six years old when she remarried.[19] Now the wife of a cavalier general, she was obliged to follow the Court into exile, and was certainly in Paris with her children, including the young John Wilmot, in

---

[16] Clarendon's *History of the Great Rebellion*, ed. W. Dunn Macray, Oxford, 1888, III, viii, pp. 30 and 94. Fuller details of some of Wilmot's Royalist activities may be found in David Underdown, *Royalist Conspiracy in England, 1649–1660*, New Haven, 1960.

[17] See H. J. Oliver, *Sir Robert Howard, 1626–1698*, Durham, N.C., 1963, p. 7; and below, p. 78.

[18] Clarendon, op. cit., III, viii, pp. 95f.

[19] *GEC's Complete Baronetage*, 1900, i, pp. 78–9.

1653–4. In August 1653 her kinsman Edward Hyde, later Earl of Clarendon, wrote from there to her husband, who was in Germany fund-raising for the King: Rochester's son, he said, was always anxious for news of him.[20] When he grew up, the poet may have remembered his feelings then; two of his own affectionate notes to his young son Charles survive.[21] Meanwhile, Lady Rochester, who was 'heartily weary of Paris' and of following her husband around Europe generally, had her older sons to fend for, and in 1656 she returned to Ditchley to contest parliament's claims on the estate.[22] She was to fight legal battles over property all her life in this struggle to keep what she had intact for her heirs.[23] In material terms she was largely successful. In human ones, her efforts were mocked by a series of bereavements. In 1658 her husband Rochester and her eldest son Henry both died—Rochester heavily in debt.[24] The other child of her first marriage, Francis, followed them in 1667 (though not before supplying two heirs, one of whom founded the Lichfield family by his marriage to an illegitimate daughter of Charles II). Her son Rochester, the poet, died in 1680 at the age of thirty-three; his wife and their only son the following year. The Dowager Countess was left with five fatherless granddaughters to keep an eye on: Sir Henry Lee's daughters Eleanor (Dryden's 'Eleanora') who became Countess of Abingdon, and Anne, who died in her mid-twenties but is remembered as the poet Anne Wharton; Rochester's daughters Anne, who became ancestress of the Earls of Warwick by her second marriage, to Francis Greville; Elizabeth, who married Edward Montague, grandson and heir of the Earl of Sandwich (under whom Rochester served in the Navy); and Malet, later Viscountess Lisburne.

20 *Calendar of the Clarendon State Papers*, ed. W. D. Macray and others, Oxford, 1863–1932, August 15, 1653.
21 See pp. 143, 229 below.
22 *Clarendon Papers*, ed. cit., May 22, 1654, and passim.
23 See for example *Verney Memoirs*, i, p. 161; *CSPD*, October 21, 1661; and p. 94 below.
24 *Clarendon Papers*, ed. cit., July 27, 1657, and passim.

It was from the Countess, if from anywhere, that Rochester inherited his intelligence, but otherwise he resembled his father. The mental collision between an early upbringing which, under his mother, was firmly religious and didactic, and a later way of life influenced by his father's friend Charles II and by a temperament whose vivacity and recklessness made him conspicuous even at the Restoration Court, is the source of much of his best work. No one saw through the Court more clearly; few people more influentially set the destructive social pace there. He notoriously reviled the King in his lampoons; his letters show that he loved him. Brutally promiscuous, and both unfaithful and cruel to even his most lasting mistress, he returned more or less regularly to his wife, and had a realistic sense of the scale of his dependence on her—a consciousness revealed in his letters and contemplated in some of his songs, especially 'Absent from thee I languish still'. The atheistic author of 'Upon Nothing' and of translations from Lucretius and Seneca—almost sublime, as Hazlitt said, in his contempt for everything that others respected[25]—spent the end of his life in lengthy correspondence and discussions with theologians, and died a convert, surrounded by clergymen.

These are famous paradoxes, and it has generally been acknowledged that they begin with his upbringing. For all its rural, aristocratic surroundings, Rochester's education was highly pressurized. He had a keen tutor in his mother's chaplain, Francis Giffard,[26] and was sent to school at Burford, where he must have lodged in the town during term.[27] At thirteen he went up to Wadham College, Oxford.[28] It was the year of the Restoration and no one seems to have required him to do much

[25] *Lectures on the English Poets*, 1818, quoted in *Rochester: the Critical Heritage*, ed. D. Farley-Hills, 1972, p. 214.
[26] *Remarks and Collections of Thomas Hearne*, ed. C. E. Doble, Oxford, 1885–1918, iii, p. 263.
[27] See Pinto, p. 5.
[28] *The Registers of Wadham College, Oxford*, ed. R. B. Gardiner, Oxford, 1889–95, i, p. 231.

work, so he must already have acquired at school most of the exceptionally good knowledge of Latin and Greek attributed to him by his early biographers.[29] At Wadham 'he broke off the course of his studies'[30] and was befriended by a Merton don, Robert Whitehall, in whose company he soon, according to Hearne, 'grew debauched'.[31] Whether because she found this out or because her educational scheme for him did not anyway allow for a long stay at the hard-drinking university, the Countess moved him on rapidly. He took his M.A. in September 1661, when he was fourteen—the Chancellor, his mother's ally Clarendon, kissing him affectionately on the cheek.[32] Two months later he was on the grand tour with a new tutor, a clever young Scottish physician, naturalist and antiquarian called Sir Andrew Balfour. With the help of a book Balfour wrote much later, Vivian de Sola Pinto has imaginatively reconstructed their leisurely journey through France and Italy,[33] in the course of which, according to Burnet, Balfour persuaded Rochester to return to his reading:

> and he often acknowledged to me, in particular three days before his death, how much he was obliged to love and honour this his governor, to whom he thought he owed more than all the world, next after his parents.[34]

On their way back in the winter of 1664, they visited Charles II's sister Henrietta, Duchess of Orleans, who gave Rochester a letter to take to her brother[35]—the first of such errands he was to do for them.[36] He arrived at Whitehall with it on Christmas Day.

[29] See for example Wood's *Athenae Oxonienses*, ed. P. Bliss, 1817, iii, p. 1229; Burnet, p. 3.
[30] Burnet, p. 4.   [31] Hearne, loc. cit.
[32] *Athenae Oxonienses*, loc. cit.
[33] Pinto, pp. 12–21.
[34] Burnet, p. 5.
[35] C. H. Hartmann, *Charles II and Madame*, 1934, pp. 135–6.
[36] See pp. 55, 56 below.

Amusing, clever, handsome, energetic, bisexual and extremely young, Rochester hardly needed the entrée his father's name gave him to the circle of Charles's friends. At seventeen, Rochester quickly became a dominant figure in a group most of whose members were in their late twenties or early thirties, and he must have sensed the advantage of his precocity: indeed, his two worst enemies at Court later were the only prominent figures who were younger than him—John Sheffield, Earl of Mulgrave, and Sir Carr Scroop—respectively, one and two years his juniors. For the moment, though, enmities were in the future and his only worry, which he shared with most of his friends, was being short of money. Poverty is a relative term, and by all but the Court's own standards men like Charles and Buckingham, however deeply in debt, were incalculably rich. But Rochester's family owned little property outright, and his mother kept a tight hold on what they had. The obvious course for someone in his position was a rich marriage, and there was a challengingly sought-after young heiress in London that spring. She was Elizabeth Malet, of Enmore in Somerset. She had an income of over £2,000 a year, and was being pursued in an atmosphere of diplomacy and high finance by a number of young men, the negotiations chiefly taking place through their fathers and her guardians.[37] She was, as events were to prove, independent and tough-minded, and the prolonged arrangements and counter-arrangements evidently both exasperated and amused her. Two years later, still unmarried, she was regaling her friends with stories of how 'my Lord Herbert would have had her, my Lord Hinchingbroke was indifferent to have her, my Lord John Butler might not have her, my Lord of Rochester would have forced her, and Sir [Francis] Popham would kiss her breech to have her.'[38]

[37] For this and the following paragraphs see J. H. Wilson, 'Rochester's Marriage', RES, xix, 1943, pp. 399–403; Greene, pp. 35–6, 41f.; and Pepys, May 28, June 6, 1665; February 25, August 26, November 25, 1666; February 4, 1667.
Pepys, November 25, 1666.

Rochester's attempt to force her happened within months of their first meeting. On May 26, 1665, she had been to dinner with Frances Stuart, the least accessible and (partly for that reason) the most sought-after woman at Court. Elizabeth's grandfather, the ageing roué Lord Hawley, who was her guardian, was taking her home in his coach at the end of the evening, when, at Charing Cross, near the Rochesters' London house, she was

seized on by both horse and foot-men and forcibly taken from him, and put into a coach with six horses and two women provided to receive her; and carried away. Upon immediate pursuit, my Lord of Rochester (for whom the King had spoke to the lady often, but with no success) was taken at Uxbridge; but the lady is not yet heard of [Pepys was writing two days later], and the King mighty angry and the Lord sent to the Tower.[39]

Elizabeth was returned to her family and Rochester, after petitioning the King,[40] was released three weeks later. Appearances had to be maintained, however, and—as he was to do in the future more than once—Charles gave the impression of banishing him from Court, by sending him on what was in fact intended as an interesting and remunerative trip abroad. A safe-looking booty-hunting expedition against the Dutch fleet was being planned by the English envoy at Copenhagen and the naval commander the Earl of Sandwich, and on July 6 Rochester was sent to join it, the King having instructed Sandwich to look after him well.[41]

The Bergen raid turned out to be a disaster. The eighteen-year-old Rochester's excitedly graphic but self-effacing account of the battle, written home to his mother 'from the coast of Norway among the rocks, aboard the *Revenge*'[42] is the longest

[39] Pepys, May 28, 1665. Pepys was writing on a Sunday and clearly refers to the events as having taken place on the previous Friday, i.e. the 26th. Wilson's '25 May' (*RES*, art. cit.) is presumably a misprint.

[40] The text of the petition is printed in Appendix I.

[41] See pp. 43f. below.   [42] ibid.

letter of his that survives, as well as the earliest. Two of his companions, as he tells her, were killed at his side; he spares her the details he later recounted to Gilbert Burnet.[43] Near the end of the battle, one of them, John Windham, who had so far been calm, began to tremble so much that he could not stand and had to be held up by the other, Edward Montague. A cannon-ball hit them both, killing Windham outright and tearing out Montague's stomach. He died an hour later. Before the battle the three young men had discussed the chances of there being any life after death—again, Rochester makes no reference to these conversations in his letter to his devout mother. He and Windham made a pact, which Montague would not take part in, that if either of them were killed and there should prove to be a 'future state', he would appear to the other to let him know. Windham never did so, and Rochester later told Burnet that this had been 'a great snare to him'.[44]

It is a fascinating glimpse into the mind of the boy who, having been brought up in the most conventional Anglican orthodoxy, was now a member of the Court of Hobbes's pupil, Charles II. Rochester's poems, and to a lesser extent his letters, were to be strewn with ideas and quotations from radical modern writers, applied often unsystematically but always with an imaginative daring so emotionally involved that it can be seen as a kind of late-Metaphysical wit. The indebtedness of his work to Hobbes is unmistakable, whether in his account of the grounds of human motivation ("'Tis all from fear, to make himself secure') in *A Satyr against Reason and Mankind*, or in his sexually persuasive misappropriation of a passage from the *Leviathan* in one of his best-known lyrics, 'Love and Life'.[45] Hobbes's argument, in the latter case, is about the conditions which lead people to 'foresight and prudence':

---

[43] Burnet, pp. 16f.   [44] ibid.

[45] See also T. H. Fujimura, 'Rochester's "Satyr against Mankind": An Analysis', *SP*, lv, 1958, pp. 576–90; and H. W. Smith, ' "Reason" and the Restoration Ethos', *Scrutiny*, xviii, 1951, pp. 118–36.

by how much one man has more experience of things past than another, by so much also he is more prudent, and his expectations the seldomer fail him. The present only has a being in nature. Things past have a being in the memory, only. But things to come have no being at all, the future being but a fiction of the mind, applying the sequels of actions past to the actions that are present. . . .[46]

Rochester's apparently elegiac poem takes up these phrases:

> All my past life is mine no more;
> The flying hours are gone,
> Like transitory dreams given o'er
> Whose images are kept in store
> By memory alone.
>
> Whatever is to come is not:
> How can it then be mine?
> The present moment's all my lot. . . .[47]

But the speaker, so far from being interested in 'foresight and prudence', is using Hobbes to provide an eloquent excuse for his infidelity:

> Then talk not of inconstancy,
> False hearts, and broken vows;
> If I, by miracle, can be
> This livelong minute true to thee,
> 'Tis all that heaven allows.

Some modern scholars have tended to over-estimate his first-hand knowledge of many philosophical works, and it is clear that his ideas were often picked up second-hand from contemporary sources: his attacks on scholasticism and on ecclesiastical corruption, for example, as well as his fascination with the idea (common in Montaigne) that human beings are,

[46] *Leviathan*, ed. A. R. Waller, Cambridge, 1904, p. 11.
[47] *Complete Poems*, p. 90.

contrary to the traditional view, morally inferior to animals, may
have been influenced by Davenant.[48] But the end of *Tunbridge
Wells* ('Bless me! thought I, what thing is man, that thus/In all
his shapes, he is ridiculous?'), the whole of *A Satyr*, several of
his lyrics—particularly 'The Fall'—and some of his translations, show him treating current orthodoxy in a sceptical,
paradoxical way which also characterizes his letters, particularly
those to Savile. The hold particular ideas had on him usually
seems related to how far they reversed the Christian notions
which had dyed his mind.[49] And his writing, so alert and so full
of nuance that there is rarely any doubt about the deliberateness
of an allusion or an ambiguity, constantly draws on the Bible and
the Anglican liturgy for phrases, using them as points of contrast, or as intensifying points of resemblance. 'I commit you to
what shall ensue,' he writes comically to his wife, quoting the
funeral service as if leaving her with his mother is like putting
her in a grave, 'woman to woman, wife to mother, in hopes of a
future appearance in glory';[50] and his love-letters, like his love-
songs, are full of liturgical allusions: to Elizabeth Barry,
'Remember the hour of a strict account, when both hearts are
to be open';[51] to Henry Savile, 'for thine is my kingdom,
power and glory, for ever and ever'.[52] Ironic half-quotations like
these are common in a great deal of Restoration writing, of
course, particularly in lyrics and in the dialogue of stage
comedies. But they are peculiarly frequent, and peculiarly
resonant, in Rochester: 'The Fall' is an elegiac poem, a small
Paradise Lost in its own right, as well as a wryly amusing
adaptation of the Eden myth to a sexual situation in which the
speaker finds himself impotent:

---

[48] See J. Treglown, 'Rochester and Davenant', *N & Q*, NS, xxiii, 1976, pp.
554–9.

[49] The *Tunbridge Wells* conclusion, for example, is an inversion of Psalm 8;
see J. Treglown, 'The Satirical Inversion of some English sources in
Rochester's poetry', *RES*, NS xxiv, 1973, pp. 46–7.

[50] p. 73.   [51] p. 99.   [52] p. 138.

How blest was the created state
Of man and woman, ere they fell,
Compared to our unhappy fate:
We need not fear another hell.

Naked beneath cool shades they lay;
Enjoyment waited on desire;
Each member did their wills obey,
Nor could a wish set pleasure higher.

But we, poor slaves to hope and fear,
Are never of our joys secure;
They lessen still as they draw near,
And none but dull delights endure.

Then, Chloris, while I duly pay
The nobler tribute of my heart,
Be not you so severe to say
You love me for the frailer part.[53]

And it was clearly in his childhood that these religious structures of myth and language became fixed in his memory. On his death-bed, he dictated a letter to Gilbert Burnet asking him to pray that God would keep his promise 'that at what time soever a sinner doth repent, he would receive him'. The words come from the first Sentence before Mattins and Evensong, but in a prayer-book version that went out of use when he was fifteen.[54]

If Rochester did not tell his mother about his religious doubts at Bergen, he kept quiet about his response to danger, too. For all his subsequent sexual domineering there was a modest side to his character, reflected in his unfashionable liking for the country and family life—it need not surprise us that his favourite

[53] *Complete Poems*, p. 86.
[54] See p. 244. The quotation comes from the 1552 Book of Common Prayer, still in use in Rochester's childhood but replaced in 1662. The 1552 version of the sentence (from Ezekiel, 18:27) begins 'At what time soever a sinner doth repent him of his sin'; the 1662 version, following the King James Bible, 'When the wicked man turneth away from his wickedness that he hath committed.' See F. E. Brightman, *The English Rite*, 1915, i, p. 129.

English author was Cowley. He was, it was to become clear, as casually brave as his father. A month after Bergen he was in battle again. Sandwich (whose son was a leading contender for marriage to Elizabeth Malet, and who therefore had no reason to exaggerate the volunteer's merits) wrote to the King that he wished he could express Rochester's character according to his great desert. He was 'brave, industrious; and of parts fit to be very useful in your Majesty's service.'[55] The following June, having spent the winter at Court, Rochester returned to sea under Sir Edward Spragge, and was involved in fierce fighting in the Channel during which almost all the volunteers on his ship were killed. He offered to take a message that had to be delivered to another ship, went and returned in a small boat under heavy fire, and came back to England amidst general acclaim.[56]

Between the two periods of active service, he had been given £750 by the King on October 31, 1665,[57] and was made a Gentleman of the Bedchamber at an annual salary of £1,000 in March.[58] These rewards seem to have been designed at least partly to give him some kind of financial eligibility to propose to Elizabeth Malet again. Whether she was impressed, now, by his prospects at Court and in the forces (he had also acquired a cavalry command),[59] or whether she was simply bored by the other candidates' formal procedures and fancied the dashingly

[55] Public Record Office, MS. SP 29, f. 132.
[56] Burnet, p. 11; CSPD, July 20, 1666, p. 559n.
[57] CSPD, October 31, 1665, p. 35.
[58] CSPD, March 21, 1666, p. 310. Pinto misdates events around this time, giving the impression that the Bedchamber appointment was a kind of reward for his marriage in January 1667. The error results from a misunderstanding of a CSPD entry for March 14, 1667: 'Lord Rochester is admitted to the bedchamber in place of the Duke of Buckingham.' (p. 560.) Rochester's own appointment as a Gentleman of the Bedchamber had been made the previous year (see above). This particular reference is clearly to an occasion when he stood in for the Duke, who kept his own place until 1674. See also p. 51, below.
[59] See CSPD, July 27, 1666, p. 582.

importunate Rochester more, she married him suddenly and unexpectedly on January 29, 1667, nearly two years after the romantic abduction at Charing Cross.[60] In a fragment preserved among manuscripts in their own hands, some of them love-poems written to each other, Rochester scrawled 'She yields, she yields—pale Envy said "Amen!"'—/The first of women to the last of men.'[61]

Plenty has been written about Rochester's subsequent life at Court and about his marriage. The early proliferation of picaresque anecdotes about his sexual exploits, fights and practical jokes has been counterbalanced by a modern tendency to generalize sentimentally about his relationship with his wife, exaggerating the consistency of both her tolerance and his remorse. For all the dating problems presented by the letters, it is clear that the marriage went through various phases and that at some times his behaviour was less generous, hers more querulous, than at others. It would be surprising if this were not true, particularly of a husband so fascinated by Montaigne's ideas about the inevitability of flux[62]—our 'frail and daily-changing' natures as he blithely called them in a letter to Elizabeth Barry[63]—and of a wife as sensitive as Elizabeth Malet. Rochester did not make a habit of keeping her letters (only two survive) but she kept many—perhaps all—of his, and it is clear from them that she wrote to him often. He rarely put a date on anything, but was as inconsistent in this respect as in all others. The dated letters are supplemented by those whose contents supply a month or a year, if only through the number of children he greets.

Their first child, named Anne ('Nan') after his mother, was baptized at Adderbury on April 30, 1669, two years after their

---

[60] *HMC*, 25, *Le Fleming*, p. 44; Pepys, February 4, 1667.
[61] Nottingham University, MS. Portland PwV 31, f. 5ʳ. The tradition that the lines were written at this time is only a guess.
[62] See for example Montaigne, *Essays*, tr. Florio, II, i, 'Of the Inconstancy of our Actions'.
[63] p. 148.

marriage. The date has previously always been given incorrectly —generally as August—and used as touching evidence that Rochester returned for the occasion from Paris.[64] He had gone there in March, ostensibly with a letter from Charles to his sister, but chiefly to escape the rows that had developed over his assault on Thomas Killigrew in the King's presence in February, and involvement in a duel soon afterwards.[65] In fact he was certainly still away when Anne was christened. More was made of the birth of his son, as the correspondence of various friends about the baptism in January 1671 shows.[66] Another daughter, Elizabeth ('Betty'), was born in the summer of 1674 and a third, Malet, in the winter of 1675–6.[67]

Rochester's more irritable letters tend not to mention the children, but the affectionate ones usually contain messages for them: 'Remember me to Nan and my Lord Wilmot', 'Pray bid my daughter Betty present my duty to my daughter Malet'; and sometimes there are presents. Such references obviously help locate the letters in time, but also contribute to one's sense of the mood and circumstances in which they were written. The children gave him opportunities he would not otherwise have had in his letters from London for a winning kind of domestic intimacy, and for the vivacious flippancy which was, it is clear from Burnet, a main source of his charm:[68] ''twas my design to have writ to my Lady Anne Wilmot to intercede for me,' he writes to Elizabeth on one occasion, 'but now with joy I find myself again in your favour, it shall be my endeavours to continue so.'[69] In some of these letters, imaginative exuberance seems to be filling the gap left by the withdrawal of the simpler tenderness which characterizes the early correspondence: 'This illustrious person is my ambassador to my son and daughter,' he writes of a messenger: 'the presents she brings are great and

[64] See for example Hayward, p. xxix.   [65] See p. 55.   [66] pp. 6of.
[67] These dates are based on those of their baptisms, recorded in the parish registers at Adderbury: Anne, April 30, 1669; Charles, January 2, 1671; Elizabeth, July 13, 1674; Malet, January 6, 1676.
[68] See Burnet, pp. 7, 13–14.   [69] p. 141.

glorious. . . . To my son she will deliver a dog of the last litter of lap-dogs so much reverenced at Indostan, for the honour they have to lie on cushions of cloth of gold at the feet of the Great Mogul,'[70] and so on. The dog was a King Charles Spaniel; the Mogul is Charles himself.

There is no shortage of wit in the earlier letters, either, but they are often more straightforwardly affectionate. They are full, too, of glimpses of the difficult circumstances the couple lived in, particularly as a result of Rochester's long absences at Court. In May 1668, a year after their marriage, he writes:

> You know not how much I am pleased when I hear from you. If you did you would be so obliging to write oftener to me. I do seriously with all my heart wish myself with you and am endeavouring every day to get away from this place which I am so weary of that I may be said rather to languish than live in it.[71]

It is to some extent a pose, but a pose that was forced on him. We know little about his day-to-day life at this time, but the official demands made of a Gentleman of the Bedchamber, though trivial, were not negligible, as is shown by a letter from Buckingham, asking him to take his place during a temporary absence.[72] And, of course, the job put him where he liked to be: at the centre of the Court's punishing round of pleasure—its ostentatious sexuality, its heavy drinking and its constant quarrels. Rochester was as aggressive as anyone there and in the year of Anne's birth he was repeatedly in trouble, not only before his trip abroad but while he was in Paris (he was involved

---

[70] p. 84.   [71] p. 52.

[72] See p. 51, below, and above (p. 16). Each Gentleman of the Bedchamber took his turn to sleep in the King's bedroom during one week of every quarter, and also waited at the King's table when he was eating in private. He was also expected to stand in for the Groom of the Stole when the Groom was unavailable to help the King get dressed in the morning. See Thomas Delaune, *The Present State of London*, 1681, quoted by Greene, p. 55.

in a fight at the opera in June),[73] and when he got back: in November he challenged a younger courtier, Mulgrave, to a duel, thereby beginning a lifelong enmity.[74] He was sexually very busy, too. Once again, we have little reliable information about who he was involved with and when, but he wrote about sex more frankly than any previous English poet, was famous for his escapades, and was soon suffering from venereal disease.

Some time in 1671 he had to extricate himself from an affair with a 'damsel of low degree' called Foster, a tart who figures briefly in one of his later satires, and who seems to have passed herself off as a courtier.[75] In March of that year Elizabeth had been in London with him and went to the theatre: it is the only evidence we have of her spending any time in town after the first year of their marriage.[76] The holiday must have been overshadowed by her husband's increasing financial difficulties. He tried hard not to use her money,[77] but the Treasury was already over two years behind with payments of his salary as a Gentleman of the Bedchamber, a matter pursued in some of his letters.[78] He was ill, too, and had to retire to the country that autumn, where his friend John Muddyman wrote to him about Foster and expressed his regret that Rochester's eyes could neither endure wine nor water.[79] It was a recurring and worsening complaint. The following autumn he undertook a cure with one of the King's doctors, Monsieur Fourcade, but wrote to his wife 'I recover so slowly and relapse so continually that I am almost weary of myself.'[80] He may have improved between then and 1676, but later the letters are increasingly full of references to bouts of illness so severe that he was prematurely rumoured dead.

There were other sources of strain on the marriage. Rochester's mother insisted on living at Adderbury, the couple's married home, and she and Elizabeth were on if anything worse terms

[73] See p. 55.   [74] Ibid.   [75] See p. 71.   [76] Greene, p. 146.
[77] See pp. 65, 127.   [78] pp. 78, 79.   [79] p. 68.   [80] p. 80.

than Rochester and his own mother-in-law, with whom
Elizabeth often chose to stay. Their increasing family must have
kept Elizabeth busy, even in their amply-staffed household, and
she found Rochester's absences intolerable. His letters were as
often as not written directly in response to her requests that he
should return, to her worries about what she has been hearing
about him (her grandfather Lord Hawley was well placed to have
been a source of gossip, communicated through his daughter,
her mother Lady Warre), or more simply about money, domestic
administration, illness and boredom. Some of his letters are
apologetic, some cajoling, some irritable. A few are practical. It
seems to have occurred to him that if he could procure the Court
appointment of the Rangership of Woodstock Park, they would
have their own house to live in, the High Lodge at Woodstock,
which was tied to the position. He was granted it in February
1674,[81] but whatever his intentions may have been he ended up
using the Lodge as a bachelor retreat which Elizabeth—as a
plaintive note to him which has survived shows[82]—was only
allowed to visit by invitation.

The Court itself was essentially a bachelor place: Charles II
was married but Rochester's closest friend, Henry Savile, was
not; Buckhurst, later Earl of Dorset, married in 1674, but
Wycherley not until 1679; Etherege probably the year after.[83]
Those who wrote to Rochester in the country are either amiably
satirical about his domestic life, or simply ignore it. He
apologizes to Elizabeth for his friends, obliquely, in a note sent
to her from Woodstock one Christmas, it is uncertain in what
year: 'since these rake-hells are not here to disturb us, you might
have passed your devotions this holy season as well in this place
as at Adderbury';[84] but he clearly loved being there with them,
hunting, racing, drinking and pursuing casual affairs, and was a
popular host. Buckingham writes to him in 1677 to let him
know he is about to arrive with his famous pack of hounds; he

[81] See p. 94.   [82] p. 167.
[83] See *Court Wits*, pp. 210–11, 217.   [84] p. 177.
3

and 'other nobles' stayed there for a fortnight.[85] Savile talks nostalgically about the debauchery of Woodstock and its contrast with the sobriety of Adderbury.[86]

Rochester had met Savile at Court in 1665, when Savile (then twenty-three or twenty-four) became a Groom of the Bedchamber to the Duke of York, whose wife's lover he is likely to have been.[87] The young men's backgrounds were similar. Savile, the younger brother of George Savile (later Marquess of Halifax), came from a prominent Royalist family in Yorkshire, had spent much of his childhood abroad and went on a European tour in 1661 with two prominent courtiers, the Earl of Sunderland and Henry Sidney.[88] Hard-drinking, attractive and irascibly irresponsible, he managed to pursue an increasingly successful career in public life without sacrificing any of the freedom of the Court group, though it is clear from Rochester's comments, in letters to him about 'the unequal choice of politics or lewdness', that Savile found it as precarious a juggling trick as Rochester's own with the Court and his family. In the early years of their friendship their lives continued to follow similar patterns, though Savile never married. He was imprisoned in March 1669 for his part in a challenge to Buckingham, soon after Rochester's assault on Thomas Killigrew at Court.[89] Around the time of Rochester's involvement with Foster in 1671, Savile made an ill-judged nocturnal foray into the bedroom of a rich young widow, the Countess of Northumberland, while they were both guests of his friend Sunderland. John Muddyman's letter to Rochester in September 1671, when he was ill in the country, describes the incident in amusingly laconic terms ('her servant coming into the room, our disconsolate lover retired overwhelmed with despair and so forth'),[90] but it caused a scandal and Savile seems to have had to lie low for some months afterwards. The first of the thirty-three letters between him and

---

[85] pp. 152f.; *HMC*, 25, *Le Fleming*, p. 141.   [86] p. 134.
[87] See *Savile Correspondence*, pp. xiv–xv.   [88] Ibid., p. xiv.
[89] Ibid., p. xv.   [90] See p. 70, below.

Rochester that survive belongs to the beginning of the same year, when Savile had to apologize for missing Charles Wilmot's christening.[91] The letter adopts the pattern of many he was to send the poet in the country, regaling him with fantasticated London gossip and reproaching him for his absence from town. Later, Rochester, in his second surviving letter to his friend, improvises amusingly in turn about the deprivations of rural life, while lightly satirizing Savile's careerism.[92]

Savile went on courting trouble. He drunkenly attacked, and subsequently fought a duel with, Rochester's enemy Mulgrave in December 1674, Rochester acting as his second;[93] insulted the Duke of York so often in late 1675 and early 1676 that he was dismissed from Court;[94] and infuriated the King by opposing 'that filthy dog Lauderdale' in 1678.[95] None of this prevented his becoming an increasingly trusted diplomatic envoy, M.P. for Newark, and finally replacing the disgraced Montagu at the Paris embassy in 1679.[96] From then on he saw little, if anything, of Rochester, though their correspondence continued until a few months before the poet's death in the summer of 1680. Savile himself died in 1687, after an operation.[97] He had been ill with V.D. for at least ten years: the later letters between him and Rochester keep up an antiphon of complaint about their respective symptoms, and his account of his stay in a sweat-shop, where he met both an old friend and a former girlfriend of Rochester's, prompted Rochester to a very funny parodic fantasy, a mock-romance about the palaces in Leather Lane and the lovers held there by enchantment in chains of mercury.[98]

If Savile's letters draw most of their life from the sheer copiousness of the scandal they purvey, some of Rochester's

[91] p. 62.   [92] p. 91.
[93] Correspondence of Arthur Capel, Earl of Essex, ed. O. Airy (Camden Society, N.S. no. 47), 1890, i, p. 281.
[94] Letters to Rachel, Lady Russell, 1854, pp. 27, 33, quoted by Wilson, p. 15.
[95] See p. 181, below.
[96] Savile Correspondence, pp. xvii–xviii; and p. 217, below.
[97] Wilson, p. 25.   [98] p. 201.

written from the country in a vacuum of individuals and events
have a more purely imaginative, stylistic existence. He wrote
Savile mock-elevated letters—for example a letter which is a
parody of a formal request for charity—just as he wrote to his
wife in the style of an obsessive gambler, or of a monarch sending
gifts through an ambassador, or in the mock-pretentious
nonsense-language he shared with Buckingham. He was, as has
often been pointed out, an actor, fond of practical jokes in which
he dressed up as other people; even when he lay dying he wrote
to one of his confessors asking him to take him into heaven in
disguise.[99] The small comic disguises adopted in some of his
letters were appreciated, as Savile's thanking him for 'two letters
of different styles' shows,[100] and they are related to Rochester's
almost instinctive use of parody in many of his poems. But it is
typical of the Court's literary dilettantism that while epistolary
style could briefly figure as a subject of discussion in their
correspondence, technical points about poetry are never mentioned. No letter to Rochester from any of his friends survives
in which any poem of his is referred to, except in relation to the
scandalous content of lampoons attributed to him. People
further from him—professional authors like Dryden, whose
patron he was for a time, and Charles Blount—talk about
individual poems of his with abject admiration, but Rochester's
own letters never allude to his writing. All the same, we have
Savile to thank for urging him to go on with it. The encouragement that survives in the letters dates from after the likely period
of Rochester's best work in the early and mid-70s. Savile writes
in August 1676, urging him to use his abilities and his leisure to
'show the world their follies',[101] and again in November 1677
pointing out that the elderly Edmund Waller and Samuel
Butler are still writing, and encouraging Rochester—partly by a
flattering allusion to his youth (he was actually thirty)—to 'take
the opportunity to show us that five-and-twenty is much a
better age for poetry.'[102]

[99] p. 246.   [100] p. 62.   [101] p. 136.   [102] p. 169.

It is difficult to date Rochester's poetry, and much of the work produced in response to all this may have consisted of the savagely personal lampoons assigned by David Vieth to the poet's last years, particularly the attacks on Scroop, Mulgrave, and a suitor of Rochester's girlfriend Elizabeth Barry, the dramatist Thomas Otway. But better poems, including 'Upon Nothing' and the memorably savage poetic self-portrait 'The Disabled Debauchee', may date from this time, as well as the strong translation of a chorus from Seneca's *Troades*, rightly praised by Blount.[103] And Savile's encouragement had almost certainly become important to their friendship long before these letters. Rochester was devoted to him. If his letters to him are often funny, some of them are as tender as the fondest ones he wrote to his wife: ''Tis not the least of my happinesses that I think you love me,' he says some time between 1673 and 1675, 'but the first of all my pretentions is to make it appear that I faithfully endeavour to deserve it. If there be a real good upon earth, 'tis in the name of friend.'[104] There are many similar declarations and although Savile's letters are less demonstrative, his unyielding pressure on the poet to leave wherever he was and join him in London or Paris shows that Rochester's affection was returned.

For obvious reasons we know little in detail about the physical relationships of the men at Charles's Court, and there is nothing to confirm or deny that such a relationship existed between Rochester and Savile. It seems certain, though, that they had a common interest in boys. One of Rochester's songs refers to 'a sweet, soft page of mine' who 'Does the trick worth forty wenches',[105] and there is a funnily compact stanza in 'The Disabled Debauchee' on a similar subject:

> Nor shall our love-fits, Chloris, be forgot,
>   When each the well-looked linkboy strove t' enjoy,

103 See *Complete Poems*, pp. 205–7, 215–16; and see p. 234, below.
104 p. 93.   105 'Love a woman? You're an ass!', *Complete Poems*, p. 51.

And the best kiss was the deciding lot
Whether the boy fucked you, or I the boy.[106]

Savile's involvement seems to be implied in two letters to him
from Rochester. Some time in October 1677, Rochester wrote
to him from the country, sending him a twenty-year-old French
musician, James Paisible, as 'The best present I can make at
this time', and signing himself, in French, 'a tired bugger who
will be, all the rest of his fucking life, your very faithful
friend.'[107] Savile's reply is discreetly unrevealing, but two years
later Rochester sent him another young Frenchman, his valet
Jean-Baptiste de Belle-Fasse, with a more openly suggestive
letter in which the idea of music itself comes to sound like a
sexual code.[108] The following spring, he refers to an accusation
made to Savile about him by—according to the often inaccurate text of *Familiar Letters* (1697)—'Mr P.' It sounds like a
blackmail attempt:

> [I] was not more surprised at the indirectness of Mr P's proceeding
> than overjoyed at the kindness and care of yours. Misery makes all
> men less or more dishonest and I am not astonished to see villainy
> industrious for bread . . . I believe the fellow thought of this device
> to get some money, or else he is put upon it by somebody who has
> given it him already.[109]

The circumstances are unknown, but it seems possible that
'Mr P.' is a misprint for 'Mr B.', and that Mr Baptist, as
Rochester called him, had tried to betray him. Whatever the
truth of the matter, the valet was back in Rochester's service at
the time of his death.[110]

However hazy the facts, some of what Elizabeth had to
contend with is easy to guess. It would be wrong to suggest that
they were estranged in the mid-70s: he was often at Adderbury,

[106] Ibid., pp. 116–17.   [107] p. 160.
[108] See p. 230.   [109] p. 243.
[110] He is mentioned in Rochester's will; see Prinz, pp. 298–302.

and she became pregnant in the autumn before the Woodstock appointment and in the spring of 1675. But two of the main problems—his violence and his infidelity—increased during this period. The violence is apparent throughout his adult life, whether in his duelling, in the hectoring tone of a few of his letters both to his wife and to Elizabeth Barry, or in the domineering machismo of poems like 'The Advice' or 'Phyllis, be gentler, I advise' and his sexual satires. It was a tendency shared by most of his friends, but it reached some sort of a personal crisis in the mid-70s in a series of actions which were not easily forgiven at Court. He was responsible for several fierce lampoons on Charles II and his mistresses, and whatever it was that impelled him to attack his benefactor—perhaps a belated rebellion against, and testing of, the dead father whose proxy Charles may have become—was eventually expressed in a physical act of vandalism. The King had had an elaborate set of chronometers built in the Privy Garden at Whitehall; they contained a mechanism in a phallic group of glass spheres. On June 25, 1675, Rochester and a few friends smashed it up.[111]

That autumn and winter he was in exile in Oxfordshire, complaining that he had lost all his friends as the result, he felt, of some unwarranted grievance against him held by the Duchess of Portsmouth.[112] His indignant letters do not seem disingenuous. He is passionately aggrieved, and there is no hint of any sense that if the particular charge was unmerited, the general hostility to him had good causes. And the following June, almost on the anniversary of the Privy Garden affair, he was back in action with a different gang of friends in Epsom.[113] Some musicians, it was said, refused to play for them, so Rochester, Etherege and two other men tossed them in a blanket. A passer-by, curious to see what the noise was about,

111 Aubrey, *Brief Lives*, ed. A. Clark, Oxford, 1898, ii, p. 34; Pinto, p. 80.
112 See pp. 106f.
113 See *Correspondence of the Family of Hatton*, ed. E. M. Thompson, 1878, i, pp. 133–4; *The Poems and Letters of Andrew Marvell*, ed. H. M. Margoliouth, 1971, ii, pp. 344–5; *HMC* 7th Report, Appendix, p. 467b.

was set on in turn and, to free himself, offered to take them to the handsomest woman in Epsom. When they showed interest, he resourcefully directed them to the house of the local constable, who 'demanding what they came for, they told him "A whore" and, he refusing to let them in, they broke open his doors and broke his head and beat him very severely.' The constable managed to break free and call the watch. Now faced with serious opposition, they calmed down. Etherege made a pacifying speech and the watch was sent away again. At this point Rochester drew his sword on the solitary constable. One of the group, a Mr Downs, was in time to hold him, the officer shouted murder, the watch returned, one of them hit Downs over the head with his staff and Rochester and his friends fled. Downs tried to defend himself, but the now incensed local men 'animadverted so severely' upon him(in Marvell's dry phrase)[114] that Downs died of his injuries. It was generally assumed that the courtiers would be charged but, as courtiers tended to do in such circumstances, they went free.

The years of these turbulent events were also the period in which Rochester's most lasting affair began. Like the letters to his wife, those addressed to Elizabeth Barry present often insurmountable difficulties of dating and content. None exists in manuscript. The genuine ones that survive are contained in the second volume of *Familiar Letters* (1697), a collection of both real and fictitious correspondence one of whose functions was to supply models of epistolary style, particularly for love-letters. Those from Rochester to 'Mrs B——' are almost certainly all authentic—Elizabeth Barry was alive and well in 1697 and probably supplied them to the editor herself, perhaps with Otway's letters printed in Volume I. But they were tidied up for the press, and all the names mentioned are abbreviated, often now beyond recognition. Rochester dated hardly any of them, and so little is known in detail about their lives at this time that it is often impossible to reconstruct the events alluded to.

[114] Margoliouth, loc. cit.

It seems likely, however, that the affair began around 1675, when she was about seventeen. He was roughly eleven years her elder. She was then trying to start her acting career, and her first role was probably the small part of Draxilla in Otway's heroic play *Alcibiades*, at the Dorset Garden, late in September 1675.[115] She was unsuccessful and seems to have left the company at the end of the season.[116] It is unlikely that Rochester saw *Alcibiades*, as he was in exile in the country then, but he could easily have met her earlier: she was brought up by Sir William Davenant and his family, with whom he was on friendly terms.[117] At all events, Rochester became Otway's patron around this time,[118] and possibly coached Elizabeth Barry as an actress between then and her successful appearance as Leonora in Aphra Behn's *Abdelazar* in July 1676,[119] a part which he may have helped procure for her.

The early months of the affair were deliriously romantic, but Rochester's long absence in the country must have quickly pushed the pair apart. Barry was no more monogamous than him, and a number of his letters are devoted either to expressing his suspicions, or to allaying hers; they may belong to 1676–7, when she was theatrically very busy[120] and when Rochester

---

115 See *The London Stage*, ed. W. van Lennep, Carbondale, Illinois, 1960–68, i, p. 239, and passim.

116 *An Apology for the Life of Mr Colly Cibber*, ed. R. W. Lowe, 1889, i, p. 159.

117 See Thomas Davies, *Dramatic Miscellanies*, 1784, iii, p. 197. For Rochester's friendship with the Davenants, see J. Treglown, 'Rochester and Davenant', *N & Q*, NS xxiii, 1976, pp. 554–9.

118 See the Preface to Otway's *Don Carlos* in the *Works*, ed. J. C. Ghosh, Oxford, 1932, i, p. 174.

119 *The London Stage*, i, p. 245. Although she is listed in the cast of Etherege's *The Man of Mode*, which opened in March, 1676, it is likely that she took over the role at a later date from another actress; ibid., p. 243.

120 She played Constantia in D'Urfey's *Madam Fickle* in November, 1676; Phaenice in Otway's *Titus and Berenice* and Lucia in his *The Cheats of Scapin* that December; Hellena in Aphra Behn's *The Rover* the following March; Emillia in D'Urfey's *A Fond Husband* in May; Clorinia in Porter's *The French Conjurer* in June; and Philisides in the anonymous *The Constant Nymph* in July. (Ibid., pp. 251–2, 256–8.)

probably wrote the poem 'Leave this gaudy gilded stage'. But by April 1677 she was pregnant. She did not appear in the 1677–8 season, and in December 1677 she gave birth to their daughter, also called Elizabeth.[121] Savile reproached Rochester with his neglect of her at this time,[122] and although he may have responded with various gifts to her[123] it seems likely that the relationship was never successfully resumed. Barry returned to the stage quickly, appearing in Otway's *Friendship in Fashion* on April 5, 1678.[124] Rochester was very ill that month, and went to Adderbury in May amidst excited gossip about his penitence and reformation.[125] The fact that Barry seems to have played few roles between then and 1679 may suggest that she had lost his patronage. Certainly he spent the summer of 1678 in the country[126] and it may have been around then that he took the child out of her care, on the pretext that Barry was unfit to look after her.[127] According to contemporary scandal, after their affair ended she had a number of flings with friends of his, including Etherege, Buckhurst and, perhaps, his cousin Henry St John.[128] Some of the bitterness which prompted, and was prompted by, these mutual revenges surfaces painfully in the letters.

Everything about Rochester's life when he was in his late twenties suggests the manic energy that was part of his attraction. It was in many ways frustrated. He had no demanding job: the military career he had begun so well was set aside, and he despised politics except as a source of gossip, and took little part in them although he had become a member of the House of Lords unconventionally early.[129] (The parliamentary speech

[121] See p. 171. [122] p. 174.

[123] See p. 171: it is not clear whether the letter preceded or followed Savile's.

[124] *The London Stage*, i, p. 269.

[125] See *HMC* 7th Report, Appendix, p. 470a; and see p. 181.

[126] See the correspondence with Savile of that period, pp. 181f.

[127] See p. 216. [128] See *Court Satires*, p. 78.

[129] He was 'called in' with Mulgrave in July 1667, when they were still under twenty-one. *HMC*, 25, *Le Fleming*, p. 51.

attributed to him by Prinz and others[130] was actually made by
Clarendon's son Lawrence Hyde, who took the Rochester title
in 1682 when it had become extinct with Charles Wilmot's
death.) He was too poor to absorb himself in building a great
house, as Buckingham was doing at Cliveden; too grand to
write for money. With no permanent claim on his many talents,
he could easily have wasted them entirely. Certainly his brief life
was littered with unfinished projects—brief, impulsive periods
of literary patronage; temporary aristocratic hobbies like carp-
breeding and chemistry;[131] uncompleted works—a collaboration
with Sir Robert Howard on a play;[132] a translation of Lucretius
(he wrote fourteen lines of the first book).[133] Of his anyway
small body of poems, many are impromptus or other pieces
apparently rapidly composed—the automatically rhyming 'Signior
Dildo', the narratively linear *Tunbridge Wells*, the argumentatively
improvisatory *Satyr against Reason and Mankind*. Samuel Johnson,
with the self-assurance of a man who has written a dictionary and
a novel, was later quick to point out that 'his pieces are commonly short, such as one fit of resolution would produce',[134]
and whatever evidence to the contrary is offered by the elegantly
constructed *A Letter from Artemisia in the Town to Chloe in the
Country*, or the lengthy adaptation of Fletcher's *Valentinian*, it is
a fair point. But the very squanderings and frustrations of this
period in his life themselves produced much of his best poetry.
Needing an outlet not only for his comic imaginative energy and
his sometimes virulent social scorn, but also for his complex
emotional response to the conflicting demands made on him by
his sexuality and his domesticity, Rochester probably wrote his
major satires and his most subtle, ambivalent songs in the
mid-70s.[135]

---

[130] Prinz, p. 296. John Adlard perpetuates the error in *The Debt to Pleasure*,
    Cheadle, Cheshire, 1974, p. 122.
[131] See pp. 142, 153.   [132] See p. 116.
[133] *Complete Poems*, pp. 34–5.
[134] *Lives of the English Poets*, ed. G. Birkbeck Hill, Oxford, 1905, i, pp. 219f.
[135] Although many of the poems are impossible to date with any certainty,

The songs, in particular, with their multiple attitudes to
infidelity, are so clearly related to his life, and so emotionally
rich under the controlled surface, that they easily overbalance
any description of Rochester himself. He was sensitive,
philosophical, torn by conflicting impulses, and so on, but he
was too buoyant, as well as too classically well-bred, to think
self-analysis admirable in itself. (Besides, such introspection as
the lyrics contain is generally complicated by being used to
some more or less selfish end, like sexual persuasion or an
excuse for inconstancy.) And the qualities of his satires are not
those of schematized moral or political thought, or even—with
one or two exceptions—of sophisticated narrative or argu-
mentative organization. They are best when they are least
argued and least responsible, letting half-instinctive, strongly
felt, often capricious or snobbish responses to people and ideas
prompt his sharply turned, vividly detailed couplets. He told
Burnet that 'to make a satire without resentments, upon the cold
notions of philosophy, was as if a man would in cold blood cut
men's throats who had never offended him',[136] and said that the
lies he wrote 'came often in as ornaments, that could not be
spared without spoiling the beauty of the poem.'[137]

This cheerful irresponsibility characterizes the more school-
boyish stories about his life, too—his disguising spies as sentries,
posted at the doors of people he wanted to satirize, with
instructions to note their movements and visitors; his setting up
as a tinker in Adderbury, and knocking out the bottoms of the

several either can be confidently assigned to particular periods or have
clear terminal dates. Vieth has been unnecessarily harshly criticized for
using these landmarks as bases of comparison by which other poems can
be conjecturally dated. Among the more or less precisely dateable poems
from this particular period are *Tunbridge Wells* (spring, 1674), *Timon*
(April–June, 1674), *A Satyr against Reason and Mankind* (before March 23,
1676) and the lyrics 'Tell me no more of constancy' and 'To a Lady in a
Letter' (both first printed in the spring of 1676) and 'Love and Life'
(first printed in 1677).

---

[136] Burnet, p. 26.   [137] Ibid.

pans people brought him to mend.[138] In the middle of this period, probably immediately after the dials-smashing episode, he pretended to be a doctor and set himself up on Tower Hill, advertising his skills in a hilariously convoluted, ironic pamphlet, and allegedly attracting women patients by his tact in always having them attended by his 'wife'—who was, according to his accomplice Thomas Alcock, Rochester himself in another disguise.[139] There are letters from this in some ways dark period, as from other times, which show him in similarly casual high spirits. In 1677 he was as popular as ever at Court, acting for the King on behalf of Nell Gwynn by bribing the Lord Lieutenant of Ireland to help her push through some claims for land,[140] and helping Buckingham out of a quarrel with the House of Lords.[141] But it was probably around this time, too, that he wrote to his 'most neglected wife' saying he had heard her continually complain these three years, and insolently pretending he had no idea what the fuss was about.[142]

The last three years of his life saw the end of his affair with Elizabeth Barry, a reconciliation with his wife, and his widely-publicized return to Christianity. It would be pleasant to make a straightforwardly happy ending out of these undeniable facts, but the evidence introduces complications. He lived between fierce extremes from 1677 to 1680, all, it seems, directly or indirectly a result of his illness. Around October 1677 he wrote from Woodstock to his wife at Adderbury, comically down-playing his ailments: 'my pissing of blood Dr Wetherley says is nothing; my eyes are almost out, but that, he says, will not do me much harm. . . .'[143] A letter of the same period to Savile begins more pathetically: 'I am almost blind, utterly lame, and scarce within reasonable hopes of seeing London again.'[144]

[138] Burnet, p. 27; Pinto, p. 139.
[139] See Thomas Alcock and John Wilmot, Earl of Rochester, *The Famous Pathologist or The Noble Mountebank*, ed. V. de S. Pinto, Nottingham, 1961, pp. 26–7.
[140] See p. 143.   [141] See p. 145.   [142] p. 170.
[143] p. 155.   [144] p. 158.

What he was suffering, he repeatedly claimed to think, were
'the torments of the stone'. Certainly, faced with his symptoms
but with no knowledge of his way of life, a doctor might have
diagnosed renal calculus. In the following century, *James's
Medical Dictionary* described the symptoms of kidney stones in
terms very similar to Rochester's complaints in these letters.
The sufferers

> make bloody urine . . . After their periodical haemorrhage, they
> become languid and paralytic in their limbs . . . But if they miss their
> usual evacuation, they are troubled with a pain in the head, a dim-
> ness of sight . . . and vertigo; whence many become epileptic, others
> bloated, blind and hydropsical; others grow melancholy or
> paralytic.[145]

On his death bed, Rochester insisted on being 'searched' for a
stone,[146] and that none was found is, of course, inconclusive.
But all his symptoms could equally well have been caused by
neurosyphilis, a notoriously mimetic form of tertiary syphilis
often confused with other illnesses, including renal stone.
Other members of Rochester's gang were suffering similarly.
William Fanshaw, who visited him regularly in his last illness,
was deformed by V.D.[147] Jane Roberts, a former girlfriend of
both Rochester and the King, died of it in 1679 after spending
some time in the same sweatshop as Fanshaw and Savile, where,
Savile wrote, 'what she has endured would make a damned soul
fall a-laughing at his lesser pains.'[148]

Rochester's illness was intermittent, and for much of the time
he was his usual self. But there are disturbing features of his
later correspondence. There is an uncharacteristically unctuous
note to his young nephew, the Earl of Lichfield;[149] there are
some badly off-balance letters to Elizabeth Barry, apparently
about her affairs with other men ('I thank God I can see very

---

[145] *James's Medical Dictionary*, 1743-5, *"Calculus"*.
[146] Burnet, p. 155.   [147] See p. 183.
[148] p. 197, and see Pinto, p. 195.   [149] p. 176.

woman in you, and from yourself am convinced I have never been in the wrong in my opinion of women');[150] there is the abrupt change of mood in one to Savile of July 1678, starting with a comical mock-romance about Leather Lane and ending with his belief that he would be dead by October.[151] Around this time he asked the philosopher Charles Blount to write to him on various theological matters, an invitation Blount took up with a diligence stultifying to modern readers, though the poet actually seems to have gone on encouraging him.[152] Savile sent him a present of various medicines in April 1679 and had to wait nearly three months for an acknowledgment.[153] Both he and Rochester were worried about a possible diminution of each other's affections around this time, and the letters alternate between anxiety and over-jaunty reassurance.[154] In December 1679, Dryden was beaten up in Rose Alley, possibly at the instigation of Rochester and the Duchess of Portsmouth, who thought Dryden was responsible for the attack on them in *An Essay Upon Satire*.[155]

By the time he died on July 26, 1680, his friends assumed he had gone mad. Fanshaw, a regular visitor who knew him well and knew, too, how syphilis could end, said so openly,[156] and much of the energy of Rochester's mother, of her chaplain Robert Parsons and of Gilbert Burnet was subsequently spent denying the charge.[157] However vehement their protestations, they cannot conceal the extremity of his condition. As early as the autumn of 1679, when Rochester began his conversations with Burnet, he was, Burnet says, 'apt to fall into hectical fits'.[158] By the time he saw him at Woodstock, in July 1680, he was 'wounded both in body and mind'.[159] Burnet may be using

[150] p. 180.   [151] p. 201.   [152] pp. 206f., 234f.   [153] pp. 216, 224.
[154] See for example, pp. 220, 224, 229.
[155] See p. 120 for discussion of this controversial subject.
[156] *Rochesteriana*, pp. 57–8.
[157] The Dowager Countess's letters to her sister from this period are contained in Appendix II.
[158] Burnet, p. 33.   [159] Ibid., p. 128.

the expression metaphorically, here, to express the poet's spiritual pain, but admits that the night he arrived (July 20) Rochester 'had a convulsion fit, and raved',[160] a statement which contradicts Parsons's claim in the funeral sermon that he was composed and sane throughout the nine weeks of his illness except for a period of about thirty hours half-way through[161]— that is, a month before Burnet's arrival. Similarly, Rochester's mother's letters to her sister during this time betray a seemingly excessive anxiety that her son's sanity should not be doubted. If Rochester was returning to his maker, he was returning to his mother too, and she naturally did all she could to avoid having the homecoming impugned. But in all her assertions, the symptoms she mentions in order to play them down are themselves damaging: he has a kind of hectic fever on him, she admits,[162] and has suffered some faint fits.[163] One night he was disordered in his head;[164] another day, he was a little disordered.[165]

In theological terms, of course, any change of personality Rochester may have suffered could only have been for the better, and anyway Fanshaw's rejection of his friend's—as he saw them—'melancholy fancies' has to be set against the apparent authenticity of Burnet's own account of the long arguments he had with the then intractable poet late in 1679—of Rochester's having been unconvinced, but of the sudden breakthrough the following spring when his mother's chaplain read him Isaiah's words about the suffering servant.[166] As Graham Greene points out in his account of these months, Christianity had dominated the poet's thoughts in one way or another all his life.[167] But clearly his almost unendurable last illness drove him out of his mind for considerable periods of time, he was under intense pressure to repent and to be seen to do so, and any decision he reached was not only influenced by these circum-

160 Ibid., p. 137.
161 Robert Parsons, *A Sermon preached at the funeral of the Right Honorable John Earl of Rochester*, Oxford, 1680, p. 33.
162 p. 249.   163 p. 253.   164 p. 250.   165 p. 253.
166 Burnet, pp. 127–43.   167 Greene, pp. 197f.

stances but reported to the outside world in a determinedly cosmetic way.[168]

His reconciliation with his wife had happened earlier. We have no details at all, but it may have been around 1678–9 that he wrote her a movingly apologetic, unostentatiously intimate letter from London to Adderbury:[169]

'Tis not an easy thing to be entirely happy, but to be kind is very easy and that is the greatest measure of happiness. I say not this to put you in mind of being kind to me—you have practised that so long that I have a joyful confidence you will never forget it—but to show that I myself have a sense of what the methods of my life seem so utterly to contradict.

I must not be too wise about my own follies, or else this letter had been a book dedicated to you and published to the world.

---

[168] See for example the correspondence between Burnet and Halifax printed in H. C. Foxcroft, 'Some Unpublished Letters of Gilbert Burnet', *Camden Miscellany*, xi, 1907, and D. L. Poole, 'Some Unpublished Letters of George Savile, Lord Halifax, to Gilbert Burnet', *EHR*, xxvi, 1911, 535–42. Halifax wrote on August 23, 1680, saying 'you will I suppose entertain yourself with giving some account of my Lord Rochester, concerning which do not think it impertinent that I give you this caution, which is, that it is not possible for you to write on a subject that requireth more care, and therefore though it looketh like a slight thing, and such a one as you would rather play with than spend much either of your time or thoughts upon it, let me beg of you to be exactly careful in it, and to file it over oftener than you have ever done anything that hath come from you.'

[169] p. 228.

The text

The main manuscript sources of Rochester's correspondence are: (1) Harleian MS. 7003, in the British Library, which contains most of his surviving letters to his wife, others to his mother and son, to Savile and other correspondents, and several letters addressed to him by Savile, Buckingham, Buckhurst, Dryden and others; and (2) the Marquess of Bath's MS. Portland II, at Longleat House, which contains eleven letters to Rochester from Savile—printed in a bowdlerized and inaccurate form in *HMC*, the copy-text of Wilson's *Rochester-Savile Letters*—and one from John Muddyman. Full references, and references to various other manuscripts used, are given in the appropriate footnotes

The main printed sources are the two volumes of *Familiar Letters: Written by the Right Honourable John late Earl of Rochester. And several other Persons of Honour and Quality* (London, 1697), which contain all of the surviving letters from the poet to Elizabeth Barry and a number to Savile. The text followed in the case of *Familiar Letters* is the 1699 edition, which comparison with such MSS as survive shows to be slightly more reliable. This and other printed texts used are, again, recorded in the notes.

In his life of the poet, Graham Greene quotes a letter supposedly from Rochester to Barry, and her supposed reply, both printed in an eighteenth-century collection of mildly pornographic epistolary short romances about historical figures, Alexander Smith's *The School of Venus* (London, 1716) and reproduced in Prinz's *Rochesteriana*, pp. 22f. Greene thinks they 'may well be genuine', though they occur in the middle of a

description of the couple's relationship which bears no resemblance to other early accounts, and are accompanied by a
series of similar exchanges of correspondence supposedly
between Barry and a number of other titled people, including
some with whom there is no particular reason to connect her.
All these letters are unmistakably fictitious.

I should explain my approach to transcription. Those letters
which survive in holograph are often idiosyncratic in spelling
and punctuation in ways which give—however impressionistic-
ally—a feeling of their authors' individuality. This is sometimes
true even of the precise orthographic forms used. Rochester
uses 'yᵉ', for example, in a mockingly archaic letter, where
otherwise (unlike many of his correspondents) he generally
writes 'the'. For reasons like this, I have transcribed the holograph manuscripts with minimal editorial interference. The only
contractions filled out are the special seventeenth-century forms
for –*mm*–, and for –*ed* (even the latter with some reluctance, as
Savile wrote all his *d*s as if they were contractions). The only
letter I modernize is *S*. Corrections and deletions are not
recorded (they are mostly illegible, and if they can be read are
uninteresting) and full stops in superscript contractions have
been omitted, but otherwise the present text reproduces as
closely as possible what appears in the originals.

Early printed texts of otherwise lost letters, on the other hand,
were all tidied up in spelling and punctuation and made to
conform to the then current conventions of typography (for
example in matters of italicization and capitalization). As these
conventions bear no relation to the writers' own practice, there
seems no point in following previous modern editors in exactly
reproducing these texts simply for the sake of a vaguely antique
appearance, so I have modernized them.

As will be clear from the Introduction, the ordering of the
letters presents almost insurmountable difficulties. A number are
dated, and many others can be assigned to a year, a month or
even a precise date by their content, or by their relationship to a

datable letter. Many, though, can only be dated conjecturally, and in some of these cases the guess is practically random. There are notes from Rochester to his wife and to Elizabeth Barry which could belong to almost any period of their respective relationships. But it would be pedantic not to attempt some kind of ordering, based on the datable material and on what is known or can be inferred about Rochester's life—facts and inferences discussed both in the Introduction and in the explanatory notes. Of the other possible procedures—alphabetical order of first words, or the order in which letters appear in manuscripts and printed collections—the former would be the more coherent.

Each of the letters below is headed with either some kind of date or a question mark, so that the reader can easily see when the positioning of a letter is authoritative and when merely conjectural. Deliberately, the conjectural placings are not always tidy. It seems more likely, on the evidence we have, that Rochester's moods often changed than that, for example, all the letters to his wife in one year were affectionate and all those in another were bad-tempered; more likely than not, also, that sometimes he wrote love-letters to both her and Elizabeth Barry on the same day. The guesses remain guesses, though, and I have not tried to make a case for them in the notes if there was no real case to make.

To make the letters comprehensible it has often been necessary to provide very full annotation, in a few cases even to the extent of providing a brief introduction. Personal and historical allusions are, of course, explained wherever possible, but at the risk of seeming ponderous I have also pointed out the sources of quotations, translated passages of Latin and French, and glossed obsolete (or otherwise misinterpretable) words and usages.

Abbreviations

Where a note simply refers to *CSPD* or *CTB*, the entry is for the date mentioned in that note. Similarly, 'passim' implies a large number of references in the volume for the period concerned. Otherwise references are given in the form '*CSPD*, February 12, 1677'. Fuller description has been avoided on the ground that these works are indexed in detail.

Place of publication is London unless otherwise stated. Full publication details are not given for standard works of reference.

A further note on the text, including prefatory material from *Familiar Letters* and *The Museum*, will be found in Appendix IV.

Burnet: G. Burnet, *Some Passages of the Life and Death of the Right Honourable John, Earl of Rochester*, 1680.

Collins: E. Bridger, ed., *Collins's Peerage of England*, 1812.

Complete Poems: David M. Vieth, ed., *The Complete Poems of John Wilmot, Earl of Rochester*, New Haven and London, 1968.

Court Satires: J. H. Wilson [ed.], *Court Satires of the Restoration*, Columbus, Ohio, 1976.

Court Wits: J. H. Wilson, *The Court Wits of the Restoration: An Introduction*, Princeton, N.J., 1948.

CSPD: *Calendar of State Papers Domestic*.

CTB: *Calendar of Treasury Books*.

DNB: *Dictionary of National Biography*.

Evelyn, *Diary*: John Evelyn. *The Diary*, ed. E. S. de Beer, Oxford, 1955.

FL: *Familiar Letters*, by Rochester and others, two volumes (*FL* i and *FL* ii), 1697, 1699 ed.

The Famous Pathologist: Vivian de Sola Pinto, ed., *The Famous Pathologist, or The Noble Mountebank, by Thomas Alcock and John Wilmot, Earl of Rochester*, Nottingham, 1961.

GEC: V. Gibbs, ed., *The Complete Peerage . . . by G.E.C.*, 1910–49.

Greene: Graham Greene, *Lord Rochester's Monkey: being the Life of John Wilmot, Second Earl of Rochester*, 1974.

Hayward: John Hayward, ed., *Collected Works of John Wilmot Earl of Rochester*, 1926.

HMC: *Reports of the Historical Manuscripts Commission*.

JHC: *Journals of the House of Commons.*

JHL: *Journals of the House of Lords.*

MS. Harl.: British Library Harleian Manuscript.

OCD: *Oxford Classical Dictionary.*

ODCC: *Oxford Dictionary of the Christian Church.*

OED: *Oxford English Dictionary.*

Ogg: David Ogg, *England in the Reign of Charles II*, Oxford, 1955.

Pepys, *Diary*: R. Latham and W. Matthews, ed., *The Diary of Samuel Pepys*, 1970–.

Pinto: Vivian de Sola Pinto, *Enthusiast in Wit: A Portrait of John Wilmot Earl of Rochester 1647–1680*, 1962.

Pinto, ed., *Rochester*: Vivian de Sola Pinto, ed., *Poems by John Wilmot, Earl of Rochester*, 1953, 2nd edn, 1964.

POAS: see Yale *POAS*.

P.R.O.: Public Record Office.

PQ: *Philological Quarterly.*

Prinz: Johannes Prinz, ed., *John Wilmot, Earl of Rochester: His Life and Writings*, Leipzig, 1927.

R.E.S.: *Review of English Studies.*

Rochesteriana: Johannes Prinz, ed., *Rochesteriana: Being Some Anecdotes Concerning John Wilmot Earl of Rochester*, Leipzig, 1926.

Rochester-Savile: see Wilson.

Savile Correspondence: W. D. Cooper, ed., *Savile Correspondence, Letters to and from Henry Savile . . . including letters from . . . George Marquess of Halifax*, 1858.

S.P.: *Studies in Philology.*

Verney Memoirs: *Memoirs of the Verney family during the Seventeenth Century*, compiled by F. P. and M. M. Verney, 1904.

Vieth: see *Complete Poems.*

Wilson: J. H. Wilson, ed., *The Rochester-Savile Letters, 1671–1680*, Columbus, Ohio, 1941.

Wood, *Athenae*: P. Bliss, ed., *Athenae Oxonienses*, by Anthony à Wood, 3rd edn, 1813–20.

Yale *POAS*: G. deF. Lord and others, ed., *Poems on Affairs of State: Augustan Satirical Verse, 1660–1714*, Yale, 1963–75.

1665-70
Fain to Borrow Money

[Rochester had spent the first weeks of June, 1665, imprisoned in the Tower for abducting Elizabeth Malet. After petitioning the King (see Appendix I) he was released on June 19 and within a month had joined the Earl of Sandwich's fleet as one of a number of well-placed volunteers. The practice of giving high rank to young men with Court influence ('King's Letter Boys') alongside more traditionally trained officers was a significant development in naval history during the Restoration. Rochester's biographers have tended to emphasize the heroic, self-redemptory aspects of this period of his life, but it should not be forgotten that, at the time, the Bergen expedition looked likely to be a safe raid from which the participants would return enriched—as Rochester's own wry admission of his disappointed hopes ('I for shirts and gould wch I had most neede of') shows. It is clear that Charles intended Rochester to be well looked after. Sandwich wrote to the King promptly to announce his arrival and to say that 'In obedience to y^r Ma:^ties Commands by my Ld Rochester I haue accommodated him the best I can' (P.R.O. MS. SP 29, f. 127); and in his journal for July 15 he notes that he has put the 18-year-old earl in a cabin on board his own ship, the *Revenge*.

[The Bergen expedition had been planned by the English envoy at Copenhagen, Sir Gilbert Talbot, with the approval of the supposedly neutral King of Denmark who was to share the

booty equally with the English. Two valuable homeward-bound
Dutch fleets—de Ruyter's from the Guinea expedition and the
Dutch East India fleet—seemed likely, relying on Danish
neutrality, to anchor shortly in a Norwegian port, probably
Bergen. The English were to surprise them there, unimpeded by
the local authorities. A message from Talbot to Sandwich (which
did not reach him until after the raid) conveys the cynicism of the
plan, particularly in relation to the town governor's role:

> you are not to be surprised if he seem to be highly displeased with
> your proceeding and that he make high complaint thereof against
> you, which nevertheless will be but in show to amuse the Hollanders
> and excuse himselfe outwardly to the world.
>
> (Quoted by Tedder, p. 128, see below.)

[In the event almost everything went wrong. There were errors
and confusions among the English from the earliest stages in
preparation, including over who was to command the expedition. Weather conditions were difficult. Neither of the expected
fleets was caught. All the same, on July 23 Sandwich 'got
certain news . . . that there was now 28 sail of the Straits and
French and Portugal ships of Holland' at Bergen, and after a long
council of war during which news arrived of a further fleet in or
near the port he detached a squadron of 20 ships (including the
Revenge, a number of fourth- and fifth-rates and fire-ships)
under the command of Rear-Admiral Sir Thomas Teddiman.
The squadron anchored outside Bergen on Monday, July 21,
sent messages to the governor and, having been favourably
received, in the words of Sir Thomas Clifford 'sailed merrily on'
and anchored close to the castle.

It seems certain that the English command, which had not
received all Talbot's messages, expected the governor of Bergen
to give active support in the planned attack. In fact, through a
mixture of reluctance and policy (a Danish fleet was expected
imminently which might enable the Danes to monopolize the

booty) he began a series of delaying negotiations which lasted
until early on Wednesday morning. During this time the Dutch
placed four ships in a line across the harbour, moved their guns
so as to train the maximum possible fire on the English, and
constructed a number of temporary forts on land.

[Rochester's account of the immediate events is well-informed
and accurate. The English attacked at about 5 a.m. The Dutch
retaliated from sea and land, and after a fierce, confined battle
lasting about three and a half hours with the wind blowing
straight out of the harbour, the English, blinded by smoke and
unable to use their fireships, were forced to retire taking one
prize with them but perhaps leaving a ketch to sink. 118 men
had been killed, including six captains and Rochester's companions Edward Montague (cousin of the Earl of Sandwich)
and John Windham, another gentleman volunteer. 239 were
wounded. The Dutch claimed about 100 casualties in all.

[Despite the bravado of his letter home, Rochester was deeply
affected by certain events in the battle which he discussed much
later with Gilbert Burnet. Burnet's often-quoted account of
this part of their conversation provides a moving supplement to
the version Rochester sent to his mother:

> when he went to Sea in the Year 1665, there happened to be in the
> same Ship with him Mr. *Mountague* and another Gentleman of
> Quality, these two, the former especially, seemed perswaded that
> they should never return into *England*. Mr. *Mountague* said, He was
> sure of it: the other was not so positive. The Earl of *Rochester*, and
> the last of these, entred into a formal Engagement, not without
> Ceremonies of Religion, that if either of them died, he should appear,
> and give the other notice of the future State, if there was any. But
> Mr. *Mountague* would not enter into the Bond. When the day came
> that they thought to have taken the *Dutch*-Fleet in the Port of
> *Bergen*[,] Mr. *Mountague* though he had such a strong Presage in his
> Mind of his approaching death, yet he generously staid all the while
> in the place of greatest danger: The other Gentleman signalized his
> Courage in a most undaunted manner, till near the end of the

Action; when he fell on a sudden into such a trembling that he could scarce stand: and Mr. *Mountague* going to him to hold him up, as they were in each others Arms, a Cannon Ball killed him outright, and carried away Mr. *Mountague's* Belly, so that he died within an hour after. The Earl of *Rochester* told me that these Presages they had in their minds made some impression on him, that there were separated Beings: and that the Soul either by a natural sagacity, or some secret Notice communicated to it, had a sort of Divination: But that Gentlemans never appearing was a great snare to him, during the rest of his life.

(Burnet, 16–18).

[The general contemporary view of the Bergen débâcle is reflected in 'The History of Insipids', a lampoon often attributed to Rochester but now thought to be by John Freke:

> The Bergen business was well laid,
>   Though we paid dear for that design,
> Had we not three days parling stay'd,
>   The Dutch fleet there, Charles, had been thine:
> Though the false Dane agreed to sell 'um,
> He cheated us and saved Skellum.

(Yale *POAS*, i, 247)

(See: A. W. Tedder, *The Navy of the Restoration*, Cambridge, 1916; R. C. Anderson, ed., *The Journal of Edward Mountagu First Earl of Sandwich*, 1928; F. R. Harris, *The Life of Edward Mountagu*, 1912.)]

From the Coast of Norway amongst the rocks aboard
the Revenge, August the 3ᵈ

Madam
I hope it will not bee hard for your Laˢᵖ to believe that it hath binn want of opportunity & noe neglect in mee the not writing to your Laˢᵖ all this while, I know noe body hath more reason to express theire duty to you, than I have, & certainely I will

never bee soe imprudent as to omitt the occasions of doing it. there have many things past since I writt last to your La^{sp} wee had many reports of de Ruyter & the Eastindia fleete but none true till towards the 26 of the last month wee had certaine intelligence then of 30 saile in Bergen in Norway, a haven belonging to the King of Denmarke but the Port was found to bee soe little that it was impossible for the greate ships to gett in, soe that my Lord Sandwich ordered 20 saile of fourth & fifth rate friggotts to goe in and take them. they were commanded by S^r [Thomas] Teddeman one of the vice Admiralls, it was not fitt for mee to see any occasion of service to the King without offering my self, soe I desired & obtained leave of my Ld Sandwich to goe with them & accordingly the thirtieth of this month wee sett saile at six a clock at night and the next day wee made the haven Cruchfort (on this side of the town 15 leagues) not without much hazard of shipwrack, for (besides the danger of Rocks wch according to the seamens judgment was greater than ever was seene by any of them) wee found the Harbour where twenty shipps were to anchor not bigg enough for seven, soe that in a moment wee were all together one upon another ready to dash in peeces having nothing but bare Rocks to save our selves, in case wee had binn lost; but it was gods greate mercy wee gott cleare & only that, for wee had noe humane probability of safety; there wee lay all night and by twelve a clock next day gott off and sailed to Bergen full of hopes and expectation, having allready shared amongst us the rich lading of the Eastindia merchants some for diamonds some for spices others for rich silkes & I for shirts and gould wch I had

Source: MS. Harl. 7003, f. 193.
Date: as heading, August 3, [1665].
the 26 of the last month: the date of Sandwich's council of war. The news had
    arrived by July 23 (see Sandwich's Journal, ed. cit., above, July 23, 1665).
30 saile: for this and other details in Rochester's fairly reliable account, see
    the general notes above.
Cruchfort: Kors Fjord, south-west of Bergen.

most neede of, but reckoning without our Hoast wee were faine
to reckon twice, however wee came bravely into the Harbour in
the midst of the towne and Castles and there Anchored close
by the Dutch men, wee had immediately a message from the
Governour full of civility & offers of service, wch was returned
by us Mr Mountegue being the messenger, that night we had 7
or ten more wch signified nothing, but mere empty delayes. it
grew darke & wee were faine to ly still untill morning, all the
night the Dutch carried above 200 peices of Cannon into the
Danish Castells & forts, and wee were by morne drawne into a
very faire halfe moone ready for both towne & ships, wee
received severall messages from breake of day untill fower of
clock much like those of the over night, intending nothing but
delay that they myght fortifie themselves the more, wch being
perceived wee delayed noe more but just upon the stroke of
five wee lett flye our fighting Coulours & immediately fired
upon the shipps, who answered us immediately & were seconded
by the Castles & forts of the towne, upon wch wee shott at all
and in a short time beat from one of theire greatest forts some
three or fower thousand men that were placed wth small shott
upon us; but the Castles were not to bee [shot] downe, for
besides the strength of theire walls they had soe many of the
Dutch Gunns (wth theire owne) wch played in the hulls & Deckes
of our shipps, that in 3 howers time wee lost some 500 men &
six Captaines our Cables were cut & wee were driven out by the
winde, wch was soe directly against us that wee could not use our
fireships wch otherwise had infallybly done our business, soe wee
came off having beate the towne all to peices without losing one
shipp, wee now lie off a little still expecting a wind that wee may
send in fireshipps to make an end of the rest, Mr Mountegue &
Thom: Windhams brother were both killed with one shott just

Mr *Mountague being the messenger:* last-minute attempts at negotiation with the
governor of Bergen were made by Edward Montague, an experienced
diplomat who had on several occasions acted as intermediary between
Charles and the Earl of Sandwich in 1660.

by mee, but God Almyghty was pleased to preserve mee from any kind of hurt, Madam I have bin tedious but begg your La^{sps} pardon who am

Your most obedient son
Rochester

I have binn as good a husband as I could, but in spight of my teeth have binn faine to borrow mony ——

Rochester ?to his wife ?*1667*

Madam

If itt were worth any thing to bee belov'd by mee you were the richest woman in ye world. but since my Love is of soe little vallue, chide y^r owne eyes for making such poore conquests; Though I am justly proude of being y^{rs}, yett give mee leave to tell you, there cannott bee more glory in y^r service than there is pleasure & true Pride in freedome; this I write to assure y^r La^{sp} 'tis nott through vanity that I affect the title of y^r servant, but that I feele a truth wth in my heart, wch my mouth rather does confess than Boast of,—That there is Left for mee, noe pleasure but in y^r smiles, noe life but in y^r favour, noe Heaven but in y^r Love; When I deserve soe ill, that you would Torment, kill & Damn mee, Madam you need but Hate mee.

husband: steward.

Source: MS. Harl. 7003, f. 262.

Date: ?1667. Although the Contents page of MS. Harl. 7003 describes it as 'The Earl to a Lady: a Love Letter', implicitly linking it with the notes to Elizabeth Barry printed in *Familiar Letters*, its presence in a collection otherwise mostly addressed to members of the family suggests that it may have been written to Elizabeth Malet, perhaps, since he calls her 'your Ladyship', soon after their marriage on January 29, 1667.

Rochester to his wife   ?1667-9

I kiss my deare wife a thousand times, as farr as imagination &
wish will give mee leave, thinke upon mee as long as it is
pleasant & convenient to you to doe soe, & afterwards forgett
mee, for though I would faine make you the Author & foundation of my happiness yet would I not bee the cause of your
constraint [or] disturbance, for I love not my selfe soe [m]uch
as I doe you, neither doe I value my [o]wne satisfaction equally
as I doe yours

                          farewell
                                    Rochester

Rochester at Newmarket to his wife   ?1667-9

                                              Newmarkett
I'le hould you six to fower I love you wth all my heart, if I
would bett wth other people I'me sure I could gett two to one,
but because my passion is not soe extensive to reach to every
body, I am not in paine to satisfye many, it will content mee if
you beleive mee & love mee.

                                    R

For my Wife

Source: MS. Harl. 7003, f. 224.
Date: ?1667-9 (a love-letter, with no reference to any children).

Source: MS. Harl. 7003, f. 226.
Date: ?1667-9 (see previous letter).
Newmarkett: the King and court went to the races at Newmarket every year
in the autumn and sometimes also in the spring.

Rochester to his wife   *?1667–9*

Persons in Absence aught to notifie Returns reciprocrally, affectionately reconsell'd with humble Redentigration; however correspondent to the Sencesibility of equivalent Appollegy; neither can I distinctly glorifie myself collaterally in superlative Transcendency with more Lustre, than by vanting myself

Your most humble Servant,
ROCHESTER.

Madam,
I humbly thank you for your kind Letter, and am in Hopes to be very speedily with you, which is ever a great Happiness to

Your humble Servant,
ROCHESTER.

To Rochester from George Villiers, Duke of Buckingham   *1667–73*

My Lorde
Being to goe a hunting tomorrow and not knowing whither I shall returne time enoughf to doe my duty to his Maiesty, I hope

Source: *The Museum*, xxxi, May 23, 1747, p. 156. Because of the spelling joke, this letter has not been modernized, though no MS survives.

Date: ?1667–9 (no reference to any children).

'The Letter to his Lady, ill spelt and full of hard Words, is no doubt a very natural Burlesque on that kind of Stile which then was and still is in use among a certain Sort of People' (*Museum* editors' preface). See the discussion of Rochester's use of parody in the letters, Introduction, p. 24.

reconsell'd: (i.e. recounselled) reconciled. The word has a strong religious association, particularly of purification after prophanation. (*OED*).

Redentigration: (i.e. redintegration) reconciliation. The word was used by Cowley, whom Rochester admired. (*OED*).

Source: MS. Harl. 7003, f. 276.

Date: 1667–73 (Rochester became a Gentleman of the Bedchamber on March 14, 1667 (*CSPD*); Buckingham lost all his Court employments early in 1674 (*DNB*).)

Buckingham: (1628–87), one of Rochester's closest friends. See pp. 145f., 151f.

your Lordship will not refuse mee the fauour to wayte for mee
that day and ly in the bedchamber at night. I am very perticular
in this matter that your Lordship may see I am a man of businesse, and take the liberty of troubling you upon this occasion becawse I had rather bee oblidged to you then any body else. I am

My Lorde

Your lordships

Most humble seruant

Buckingham.

Sunday at night.

Rochester in London to his wife at Adderbury   *May, 1668*

You know not how much I am pleased when I heare from you,
if you did you would bee soe oblidging to write oftner to mee, I
doe seriously wth all my heart wish my selfe wth you, & am
endeavouring every day to get away from this place which I am
soe weary of, that I may be said rather to languish than live in
it; My Lady Warr intends to honour you with a visitt on monday
come sennight (she saies), in the meane time pray behave y^r
selfe well, & let me heare of noe miscarriages, if I doe, my
partiallyty to you will make mee apt to lay them to y^r maide
Joane, as I have before, rather than to you. here is noe newes

wayte for mee: i.e. carry out my Court-attendance duties.
ly in the bedchamber: one Gentleman of the Bedchamber was required every
   night to sleep in the same room as the King; see p. 19.

Source: MS. Harl. 7003, f. 216.
Date: May, 1668 (see note on the Duchess of Monmouth, below).
Lady Warr: Rochester's mother-in-law had married Sir John Warre after the
   death of her first husband, Elizabeth's father, John Malet in 1656.
monday come sennight: Monday week.
miscarriages: in view of the rest of the sentence, perhaps simply 'accidents', in
   general.

but that the Dutches of Rich[mond] will loose an eye the Dutchess of Mun[mouth] has put out her thigh, my Ld Hawley is to bee married to my Lady Munnings, hee drinks puppydogg water to make himselfe handsome but shee they say having heard hee had a clapp, has refused to enter into conjugall bonds till shee bee better assur'd of his soundness.

Remember mee to Mrs Baxter

For the Countess of Rochester
at Adderbury neare Banbury
Oxfordshire.

Rochester to his wife   ?

I am sorry, Madam to heare that you are not well & as much troubled that you should beleive I have not writt to you all this

the Dutches of Rich[mond]: Frances Stuart, one of the most hotly pursued Court women, became the Duke of Richmond's third wife in 1667. She was disfigured by an attack of smallpox in March, 1668 which badly affected one of her eyes. (See Pepys, *Diary*, March 30 and August 30, 1668.)

the Dutchess of Mun[mouth]: Anne, Duchess of Monmouth, dislocated her hip while dancing at her lodgings on May 9, 1668. (See Pepys, *Diary*, May 9 and 15, 1668.) She was permanently lamed.

Ld Hawley: Elizabeth's maternal grandfather Francis, 1st Baron Hawley, was 60 in 1668. I have not been able to find any other reference to his pursuit of Lady Munnings or Mannings.

puppydogg water: 'puppy-water' was used, though not internally, as a cosmetic. Pepys complains (March 8, 1664): 'Up, with some little discontent with my wife upon her saying that she had got and used some puppy-dog water, being put upon it by a desire of my aunt Wight to get some for her; who hath a mind, unknown to her husband, to get some for her ugly face.'

Mrs Baxter: unidentified.

Source: MS. Harl. 7003, f. 218.
Date: uncertain.
5

while, I who am not used to flatter doe assure you, that if two
letters from mee came not to y^r hands this last weeke & that
before, they have miscarried; nothing is soe much my business
now as to make hast to waite on you, I thinke in that I comply
wth your commands as I doe with the hearty inclinations of

Your humble servant

Rochester

For the Countess of Rochester

Rochester at Adderbury to his father-in-law, Sir John Warre   1667-9

S^r

I was forc't by the news of my wives being not well to post out
of towne before I could have the opportunity of waiting on you,
wch I confess was a fault I should not otherwise have bin guilty
of, & I therefore purpose at the beginning of the next weeke to
returne, that I may receive y^r pardon, & put you in minde of
performing y^r promise, & shew you the way hither, where
(upon my word) is one very much transported wth the thoughts
of being soe happy as to see you & for my owne part I begg you
to beleive that noe man does more heartily desire any good in
this world, than I doe the honour of your freindshipp & kindnes
nor can any one have a greater value & service for you than has

Your humble servant

Rochester

Satturday

These For Sr John Warr.

Source: MS. Harl. 7003, f. 258.
Date: 1667-1669 (after Rochester's marriage, before Sir John's death).
Sir John Warre: see p. 52, *Lady Warr.*
waiting on you: paying you a visit.
hither: to Adderbury.

Rochester to his wife at Adderbury   ?*1669*

I am very glad to heare news from you & I thinke it very good
when I heare you are well, pray bee pleas'd to send mee word
what you are apt to bee pleas'd with, that I may shew you how
good a husband I can bee; I would not have you soe formall as
to Iudge of the kindness of a letter by the length of it but beleive
of every thing that it is as you would have it.

For the Countess of Rochester att
Adderbury neare Banbury in
Oxfordshire

Rochester in Paris to his wife   *April 12, 1669*

I should be infinitely pleased (Madam) with the newes of your
health hitherto I have not bin soe fortunate to heare any of you
but assure y^r selfe my wishes are of your side as much as is

Source: MS. Harl. 7003, f. 231.
Date: ?1669. Rochester's enquiries about his wife's health possibly link the
letter with the previous and following ones.

Source: MS. Harl. 7003, f. 199.
Date: as letter, April 22 new style: i.e. April 12 in England. Rochester made
himself unwelcome at Court in February, 1669, when he attacked Thomas
Killigrew in the presence of the King. He was received back into favour
but almost immediately got into trouble again by becoming involved in a
duel between the Duke of Richmond and James Hamilton. He set out for
Paris on March 12, taking a letter from the King to his sister, the Duchess
of Orleans (see p. 61), and was still there on July 15. Some time in June he
was involved in a fight at the Opera (Pinto, p. 72). He was back in London,
quarrelling with the Earl of Mulgrave, in November. (See Pepys, *Diary*,
February 17, 1669: *HMC*, 7th Report, Appendix, 531a, 488b; Greene,
p. 77.)
your health: a reference to the birth of their first child, Anne, who was
baptized on April 30. (See p. 17.)

possible, pray only that they may bee effectuall, and you will not
want for happiness

Paris the 22 of Aprill
French Stile

For the Countess of Rochester

Rochester in London to his wife at Adderbury   *July, 1670*

[Henrietta, Duchess of Orleans, was the fifth daughter of
Charles I by Queen Henrietta Maria, and a favourite of both the
English and French courts, particularly with Charles II. Despite
rumours of a possible marriage with Louis XIV she was married
in 1661 to Philippe, Duke of Anjou and now Duke of Orleans.
The Duke, a homosexual, became a notoriously jealous husband
whose sometimes well-founded suspicions were encouraged by
his lover the Chevalier de Lorraine, who hoped to estrange the
couple. These marital difficulties were exacerbated when
'Madame' became the chief agent between the English and
French courts during their negotiations in the late '60s. After her
visit to Dover in 1670 the Duke became increasingly annoyed by
her secret meetings with Louis XIV, and suspicious of the
reasons for his gratitude to her. He took her into retirement at
St Cloud on June 24. On the 26th they were called to Versailles
by Louis; but finding his wife in a secret conversation with the
King, Philippe immediately carried her off home again.

[Despite generally poor health, Madame insisted on bathing in
the Seine against her doctor's advice and on June 29, after
drinking chicory water, she suffered violent pains and vomiting.
These events are recorded in a letter from Ralph Montagu, the
English Ambassador in Paris, whose account is very closely
followed by Rochester:

Source: MS. Harl. 7003, f. 202.
Date: early July, 1670 (see above).

Paris,
June 30, 1670. Four in the morning.

My Lord,—I am sorry to be obliged by my employment, to give you
an account of the saddest story in the world, and which I have
hardly the courage to write. Madame, on Sunday the 29th of this
instant, being at St. Clou with a great deal of company, about five
o'clock in the afternoon called for a glass of chicory water that was
prescribed for her to drink, she having for two or three days after
bathing found herself indisposed. She had no sooner drunk this but
she cryed out she was dead, and fell into Madam Mechelbourg's
arms, desired to be put to bed, and have a confessor. She continued
in the greatest tortures imaginable, till 3 o'clock in the morning,
when she dyed; the King, the Queen, and all the Court being there,
till about an hour before . . .

(Quoted by J. Cartwright (Mrs Julia Ady) in *Madame:
a Life of Henrietta . . . Duchess of Orleans*, London, 2nd edn,
1900, p. 358.)]

Pray doe not take itt ill that I have writt to you soe seldome
since my comming to towne, my being in waiting; upon the sad
accident of madam's death, (for wch the King endures the
highest affliction immaginable) would not allow me time, or
power to write letters, you have heard the thing, but the
barberousness of the manner you may guess att by my relation:—
Mounsieur since the bannishment of the Chevallier de Lorrain
(of wch hee suspected Madame to have bin the Authour) has ever
behav'd himselfe very ill to her in all things, threatning her upon
all occasion that if shee did not gett Lorrain recall'd, she myght
expect from him the worst that could befall her; it was not now
in her power to performe what hee expected, soe that shee
returning to Paris, hee immediately carries her away to S^nt Cloud
where having remain'd fifteen dayes, in good health she having
bin bathing one morning, and finding her self very dry call'd

madam: Henrietta, Duchess of Orleans (see above).
Mounsieur: the Duke.
the bannishment, etc.: in February, 1670. See J. Cartwright, op. cit. pp. 308f.

for some succory water (a cordiall julepp she usually tooke upon
these occasions) and being than very merry discoursing wth
some of the Ladyes that were wth her shee had noe sooner
swallow'd this succory water but immediately, falling into
Madam de Chatillons armes, she cryed she was dead, and
sending for her confessour after 8 howers infinite torment in her
stomack and bowells shee died, the most lamented (both in
france & England) since dying has bin in fashion, but I will not
keepe you too long upon this dolefull relation it is enough to
make most wives in the world very melancholy, but I thanke
you for my cheeses, my sugar of roses, & all my good things,
pray lett it not bee necessary for mee to put you too often in
mind of what you ought not to bee less forward in doing than I
in advising, I hope you will give mee noe occasion to explaine
my selfe, for if I am putt upon that you will find mee very
troublesome, I receiv'd noe letter from you wth an inclos'd to y^r
mother nor doe I beleive you writt any, besides I finde by
another circumstance that the returnes of letters betwixt London
and Adderbury are very tedious; if you write to mee, you must
direct to Lincolnsendfeild the house next to the Dukes playhouse
in Portugall row, there lives yr humble servant Rochester, I
writ a letter to the ranger I would faine know if hee received it
and whither I am like to receive an answer or noe, pray send
mee some ale and rem[em]ber mee to nan, shee has a present

succory water: chicory water, a cooling drink.
julepp: julep, a sweet medicinal drink.
Madam de Chattillon: the Duchess of Mecklembourg, constant companion
   of Henrietta.
sugar of roses: sugar roset, a confection made with essence of roses. Sixteenth-
   century herbals refer to its qualities as a cure for 'chollerick vomiting'.
   (*OED.*)
Lincolnsendfeild: Lincoln's Inn Fields.
Dukes Playhouse: in Portugal Row, by Lincoln's Inn.
nan: their daughter Anne.
shee: unclear. Anne could not have been a godmother, yet. Perhaps Rochester
   meant to write 'from her godmother', or perhaps the bearer of the letter
   was Anne's godmother and is the 'shee' referred to.

for her godaughter but I doe not know w^ht it is, send mee word
and if it bee not as it should bee, Ile send another—

tarara—

For the Countess of
Rochester att Adderbury
neare Banbury Oxfordshire

tarara—: 'tara' is an exclamation, like 'tantara'. It is used in *The Rehearsal*
(IV.i), attributed to Buckingham but probably written jointly by several
of the Court circle. (*OED, Tara, int.*)

1670–71
Staying Much with his Lady

*To Rochester at Adderbury from Charles
Sackville, Lord Buckhurst in London*   *December 24, 1670*

Saturday 24

his majesty is graciously pleased to make mee his Leiuetenant
generall against the world the flesh and the deuil a thursday I
shall begin my march, and in the mean time am resolued to
behaue my self so discreetly, that the Enemy as vigilant as hee is
shall haue no suspition of the quarrell; I must confess tis with
some unwilingness; I begin a war against a prince I haue so long
seru'd under but since 'pax queritur bello' and this short dispute

Source: MS. Harl. 7003, f. 268.
Date: December 24, 1670 (see below).
Charles Sackville, Lord Buckhurst: (1638–1706), later Earl of Middlesex and
Earl of Dorset, one of Rochester's closest friends.
his Leiuetenant generall . . .: Buckhurst was to represent Charles II as god-
father to Rochester's son, Charles Wilmot, at his baptism on January 2,
1671.
the world the flesh and the deuil: in the Anglican Baptism service, the god-
parents, in the name of the child, renounce 'the devil and all his works, the
vain pomp and glory of this world, with all covetous desires of the same.'
Everyone knew this promise by heart, having learned it in the Catechism,
where it appears in a form slightly closer to Buckhurst's quotation: 'I
should renounce the devil and all his works, the pomps and vanity of this
wicked world, and all the sinful lusts of the flesh.'
the Enemy: the Devil (another reference to the Catechism: 'I pray unto
God . . . that he will keep us . . . from our ghostly enemy').
pax queritur bello: a conflation of two Latin tags: 'paritur pax bello'
(Cornelius Nepos, *Epaminondas*, v) and 'saevis pax quaeritur armis'
(Statius, *Thebais*, vii, 554). Both can be roughly translated in the same way:
'peace is procured by war.'

is like to purchase a firmer peace hereafter I will obey my king
and my deare deare L Rochester
Your most humble and faithfull seruant,
C. Buckhurst.

For the Earle of Rochester

*To Rochester at Adderbury from Charles
Sackville, Lord Buckhurst, in London*   *December 28, 1670*

My Dear Lord   Wensday
I am just now comanded not to stir till after thursday for wee
are like to haue warm doings in the house, about Couentryes
nose; I look upon myselfe as a greater sufferer then hee in this
busines; since it takes from the greatest satisfaction I can euer
haue in this world my dear Lord Rochesters company, but my
conscience will not giue me leaue to defer my Journey any
longer than Saturday pray let your coach meet us at Alesbury, I

Source: MS. Harl. 7003, f. 270.
Date: December 28, 1670. (The Wednesday after the previous letter.)
till after thursday: parliament adjourned from Thursday December 29 to
  Tuesday January 3. (JHC.)
Couentryes nose: Sir John Coventry, M.P. for Weymouth, had asked, during
  the course of a parliamentary discussion of a governmental proposal to
  tax playhouses, 'whether did the king's pleasure lie among the men or the
  women that acted.' On December 21, while on his way home from
  supper, he was taken out of his carriage by a gang led by Sir Thomas
  Sandys, who tied him up in his cloak and cut his face, slicing his nose to
  the bone. The 'warm doings in the house' did not in fact occur until a
  week after parliament reassembled after its recess. The wounding was
  discussed angrily on January 10, and a bill for banishing Coventry's
  assailants was read, revised and passed over the rest of the month. They
  were never captured. (DNB; JHC, January 10–25, 1671.)
Alesbury: Aylesbury, Buckinghamshire, two-thirds of the way from London
  to Adderbury.

hope both you and my L Wilmot will pardon my leauing him
thus long in a danger you are niether of you as yet sensible of
Your most humble seruant
C. Buckhurst

For the Earle of Rochester

To Rochester from Savile in London   *January 26, 1671*

London. Ian: ye 26th 1670
My Lord of Rochester has soe much obliged mee by two letters
of different stiles that I know not whether I ought to applaud
most his good parts, or his good Nature, I am sure they neither
of them need any thing that I can say of them; in his L^{ps} last
letter my brother thinkes himself as much concerned as I &
therefore does joyne with mee in most humble thanks. As to y^e
former, my most deplorable excuse was made why I was not at
ye Christning of my Ld Wilmot by my Ld Buckhurst & Sedley,
it is a ceremony I was sorry to misse but yr L^p staying much
with y^r Lady will I presume once a yeare furnish us with such
solemnityes, & for ye next I hope I shall have noe reason to
fayle paying my attendance, in ye mean time ye L^{ps} has been

my L Wilmot: Rochester's baby son. (See previous letter.)
a danger: like the reference to Buckhurst's 'conscience', a joke about Charles
  Wilmot's moral vulnerability before baptism.

Source: MS. Harl. 7003, f. 296.
Date: as heading, January 26, 1671 (1670/1).
of different stiles: perhaps a letter like the one to his wife on p. 51.
my brother: George Savile (1633–95), Viscount (later Marquess of) Halifax.
ye Christning of my Ld Wilmot: see previous two letters.
Buckhurst & Sedley: Charles Wilmot's godfathers Lord Buckhurst (see
  previous letters) and Sir Charles Sedley, a courtier and dramatist and
  another of Rochester's close friends.

extreamly wanting heere to make friends at ye custome house
where has been lately unfortunately seized a box of those leather
instruments y^r L^p carryed downe one of, but these barbarian
Farmers prompted by ye villanous instigation of theire wives
voted them prohibited goods soe that they were burnt without
mercy notwithstanding y^t Sedley & I made too journeys into y^e
Citty in theire defence, by this my L^d, you see what things are
done in y^r absence, & then pray consider whether it is fitt for
you to bee blowing of coales in the country when there is a
revenge due to ye ashes of these Martyrs. Y^r L^p is chosen
Generall in this warr betwixt the Ballers & ye farmers nor shall
peace by my consent ever bee made till they grant us our wine
and our D^s custome free. My Ld Vaughan is come to towne &
has brought out of Wales severall new arguments concerning
some points you wott of, in fine here are soe many reasons for
y^r L^{ps} returne hither that I know not how you can stay a moment
where you are without breach of justice to your profession and
of kindnesse to y^r friends who linger in your absence though

those leather instruments: dildoes.
Farmers: customs officers.
the Ballers: a group of young courtiers. See Pepys, *Diary*, May 30, 1668:
> over to Fox-hall and there fell into the company of Harry Killigrew,
> a rogue, newly come back out of France but still in disgrace at our
> Court, and young Newport and others, as very rogues as any in the
> town, who were ready to take hold of every woman that came by
> them. And so to supper in an arbor; but Lord, this mad bawdy talk
> did make my heart ake. And here I first understood by their talk the
> meaning of the company that lately were called 'Ballers', Harris
> telling how it was by a meeting of some young blades, where he was
> among them, and my Lady Bennet and her ladies, and there dancing
> naked, and all the roguish things in the world. But Lord, what loose
> cursed company was this that I was in tonight; though full of wit and
> worth a man's being in for once, to know the nature of it and their
> manner of talk and lives.
My Ld Vaughan: John Vaughan (1640–1713), later third Earl of Carbery,
MP for Camarthen. Pepys called him 'one of the lewdest fellows of the
age, worse then Sir Ch. Sidley [i.e. Sedley]' (*Diary*, November 16, 1667).
He married Savile's niece, Anne Savile, as his second wife, in August,
1682. (*DNB*.)

they can not properly bee said to thirst after you, being perpetually drinking y^r health, noe man oftner nor in greater
glasses then my L^d of Rochesters most everything he would
have mee

Hen. S.

These to ye R^t Honble the Earle of Rochester humbly present

Rochester to his wife at Adderbury   *1671-2*

You have order'd the matter soe well that you must of necessity
bee att the place you intend before I can give you an answer to
y^r letter, yett meethinks you ought rather to have resolv'd in the
negative since it was w^{ht} I desir'd of you before, but the happy
conjunction of my mother and you can produce nothing but
extreme good carriage to mee as it has formerly done; you shew
y^r selfe very discreet and kind in this and in other matters, I wish
you very well, & my mother, but assure you, I will bee very
backward in giving you the trouble of
Your humble servant
Rochester

For the Countess of Rochester,
att Adderbury neare Banbury;
Oxfordshire
my wife.

Source: MS. Harl. 7003, f. 235.

Date: ?1671-2 (see following letter).

the place you intend: the gist seems to be that the Countess has written from
    Enmore (her Somerset home) to tell Rochester she is on her way to
    Adderbury and to a reconciliation with his mother, the failure of which is
    discussed in the letter on p. 74.

good carriage: i.e. kind treatment (*OED, Carriage, sb.,* 14). In view of the end
    of the letter, this and what follows is presumably ironic.

my wife: as distinct from the Dowager Countess, his mother.

Rochester to Joseph Williamson   *1671*

I was att the office to desire a favour of you, it is that you will gett a mandamus drawne for Mr Robert parsons to bee chosen an Esquire Bedell, the King has promis'd it, but in regard it requires haste, I would intreate you it might bee ready for signing to night; I am your very humble servant

                        Rochester.

For Mr Williamson

Rochester in London to his wife at Adderbury   ?*1671–2*

Madam

It was the height of Complyance forc't mee to agree y^r La^{sp} shoult come into Oxfordshire if it does not please you 'tis not my fault, though much my expectation; I receive the compliment you make in desiring my company as I ought to doe; But I have

Source: P.R.O., MS. S.P. Dom. Car. II, 281A, no. 231.
Date: 1671 (pencilled date on MS, consistent with Parsons's appointment at Adderbury—see below—and Williamson's not yet having been knighted).
Joseph Williamson: (1633–1701), then Arlington's busy and influential secretary, and in 1674 his successor as Secretary of State. He was knighted in January, 1672. (*DNB*.)
mandamus: writ issued in the King's name.
Mr Robert parsons: (1647–1714) became Rochester's mother's chaplain after taking his M.A. in April, 1670, and acted as curate at Adderbury. He preached Rochester's funeral sermon in 1680. Rochester's letter, which may have been prompted by an anxiety to restore good relations with his mother (see previous and following letters), does not seem to have had any result, though other requests were made to Williamson on Parsons's behalf by his friends. (*CSPD*, August 21, 1671, p. 439.)
Esquire Bedell: title of a ceremonial university office.

Source: MS. Harl. 7003, f. 201.
Date: ?1671–2. See *the little I get here*, below.
into Oxfordshire: i.e. to Adderbury from Enmore; see p. 64.

a poore living to gett that I may bee less Burdensome to y^r La^{sp}; if y^r La^{sp} had return'd moneys out of Somerts for the Buying those things you sent for they myght have bin had by this time, But the little I gett here will very hardly serve my owne turne, however I must tell you that 'twas Blancourt's fault you had nott Holland & other things sent you a fortnight agoe, next weeke I goe into the West & att my returne shall have the Happiness of waiting on y^r La^{sp}

Rochester in Bath to Savile in London   *June 22, ?1671*

Whither Love, Wine, or Wisdome (wch rule you by turnes) have the present ascendent, I cannott pretend to determine att this distance, but good Nature wch waites about you with more dilligence than Godfry himselfe, is my security that you are not unmindfull of y^r Absent freinds; to bee from you, & forgotten by you att once, is a misfortune I never was Criminall enough to

the little I get here: payments on Rochester's annuity as a Gentleman of the Bedchamber were heavily in arrears. See his pleas to the Treasury in 1672, pp. 78–9 and notes.

Blancourt: a servant of Rochester's family's (see pp. 127, 249).

Holland: a kind of linen.

the West: to Elizabeth's Somerset estates.

Source: MS. Harl. 7003, f. 256.

Date: June 22, ?1671. The reference to 'the black and fair countesses', see below, suggests 1671, which is one of only three years (1671, 1673, 1674) in the relevant period when Rochester could have been in Bath on June 22, his rough whereabouts on the same date in other years being known to have been somewhere else (see Wilson, p. 80). Wilson opts for 1674 because early printed texts of 'A Pastoral Dialogue between Alexis and Strephon' suggest that Rochester visited Bath some time that year, but Vieth believes the poem to have been written earlier (*Complete Poems*, p. 172).

Godfry: a servant.

merritt, since to the Black & faire Countesses, I villanously betray'd the dayly addresses of y^r divided Heart; you forgave that upon the first Bottle & upon the second on my Conscience would have renounc'd them and the whole sex; oh that second bottle Harry is the sincerest, wisest, & most impartiall down-wright freind we have, tells us truth of our selves, & forces us to speake truths of others, banishes flattery from our tongues and distrust from our Hearts, setts us above the meane Pollicy of Court prudence, wch makes us lye to one another all day, for feare of being betray'd by each other att night; And before god I beleive the errantest villain breathing is honest as long as that bottle lives and few of that tribe dare venture upon him att least among the Courtiers & statesmen; I have seriously considerd one thinge, that of the three Buisnisses of this Age, Woemen, Polliticks & drinking, the last is the only exercise att wch you & I have nott prouv'd our selves Errant fumblers; if you have the vanity to thinke otherwise, when we meete next lett us appeale to freinds of both sexes & as they shall determine, live & dye sheere drunkards, or intire Lovers; for as wee mingle the matter, it is hard to say wch is the most tiresome creature, the loving drunkard or the drunken Lover.

[I]f you ventur'd y^r fatt Buttocks a gallopp to Portsmouth, I doubt not but through extreame galling you now lye bedridd of the piles or fistula in Ano, & have the Leasure to write to y^r Country aquaintance, wch if you omitt I shall take the liberty to

---

the Black and faire Countesses: Wilson (p. 81) plausibly suggests the Countesses of Falmouth and Northumberland, both associated with Savile's friend and patron the Duke of York in 1671. For Savile's sally into the bedroom of the recently widowed Lady Northumberland see the following letter. She married Ralph Montagu in August 1673. Lady Falmouth married Rochester's and Savile's friend Buckhurst in June 1674. *Black* means dark-haired.

Pollicy: cynical political cunning.

venture upon: attack.

fistula in Ano: anal ulcer.

conclude you very proude: such a Letter should bee directed to mee att Adderbury neare Banbury, where I intend to bee within these three dayes.

Bathe the 22 of June from
Your obedient humble servant
Rochester

For Mr Henry Savile

To Rochester at Adderbury from John Muddyman
in London   *September, 1671*

My dear Lord Rochester,
I am very [sorry you] find your eyes can neither endure wine nor water: I haue beene soe employd about your business here in towne that I haue not had the leisure to write to you all [this] while, but I hope when you come you will find all things in soe very good order, that you will giue that small omission to my great merit and dilligence in promoting the good old Cause. I presume Killegrew (whose talent is description) has given you to understand what a diner and day you lost when you left us at Gyroes. I confess your suddain start surprised me as much as Harry Savile's attempt upon My Lady Northumberland: but

Source: Bath MS., Portland Papers, ii, f. 236.
Date: September, 1671. (See note on *Lady Northumberland,* below.)
John Muddyman: not, *pace* Wilson (p. 7), the journalist Henry Muddiman, but his cousin, son of Sir William Muddiman. (J. G. Muddiman, *The King's Journalist,* London, 1923, pp. 85–6.)
your eyes: See Introduction, pp. 20, 33.
the good old Cause: usually the Parliamentary, but here, ironically, the Cavalier cause and specifically the fortunes of Rochester's family.
Killegrew: either the dramatist Thomas Killigrew, or his son Harry.
Gyroes: Garraway's Coffee House. The Savile-Northumberland incident is mentioned in 'Queries and Answers from Garraway's Coffee-House'. (*Poems on State Affairs,* 1716, iii, 67.)
Lady Northumberland: Elizabeth, widow of Joceline Percy, Earl of Northumberland, who had died in May, 1670. She was much sought-after,

possible that story is not vulgar enoug in your parts for a simile
yet; if you have mett with it already you may skipp it here if not

---

and remarried in 1673 to Ralph Montagu, the Earl of Montagu, having
'mist her ayme of Dutchess of Yorke' but having rejected the young Duke
of Somerset. (*G.E.C.*, Northumberland.)

The story of Savile's attempted seduction of the Countess is repeated
in a letter of September 12, 1671, from the Attorney-General Sir Heneage
Finch to his son:

You will not wonder that we yet hear nothing from my Aunt Rumsey,
if the Northamptonshire story have reached to Ragley. It seems my
Lord Lieutenant and Lady Clanbrazil called in at Woborn, from whence
the whole company went to Althorp to my Lord Sunderlands, and
with them Mr. Henry Savil, who hath long been countenanced by my
Lady Northumberland, whether as her dead Lord's friend or as
envoyé and *ambasciatore d'amore* from a great person [the Duke of
York] nobody knows, but he presumed so farr upon it that at Althrop,
having gotten from my Lord Sunderland a master key on pretence of
going into the billiard, he made use of it at one of clock at night to
enter into my Lady Northumberland's chamber in his shirt and
nightgown, and there kneeling down by the beside told her, Madam,
I am come with great confusion of face to tell you that now which I
durst not trust the light with, the passion with which I serve and
adore you. She with amazement rung the bell, but not daring to trust
to that leaps out of her bed and at another door which H. Savil was
not aware of, opens a way into the gallerye, through which she ran
barefoot and knockt at the chamber door where my Lord Ashby's
lady was lodged and made a shift to gett into bed to her, leaving H.
Savil to meditate how to come off of this adventure. He presently
retires to his lodging and writes a letter to my Lady Northumberland
in which he would [have] turned all this to ridicule as if the house
had been haunted. On the other side my Lady, as if it had been really
so, scarce recovered so much breath and spirit by morning as to be
able to tell her story. As soon as it was known and understood H.
Savil was by the generall consultation to which all the house was
presently summoned that the place would quickly grow too hott for
him, and steals down into the stable and rides away post. Newes of
his flight being brought up Mr. Russel [the Countess's brother-in-
law] and some others pursue him to London, but find him not. Some
say he is gon into France and Mr. Russel follows him. The whole
Court and town abhors the insolence and wish the Avenger of
Honour may overtake him and prosper in his chastisement.

(*HMC*, 71, *Finch*, ii, 3–4.)

read it as I heard it: The Lady was at my Lord Sunderlands and the knight errant lodg'd in a conuen[ient] apartment, from whence in the dead night tempted by his euill genius, or the earthy part of his loue, hee mad[e] a sally into her bed chamber: hauing the day before stole a way the bolt soe that there was nothing but a latch to lift: but whither offering any ruder proofes of his passion or contenting himselfe with a simple, though unseasonable declaration of it: her scrupulous virtue was soe alarumd that shee rang a litle bell that hung unfortunatly at her beds head with that Violence as if not only a poore louers heart but the whole house had been on fire: Wherupon her seruant coming into the roome our disconsolate louer retird ouerwhelmd with despayer and so forth. The famyly breath nothing but battell murther and suddain death; soe that either way wee are like to loose a very honest fellow. But I hope shall gaine this wholsome document, how necessary it is for euery man to stick to his owne calling. This side shall carry you within the rayles of Couent garden where you shall behold the furious combat of Ashton and Etheridg which ended hapily in a fall on Ashtons part company interposing, and not suffering um to renew fight. Now my lord as to a concerne of your owne: Fate

---

Lord Sunderlands: Althorp, seat of Robert Spencer (1640–1702), second Earl of Sunderland. It was a lively house to stay in. Sunderland frequently entertained royal mistresses, and his wife was an enterprising hostess: at Euston, the country house of Lord Arlington, some time in 1671 she arranged a mock-wedding between Louise de Kérouaille and the King. (*DNB*.)

The famyly: see Heneage's letter, above.

document: lesson, warning (*OED*).

calling: social station. (*OED, Calling,* 10.)

This side: of the page. (A new side is begun here.)

furious combat of Ashton and Etheridg: Etherege was a keen duellist. His opponent on this occasion was Edmund Ashton, a lieutenant-colonel in the Life Guards, who was notoriously small. (See *Letters of Sir George Etherege,* ed. F. Bracher, California, 1974, pp. xvii, 113.)

has taken care to vindicate your proceeding with Foster; whoe
is discouerd to bee a damsell of low degre, and very fit for the
latter part of your treatment: noe northerne lass but a mere
dresser at Hazards scoole: her uncle a wyght that wields the
puisant spiggot at Kensington: debaucht by Mr. Buttler a
gentleman of the cloak and gallow shoe—an order of knighthood, uery fatall to mayndenhead. But I forget to tell you what
a rout this adventure of Savile's has causd among all the lady's
drolles: the ladyes will now not conuerse with old Waller,
without their women in the rome: Some haue submited to be
searcht by a Jury of midwiues as Robin Spencer Harry Norwood
Nick Armorer Lord Hawley and are upon due examination
restord to all their rights and priuiledges, but the rest are all

Foster: one of the women named in *A Letter from Artemisia in the Town to
Chloe in the Country* (ll. 175–188) as making fools of their men: 'Foster
could make an Irish lord a Nokes.' Nothing else is known about her, or
about Rochester's affair with her.

dresser: maid employed as a dresser.

Hazards: fortune's.

a wyght that wields the puisant spiggot: i.e. a tapster, or barman. For the
hudibrastic mock-romance style, cf. p. 201 and see Introduction, p. 24.

Mr. Buttler: unidentified.

a gentleman of the cloak and gallow shoe: i.e. someone unfashionably dressed.
Cloaks were associated with Puritanism (*OED, Cloak,* 2b). *Gallowshoe* (or
goloshoe, galosh, etc.) was a name applied to various kinds of footwear, but
particularly, as now, to bad-weather outer shoes—in the Restoration, a
poor man's alternative to hiring a coach. (See *OED, Galosh.*)

rout: retreat *or* fuss. (*OED, Rout, sb.,* 2; 8.)

drolles: amusing companions.

Waller: Edmund Waller, the poet, then aged 65.

Robin Spencer: presumably the Countess's host, the Earl of Sunderland
himself (see above).

Harry Norwood: Colonel Henry Norwood, an Officer of the King's Bedchamber until 1673, and later M.P. for Gloucester. (Pepys, *Diary,*
February 9, 1666; *HMC,* 36, *Ormonde,* vii, 30.)

Nick Armorer: Sir Nicholas Armorer, member of the Irish Parliament. (See
CSPD, June 6, 1671.)

Lord Hawley: Rochester's wife's grandfather, Francis Hawley, then in his
lively sixties. See also p. 52, where Rochester talks of his having planned
to marry again but having been forestalled by his intended's suspicions
that he had a clap.

turnd to grass this hard season: Bartholmey and Southwark
fares being done tis thought twill goe very hard with most of
um this winter. My lord having almost pumpd my selfe drye of
all my news to seru[e] your Honor I take leaue to rest

Your Most humble seruan[t]
to Comand
John Muddyman

Bartholmey and Southwark fares: St. Bartholomew's fair began on August 24,
Southwark fair in mid-September. (Pepys, *Diary*, September 11, 1660;
September 25, 1663, etc.)

1672–73
Run Away Like a Rascal

Rochester to his wife at Adderbury   *Early 1672*

Runn away like a rascall without taking leave, deare wife, it is
an unpollish't way of proceeding wch a modest man ought to be
asham'd of, I have left you a prey to your owne immaginations,
amongst my Relations, the worst of damnations; but there will
come an hower of deliverance, till when, may my mother bee
mercifull unto you, soe I committ you to what shall ensue,
woman to woman, wife to mother, in hopes of a future appearance
in glory; the small share I coud [?not] spare you out of my
pockett I have sent as a debt to Mrs Rouse within a weeke or ten
dayes I will returne you more, pray write as often as you have
leisure to

Y^r

Rochester.

Source: MS. Harl. 7003, f. 192.
Date: Early 1672 (see *my neice Ellen*, below).
your owne immaginations, etc.: cf. the jingle at the end of the letter on p. 101,
    'If you are pleased, I am pleased; were my mother pleased, all were
    pleased, which God be pleased to grant'.
I committ you, etc.: a parody of the funeral service: 'we therefore commit his
    body to the ground: earth to earth, ashes to ashes, dust to dust; in sure
    and certain hope of the Resurrection to eternal life'. The phrase
    'appearance in glory' is also liturgical, coming from the Epistle for Easter
    Day: 'then shall ye also appear with him in glory'.
Mrs Rouse: probably the wife of Dudley Rouse, Receiver (i.e. treasurer) for
    both Windsor Castle and the County of Oxfordshire (*CTB*, 1669–72,
    passim.)

remember mee to Nan, & my Ld Willmott.

you must present my service to my Cosins, I intend to bee att the
deflowring of my neice Ellen if I heare of it. Excuse my ill paper
& my ill manners to my mother they are both the best the place
& age will [a]fford

For my wife.

Rochester to his wife   ?

Wood & firing, wch were the subject matter of y^r last, I tooke
order for before, & make noe question but you are serv'd in
y^t affaire before this, Mr Cary seldome fayling in any thing hee
undertakes when you have other service for mee you will
informe mee of itt & nott doubt of the utmost observance from
                         Yr h[umble] s[ervant]
                              R[ochester]

For the Countess of Rochester.

Nan: their daughter, Anne.
Ld Willmott: their son, Charles.
my Cosins: probably the Lees (see below). 'Cousins' was a flexible term.
my neice Ellen: Eleanor Lee, elder daughter of Rochester's step-brother Sir
    Henry Lee, became engaged to James Bertie, Lord Norreys, later Earl of
    Abingdon, in the winter of 1670–1 and married him at Adderbury on
    February 1, 1672. (*GEC*, Abingdon; *Verney Memoirs*.) She died in 1691
    at the age of 33 and was commemorated by Dryden in 'Eleonora'.

Source: MS. Harl. 7003, f. 233.
Date: uncertain.
Mr *Cary:* John Cary, an Oxfordshire squire and friend of the family who
    frequently acted on behalf of Rochester's mother. (*Verney Memoirs*,
    passim.)

Rochester to his wife at Adderbury   *?*

[I] cannot deny to you that Heroick resolutions in woemen are things of the wth I have never bin transported wth greate admiration nor can bee if my life lay on't for I thinke it is a very impertinent virtue, besides considering how men & woemen are compounded, that as heate and cold, soe greateness and mean[n]ess are necessary ingredients that enter both into the making up of every one that is borne, now when heate is predominant we are termed hott, when cold is wee are call'd cold; though in the mixture both take theire places, els our warmeth would bee a burning, & our cold an excessive freezing, soe greateness or virtue that sparke of primitive grace is in every one alive, & likewise meaness or vice that seede of originall sin is (in a measure) alsoe; for if either of them were totally absent, men & woemen must bee perfect angells, or absolute divills, now from the preheminence of either of these quallityes in us wee are termed good or bad; but yett as contrarietyes though they both reside in one body, must they ever bee opposite in place, thence I inferr that as heate in the feete makes cold in the head, soe may it bee wth probabilyty expected too, that greateness & meaness should bee as oppositely seated, & then a Heroick head is liker to bee ballanc't wth an humble taile, besides reason, Experience has furnish'd mee with many Examples of this kinde, my Lady Morton nell Villers, & twenty others, whose honour was ever soe exessive in theire heads that they suffered a want of it in every other part; thus it comes about

Source: MS. Harl. 7003, f. 247.
Date: uncertain.
For the parodic style of the letter, a burlesque of contemporary philosophical and scientific discourse, see Introduction (p. 24).
meaness: inferiority.
Lady Morton: Marjory, second wife of the spendthrift William Douglas, Earl of Morton. (Pepys, *Diary*, April 26, 1669.)
nell Villers: sc. 'Nell, Villiers'. Nell is Nell Gwynn; Villiers is Barbara Villiers, Duchess of Cleveland.

madam that I have noe very greate estime for a high spirited
Lady; & therefore should bee glad that none of my freinds
thought it convenient to adorne theire other perfections with
that most transcendent Accomplishment; it is tollerable only in
a waiting gentlewoman, who to prove her selfe lawfully
decended from Sr Humphry her greate Uncle, is allow'd the
affectation of a high spiritt, & a naturall inclination towards a
gentile convers; This now is a letter, & to make it a kinde one I
must assure you of all the dotage in the world, & then to make
it a civill one, downe att the bottom wth a greate space betweene
I must write

Madam

I have too much respect for you to come neare you whilst I am
in disgrace, but when I am a favorite againe I will waite on you;
Your most humble servant
Rochester.

For the Countess of Rochester att Adderbury.

Rochester to his wife   ?

I could scarce guess what measures you would take upon the
Letter I sent you, & therfore have sent this second epistle
together wth my Coach, humbly requesting you to doe therin as

a waiting gentlewoman: perhaps Rochester is thinking of Foster (p. 71).

Source: MS. Harl. 7003, f. 206.
Date: uncertain.

in your wisdome shall seeme meete, I being wth greate advised-
ness most excellently your humble servant

Rochester

My humble duty to mother, & my service to My Cozens.
For the Countess of Rochester

Rochester to his wife   ?

The Difficultyes of pleasing y^r La^{sp} doe encrease soe fast upon
mee, & are growne soe numerous that to a man less resolv'd
than my self never to give itt over, itt would appeare a madness
ever to Attempt itt more, but through your frailtys myne ought
nott to multiply; you may therfore secure y^r self that it will not
bee easy for you to put mee of[f] of my constant resolutions to
satisfy you in all I can; I confess there is nothing will soe much
contribute to my assistance in this as y^r dealing freely wth mee,
for since you have thought itt a wise thing to trust mee less and
have reserves itt has bin out of my powr to make the best of my
proceedings effectuall to what I intended them; att a distance I
am likeliest to learn y^r mind, for you have nott a very oblidging
way of delivring itt by word of Mouth, if therfore you will
lett mee know the perticulars in which I may bee usefull to you,
I will shew my readiness as to my owne part, & if I faile of the
success I wish, itt shall not bee the fault of

Your humble servant
Rochester

I intend to bee att Adderbury some time next weeke

For the Countess of Rochester
my wife

My Cozens: see p. 73.

Source: MS. Harl, 7003, f. 243.
Date: uncertain.
my wife: as distinct from the Dowager Countess, his mother.

To Rochester at Enmore from Sir Robert Howard in London   *1672*

Trea[su]ry Chamber, Aug. 29'h 1672.

My Lord:
I will not dispute whither you or I shall receiue the most
aduantage to our freindship but I am soe well satisfied with my
share that I resolue to Continue the Contract, and will performe
all that's in my pow'r to preuent your hauinge the least equitable
cause to breake it, and in order to soe iust and aduantegeous
disigne, I will wish as much speed as I can endeauor to serue
you in the particulars of your wages and pension, I cannot
promise soe derectly as I wish, for the Kings affaires are at this

Source: MS. Harl. 7003, f. 289.
Date: as heading, August 29, 1672.
Sir Robert Howard: (1626–1698) Secretary to the Treasury and an old friend
  of Rochester's family. Rochester's contribution to his never-completed
  play *The Conquest of China* (see p. 116) may have been a reward for his
  official help over Rochester's pension (see below and see J. Treglown,
  'The Dating of Rochester's "Scaen" ', *R.E.S.*, N.S. xxx, 1979, pp. 434-6).
the Contract: i.e., their friendship.
your wages and pension: although a number of money warrants in Rochester's
  favour were authorized by the Treasury during 1671 and 1672, he had the
  same difficulty as other Treasury creditors of the time in cashing them.
  Certainly there were heavy arrears on his annuity as a Gentleman of the
  Bedchamber, acknowledged to be £3,375 on March 18, 1672, but reduced
  by £250—presumably as a result of his pleas to Howard and to the
  Treasurer, Clifford (see next letter)—on September 28. (*CTB.*) Rochester's
  biographers have tended to assume that records of Treasury warrants
  imply actual payment, so it is worth emphasizing that this £250 reduction
  bears no relation to the various warrants for £1,000 and £500 made out
  to him during 1671 and 1672, but never successfully encashed. For
  details of the general Stop of the Exchequer, see the Introduction to
  CTB for this period.
the Kings affaires . . . very pressinge: 1672 was, for example, the year of the
  Stop of the Exchequer, by which many of the chief bankers in London,
  from whom the King had borrowed £1,300,000, were made bankrupt:
  see above.

time very pressinge, but I will doe all that is possible to assure
you of the truth of what I professe to be soe really.

Yo^r most faithfull freind and
humble seruant
Ro. Howard

For the Earle of Rochester these
Leave this at the post house in Taunton to be sent to Enmore
in Somersetshire.

To Rochester from Thomas, Baron
Clifford of Chudleigh   *September 7, 1672*

Whitehall Sept. 7. 72

My Lord
I thanke yr L^{d}ship for your [o]bliging letter to me, I will ever
to my power doe you service, this resolution is not newly taken
vp but I have had it ever since I had the honor first to know
you, we did this day set in our weekely bill 500£ for yr L^{d}ship
you must direct some body to follow it and empower him to
receiue the money, the season of the year is such that I know
you will not be long from vs noe one shall be gladder to see you
then My Lord

Yr Lordships
Most Affectionate and
most obedient servt
Clifford

My Ld Rochester

Source: MS. Harl. 7003, f. 302.
Date: as heading, September 7, 1672.
Thomas Clifford: (1630–1673) treasurer of the King's household from 1668
    until his death. He became Lord High Treasurer in November, 1672.
    (DNB.)
500£ for yr L^{d}ship: see p. 78. The warrant Clifford refers to was issued on
    September 9, but seems to have been cancelled subsequently. (CTB,
    September 9, 1672.)

Rochester in London to his wife in the country   *?1671–4*

Madam

I am extreamly troubled for the sickness of y^r son as well in consideration of the affliction it gives you, as the dearness I have for him myself; you have I heare done mee the favour to expect me long in the Country where I intended to have bin long agoe, but Court affaires are more hardly sollicited now then ever, and having follow'd them till I had spent all my owne money & y^rs too, I was forc't to stay somthing longer here till I had contriv'd a supply, wch being now dispatch'd I have nothing to hinder mee from what I heartily desire wch is to waite on y^r La^sp at Adderbury

I am y^r humble servant
Rochester

For my Wife

Rochester in London to his wife at Adderbury   *?September, 1672*

Deare Wife

I recover soe slowly, and relaps soe continually that I am allmost weary of my self, if I had the Least strength I would come to Adderbury, but in the condition I am, Kensington and back is a voyage I can hardly support; I hope you excuse my sending you

Source: MS. Harl. 7003, f. 241.
Date: ?1671–4 see below.
  For the mock-royal style of this letter, with its reference to 'supply', cf. Introduction, p. 24.
the sickness of y^r son: cf. p. 82, which was written between 1671 and 1674.
sollicited: conducted (*OED, Solicit, v.,* II. 8).

Source: MS. Harl. 7003, f. 214.
Date: ? September, 1672. (Rochester's having to fetch his money seems to relate to the letter on p. 79.)
till I am well enough to fetch it: see p. 79.

noe money, for till I am well enough to fetch itt my self they will not give mee a farthing, & if I had not pawn'd my Plate I believe I must have starv'd in my sickness, well god Bless you & the Children whate[ver] becomes of

Y^r humble servant

Rochester

If Mrs Catford be gone pray enclose this Letter wth the first you send.

For my Wife.

Rochester to his wife   ?

Wonder not that I have not writt to you all this while for it was hard for mee to know what to write, upon severall accounts, but in this I will only desire you not to bee too much amaz'd at the thoughts my mother has of you, since being meere immaginations they will as easily vanish as they were groundlessly created, for my owne part I will make it my endeavour they may, what you desired of mee in your other letter shall punctually bee perform'd; you must I think obey my mother in her commands to waite on her at Alesbury as I tould you in my last letter, I am very dull at this time & therefore thinke it pitty in this humour to testify my selfe to you any farther only deare wife I am your humble servant

Rochester

These For the Countess of Rochester.

Mrs Catford: unidentified.

Source: MS. Harl. 7003, f. 209.
Date: uncertain.
Alesbury: Aylesbury, Buckinghamshire.

Rochester in London to his wife   *October 18, ?1672*

From our Tubb att M^ns Fourcards this 18nt of Octob:

Wife; Our gutt has allready binn griped, & wee are now in bed
soe that wee are not in a condition of writing either according to
thy merritt or our desert, wee therefore doe command thy
benigne acceptance of these our letters in what way soever by us
inscribed or directed, willing thee therewithall to assure our sole
daughter & heire issue female, the Lady ann part. of our best
respects, this with your care & dilligence, in the erection of our
furnaces is att present the utmost of our will & pleasure —

Rochester in London to his wife in the country   *1671–4*

It were very unreasonable should I not love you whilst I beleive
you a deserving good Creature, I am allready soe weary of this

Source: MS. Harl. 7003, f. 189.

Date: as heading, October 18, [?1672]. The connection between Rochester's
   having his gut griped and the previous letters to his wife suggests 1672, a
   date broadly confirmed by the reference to his 'sole daughter & heire issue
   female' (after Anne's birth in 1669 and Charles's in 1670–1, but before
   Elizabeth's in 1674).

M^ns Fourcards: not, *pace* Prinz and subsequent editors and biographers,
   'Mrs Fourcard', but Monsieur Florence Fourcade or Forcade, one of the
   king's surgeons. (*CSPD*, June 3, 1675; May 1, 1678.)

griped: griping was a method of operating on a stone by squeezing it
   between finger and thumb. For Rochester's belief that he was suffering
   from a stone see Introduction, p. 34.

Lady ann: their daughter.

part: (mock-legal) party. This is another letter in mock-royal style.

Source: MS. Harl. 7003, f. 190.

Date: 1671–4 (after Charles's birth, before Elizabeth's).

place That upon my word I could bee Content To pass my winter att Cannington, Though I apprehend the toediousness of itt for you, pray send mee word What lyes in my power to doe for y^r service and ease here or wherever els you can impl[o]y mee and assure y^r selfe I will neglect your concerne noe more than forgett my owne; Twas very well for y^r son as ill as you tooke it that I sent him to adderbury, for it proues att last to bee the kings evill that troubles him & hee comes up to London this weeke to bee touch't; my humble service to my Aunt Rogers, & Nanne.

I write in bed & am affraid you can't reade it.

Rochester at Battersea to his wife at Adderbury   ?

If you heare not from mee it is not that I either want time or will to write to you, I am sufficiently at leasure & thinke very

Cannington: one of Elizabeth's family estates in Somerset, a few miles from Bridgwater.

y^r son: cf. p. 80, on Charles Wilmot's illness.

the kings evill: scrofula, which was supposed to be curable by the monarch's touch. The practice of touching for the king's evil continued from the reign of Edward the Confessor to the death of Queen Anne in 1714, reaching its height as an expression of monarchist fervour during the reign of Charles II. Evelyn records an occasion when 'There was so greate & eager a concourse of people with their children, to be touch'd of the *Evil,* that 6 or 7: were crush'd to *death* by pressing at the *Chirurgions* doore for Tickets. &c.' (E. S. de Beer, ed., *The Diary of John Evelyn,* 6 vols., 1955. March 28, 1684.)

Aunt Rogers: unidentified.

Nanne: Rochester's eldest daughter, Anne.

Source: MS. Harl. 7003, f. 239.
Date: uncertain, but see below.

often of you, but you would expect an account of w^ht has
befall'n mee, wch is not yett fitt for you to know, only thus much
I will tell you, it was all in vindication of you; I am now at
Battersy & have binn this weeke here, wounder not if you
receive few letters from mee, & bee satisfied wth this that I
thinke continually of you & am your

Rochester

For the Countess of Rochester at Adderbury neare Banbury
Oxfordshire
putt it in the Banbury bagg
wth care

Rochester to his wife   *1671–4*

Madam,
This illustrious person is my ambassador to my son and daughter.
The presents she brings are great and glorious and I hope will
gain her an equal reception. To my son she will deliver a dog of

---

w^tt has befall'n m^e: Rochester was so often in trouble of one kind or another
    that it is impossible to be sure what this refers to, but 'in vindication of
    you' suggests a duel, perhaps the one with Lord Dunbar narrowly
    prevented by the Earl Marshal on March 21, 1673. (*JHL*.)
Battersy: Rochester's uncle and aunt, Sir Walter and Lady St. John, lived in
    the manor house at Battersea.

Source: The Museum, xxxi, May 23, 1747, p. 157.
Date: 1671–4 (references to one daughter and a son).
this illustrious person: the bearer of the letter.
my son and daughter: Charles and Anne, see p. 18.
a dog: William Wissing painted a portrait of Charles Wilmot sitting with a
    King Charles Spaniel on his knee. (See Greene, p. 154.)

the last litter of lap-dogs so much reverenced at Indostan for the honour they have to lie on cushions of cloth of gold at the feet of the Great Mogul. The dog's name is Omrah. To my daughter I have sent the very person of the Duchess la Vallière, late mistress to the King of France, dried up and pined away to a very small proportion by fasting.

Indostan: Travel books like Bernier's *Travels in the Mogul Empire*, first published in an English translation in 1671, contained descriptions of the great Mogul's wealth which may have suggested these ideas to Rochester, who had not himself been outside Europe. Indostan is a satirical name for Whitehall, here, and the Great Mogul is Charles II. The King's love of dogs was the subject of much contemporary comment. Evelyn records that 'He tooke delight to have a number of little spaniels follow him, & lie in his bed-Chamber, where often times he suffered the bitches to puppy and give suck' (*Diary*, February 6, 1685).

Omrah: a lord of a Mohammedan court, especially that of the great Mogul. Bernier discusses the functions and status of the omrahs in some detail.

the Duchess la Vallière: Louise de la Vallière (1644–1710), Louis XIV's mistress from 1661, was superseded by Mme. de Montespan in 1667. She remained mistress *en titre* until 1674, when she entered a convent. (See John B. Wolf, *Louis XIV*, 1968; Philippe Erlanger, *Louis XIV*, translated by Stephen Cox, 1970.) Presumably Rochester had sent Anne a doll, perhaps a *pandore*, or fashion doll, of the kind which preceded French fashion prints as a means of advertising the latest designs, fabrics and styles of coiffure. (See Madge Garland, *The Changing Form of Fashion*, 1970, pp. 82–5.)

1673-75
Imminent Peril of Sobriety

To Rochester at Adderbury from Dryden in London   April–May, 1673

My Lord

I have accused my self this moneth together for not writeing to you; I have called my self by the names I deserved of vnmannerly and vngratefull. I have been uneasy, and taken vp the resolutions of a Man who is betwixt Sinn and Repentance, convinc'd of what he ought to do, and yet unable to do better. At the last I deferred it so long, that I almost grew hardened in the neglect; and thought I had suffered so much in your good opinion, that it was in vain to hope I could redeem it. So dangerous a thing it is to be inclined to sloath, that I must confesse once for all, I was ready to quit all manner of obligations And to receive, as if it were my due, the most handsom Compliment, couched in the best language I have read, and this too from my Lord of Rochester, without showing my self sensible of the favour. If your Lordship cou'd condescend so farr to say all those things to me, which I ought to have sayd to you, it might reasonably be concluded, that you had enchanted me to believe those praises, and that I owned them in my silence. Twas this consideration

Source: MS. Harl. 7003, f. 293.

Date: April–May, 1673; see notes on *an Ill Dedication* and *the Great Duke of B——,* below.

vngratefull: Rochester was a patron of Dryden's at this time, and according to the Dedication of *Marriage A-la-Mode* made some 'amendment' to the play 'e're it was fit to be presented'. (Dryden, *The Dramatic Works,* ed. M. Summers, 1932, iii, 189.)

that mov'd me at last to put off my Idlenesse. And now the
shame of seeing my self overpayed so much for an ill Dedication,
has made me almost repent of my Addresse. I find it is not for
me to contend any way with your Lordship, who can write
better on the meanest Subject than I can on the best. I have
onely ingag'd my selfe in a new debt, when I had hop'd to
cancell a part of the old one; And shou'd either have chosen
some other patron whom it was in my power to have oblig'd by
speaking better of him than he deserv'd, or have made your
Lordship onely a hearty Dedication of the respect and Honour I
had for you, without giveing you the occasion to conquer me,
as you have done, at my own weapon.

My onely relief is, that what I have written is publique, and I
am so much my own friend, as to conceale your Lordships
letter. for that which would have given vanity to any other
poet, has onely given me confusion; You see, my Lord, how farr
you have pushed mee; I dare not own the honour you have done
me, for feare of showing it to my own disadvantage. You are
that Rerum Natura of your own Lucretius, Ipsa suis pollens

---

an ill Dedication: Dryden's *Marriage A-la-Mode,* registered on March 18,
carries a long dedication to Rochester thanking him for his financial and
artistic help and for recommending the play to the King, whose approval
helped its theatrical reception. Dryden goes on, with his usual lavishness,
to praise Rochester's wit and honour, to suggest that the high status of
writers at Court is entirely due to him, and to claim that indeed he
resembles God in having 'made' Dryden: 'I became your Lordship's (if
I may venture on the Similitude) as the world was made, without knowing
him who made it; and brought onely a passive obedience to be your
Creature.' (Summers, ed. cit., iii, 190.)

You are that Rerum Natura . . . : 'your own Lucretius' flatters Rochester, who
certainly began a free translation of the 7000–8000 line *De Rerum Natura,*
but seems to have got no further than line 50. Dryden's quotation of i, 48
(literally 'itself [i.e. divinity/Rochester] mighty by its own power, not at
all in need of us'), was elegantly rendered by Rochester in his second
fragment:

> The gods, by right of nature, must possess
> An everlasting age of perfect peace;

opibus, nihil indiga nostri: You are above any Incense I can give
you; and have all the happinesse of an idle life, joined with the
good Nature of an Active. Your friends in town, are ready to
envy the leysure you have given your self in the Country:
though they know, you are onely their Steward, and that you
treasure up but so much health as you intend to spend on them in
winter. In the meane time you have withdrawn your selfe from
attendance, the curse of Courts. You may thinke of what you
please, and that as little as you please, (for in my opinion),
thinking it selfe, is a kinde of paine to a witty man; he finds so
much more in it to disquiet, than to please him. But I hope your
Lordship will not omitt the occasion of laughing at the Great
Duke of B—— who is so uneasy to [him]self by pursuing the
honour of Lieuetenant Generall which flyes him, that he can
enjoy nothing he possesses. Though at the same time, he is so
unfit to command an Army, that he is the onely Man in the
three Nations who does not know it. Yet he still picques him
self, like his father, to find another Isle of Rhe in Zealand:
thinkes this dissapointment an injury to him which is indeed a
favour; and will not be satisfyed but with his owne ruine, and

> Far off removed from us and our affairs;
> Neither approached by dangers, or by cares;
> *Rich in themselves, to whom we cannot add;*
> Not pleased by good deeds, nor provoked by bad.
>
> (*Complete Poems*, p. 35; my italics.)

attendance: 'The action or condition of an inferior in waiting upon the
leisure, convenience, or decision of a superior' (*OED*).
witty: in the common Restoration sense of 'intelligent and sensitive'.
the Great Duke of B—— etc.: Buckingham hoped to take a leading part in
an invasion of Holland by the Zuyder Zee, a plan approved by Charles.
He was appointed Lieutenant-General to the Duke of York on May 13,
but failed to raise many troops. The scheme was inevitably compared with
the disastrous expedition his father led to France on June 27, 1627,
ignominiously defeated at the Ile de Ré on July 10. (*CSPD* May 13, 19,
and July 3, 7, 1673; Winifred, Lady Burghclere, *George Villiers, Second
Duke of Buckingham, 1628–1687*, 1903, pp. 275–7.)
Zealand: Sjaelland, Denmark.

with ours. Tis a strange quality in a man to love idlenesse so well
as to destroy his Estate by it; and yet at the same time to pursue
so violently the most toilesome, and most unpleasant part of
businesse. These observations would easily run into Lampoon,
if I had not forsworn that dangerous part of wit, not so much
out of good nature, But least from the inkhorn vanity of poets,
I should show it to others, and betray my self to a worse mis-
chief than what I designed my Enemy. This has been lately the
case of Etherege, who translating a Satyre of Boileau's, and
changing the French names for English, read it so often that it
came to their eares who were concerned; and forc'd him to
leave off the design e're it were half finished. Two of the verses
I remember.

> I call a spade a spade; Eaton a Bully
> Frampton a pimp, and Brother John a Cully.

But one of his friends, imagined these names not heroique
enough for the dignity of a Satyre, and changed them thus.

These observations would easily run into Lampoon: as they did, eight years later,
   in the character of Zimri in Dryden's *Absalom and Achitophel.*
inkhorn: 'literary' in a pejorative sense.
Boileau: Etherege's version is not otherwise known. The lines he is said to
   have imitated come from Boileau's *Satire* I, lines 51–4:

> Je ne puis rien nommer, si ce n'est par son nom,
> J'appelle un chat un chat, et Rolet un fripon,
> De servir un Amant, je n'en ai pas l'adresse.

Eaton: probably Sir John Eaton or Ayton, Gentleman Isher to Charles II.
   (*HMC* 70, *Pepys*, p. 255; and cf. Marvell's *Last Instructions to a Painter*,
   line 855.)
Frampton: Tregonwell Frampton (1641–1727). He is mentioned again as a
   pimp in 'The Lovers' Session' (1687), l. 55 (*Court Satires*, p. 178).
Brother John: presumably a brother of Tregonwell Frampton.
Cully: dupe.

I call a Spade a Spade; Dunbar a Bully
Brounckard a Pimp and Aubrey Vere a Cul[ly]

Because I deale not in Satyre, I have sent your Lo[rdship] a
Prologue and Epilogue which I made for our p[layers] when they

Dunbar: Robert Constable, 3rd Viscount Dunbar, with whom Rochester had
recently quarrelled (see p. 83). In February 1671, he and the Dukes of
Monmouth and Albermarle murdered a beadle named Peter Vernell,
'praying for his life upon his knees'. They were all pardoned. The scandal
is mentioned in a number of satires, particularly 'On the Three Dukes
Killing the Beadle' (Yale *POAS*, i, 172f.).

Brounckard: Henry Brouncker, cofferer to Charles II and Gentleman of the
Bedchamber to the Duke of York, for whom he acted as a pimp. Marvell
lists him among the procurers in *Last Instructions to a Painter* (l. 175).

Aubrey Vere: Aubrey de Vere, 20th Earl of Oxford. He was so much a
'cully' that his wife Diana was said to have been able to persuade him that
it was possible for a woman to conceive without a man. (See 'Satire',
ll. 47–8, in *Court Satires*, pp. 81f.)

our p[layers]: the details of the King's Players' visit to Oxford have been the
subject of inconclusive discussion (see C. E. Ward, ed. *The Letters of John
Dryden*, Durham, North Carolina, 1942, p. 147, and James Kinsley, ed.,
The Poems of John Dryden, Oxford, 1958, iv, 1947). The prologue and
epilogue in question were first printed in *Miscellany Poems* (1684). Dryden's
joke about his flattery is necessary, as it might have occurred to Rochester
that what Dryden had to say to the dons is very similar to the praise he had
just lavished on his patron in the dedication to *Marriage A-la-Mode* (see
above). Dryden describes the dons, as he had described Rochester, as
divinities who send out mere poets as ambassadors to the human race. He
says poets correct their 'manners' by those of the dons (in the dedication
to Rochester he says the pattern is the Court) and asserts that 'Poetry,
which is in *Oxford* made/An Art, in *London* onely is a Trade', where in the
dedication he says this is precisely what Rochester's influence prevented it
from becoming. But the lines Dryden must have been most nervous about
sending—if, indeed, they appeared at all in the MS. he let Rochester see—
might easily, with their allusion to Lucretius, be interpreted as an attack on
him and his friends (though they are overtly aimed at town wits, rather
than Court wits):

> There [in London] Haughty Dunces whose unlearned Pen
> Could ne'er Spell Grammar, would be reading Men.
> Such build their Poems the *Lucretian* way,
> So many Huddled Atoms make a Play,
> And if they hit in Order by some Chance,
> They call that Nature, which is Ignorance.
>
> (Kinsley, ed. cit. i, 370.)

went down to Oxford. I heare, [some say they] have succeeded; And by the Event your Lordship will judge how easy 'tis to passe any thing upon an University; and how grosse flattery the learned will endure. If your Lordship had been in Town, and I in the Country, I durst not have entertain'd you, with three pages of a letter; but I know they are very ill things which can be tedious to a man who is fourscore miles from Covent Garden. Tis upon this Conference that I dare almost promise to entertain you with a thousand bagatelles every week; and not to be serious in any part of my letter, but that wherein I take leave to call my selfe

Your Lordships most obedient servant
John Dryden.

Tuesday
For The Right Honourable The Earl of Rochester.

Rochester at Adderbury to Savile in London   *1673–4*

Dear Savile,
Do a charity becoming one of your pious principles, in preserving your humble servant Rochester from the imminent peril of sobriety, which, for want of good wine more than company (for I drink like a hermit betwixt God and my own conscience) is very like to befall me. Remember what pains I have formerly taken to wean you from your pernicious resolutions of dis-

bagatelles: trifles.

Source: FL i, p. 1. For modern spelling, see p. 39.
Date: 1673–4. Rochester's references to Savile's statesmanship and 'foreign interest and intelligence' suggest a date after his election as M.P. for Newark in 1673, which followed his tour as Envoy to France in 1672. The light-hearted tone of the letter distinguishes it from the embittered correspondence of the period 1675–6. The letter is a parody of a request for charity. See Introduction, p. 24.

cretion and wisdom. And, if you have a grateful heart (which is a miracle amongst you statesmen), show it by directing the bearer to the best wine in town, and pray let not this highest point of sacred friendship be performed slightly, but go about it with all due deliberation and care, as holy priests to sacrifice, or as discreet thieves to the wary performance of burglary and shop-lifting. Let your well-discerning palate (the best judge about you) travel from cellar to cellar and then from piece to piece till it has lighted on wine fit for its noble choice and my approbation. To engage you the more in this matter, know, I have laid a plot may very probably betray you to the drinking of it. My Lord —— will inform you at large.

Dear Savile, as ever thou dost hope to out-do Machiavel or equal me, send some good wine! So may thy wearied soul at last find rest, no longer hovering 'twixt th' unequal choice of politics and lewdness! May'st thou be admired and loved for thy domestic wit; beloved and cherished for thy foreign interest and intelligence.

Rochester.

Rochester at Adderbury to Savile in London   *1673-5*

Adderbury Teusday the 8th

Tis not the least of my happiness that I thinke you love mee, but

shop-lifting: antedates *OED*'s first example, 1698.
from piece to piece: a piece is a cask of wine.
no longer hovering: cf. Rochester's 'fluttering soul' in 'The Imperfect Enjoy-
     ment', lines 11-12.
intelligence: news.

Source: MS. Harl. 7003, f. 252.
Date: 1673-5. Louise de Kérouaille was created Duchess of Portsmouth in
     August, 1673; Rochester fell out with her in the summer of 1675 (see
     pp. 106f.). Wilson constructs an elaborate argument for a precise date—

the first of all my pretentions, is, to make itt appeare that I faithfully endeavour to deserve it, if there bee a reall good upon Earth 'tis in the Name of freind, without wch all others are meerly fantasticall, how few of us are fitt stuff to make that thing, wee have dayly the melancholy experience; However Deare Harry let us not give out nor despaire of bringing that about wch as it is the most difficult & rare accident of life, is allsoe the Best, nay perhaps the only good one; this thought has soe intirely possest mee since I came into the Country (where only one can think, for you att Court thinke not att all or att least as if you were shutt up in a Drumme, you can thinke of nothing but the noise is made about you) y^t I have made many serious reflections upon it and amongst others, gather'd one Maxim wch I desire should bee communicated to our freind Mr Guye that wee are bound in morallity and common Honesty to endeavour after competent riches, since it is certain that few men (if any) uneasy in their fortunes have prov'd firme & clear in their freindshipps; a very poore fellow is a very poore freind, and not one of a thousand can bee good natur'd to another who is nott pleas'd within himself; but while I grow into Proverbs, I

Tuesday, September 8, 1674—on the assumption that the reference to 'the doggdayes' must refer to July, August or September. But the period taken as the literal span of the dog-days in contemporary almanacs ends in early or mid-August (*OED, Dog-day*), and in any case Rochester may simply have been using the expression in its common figurative sense, meaning a bad time.

all others: i.e. all other 'goods'.

Mr Guye: Henry Guy (1631–1710), the politician, was a close friend both of Savile and of the King (he became a Groom of the Bedchamber in 1679). He conducted his affairs on the principle of court-dealings he recommended to Henry St. John: 'to be very moderate and modest in applications for friends, and very greedy and importunate in his own behalf.' Having obtained the estate at Great Tring on Henrietta-Maria's death in 1669, he built a magnificent house there, designed by Wren. On his death in 1710 he was believed to be worth £100,000. (*DNB; Savile Correspondence*, passim. See also p. 82.)

competent: appropriate (to our status). (*OED, Competent, a.,* 2.)

forgett that you may impute my philosophy to the Doggdayes &
living alone; to prevent the inconveniencyes of sollitude and
many others; I intend to goe to the Bath on sunday next in
visitation to my Ld Treasurer, bee soe Pollitick or bee soe kind,
(or a little of both wch is better) as to stepp down thither, if
famous affayrs att Windsor doe not deteyne you; Deare Harry I
am

Your hearty faithfull affectionate
humble servant
Rochester

If you see the Dutch: of P. very often take some opportunity to
talke to her about what I spoake to you att London.

For Mr Henry Savile
Leave itt att the Porters Lodge in Whitehall, desiring them to
deliver itt wth care & speede

Rochester at Adderbury to his wife at Enmore   *?1673–4*

The alteration of my mothers former resolutions (who is

the *Doggdayes:* see note on the date of the letter, above.
living alone: presumably his family had gone to Enmore. The letter may be
  contemporary with the following one.
my Ld Treasurer: Thomas Osborne, Earl of Danby (1631–1712), made Lord
  Treasurer on 19 June, 1673; he had a house in Bath. (*DNB.*)
the Dutch: of P.: the Duchess of Portsmouth, one of Charles's mistresses: see
  above.

Source: MS, Harl. 7003, f. 196.
Date: ?1673–4 (see below).
  The letter refers to Rochester's mother's tenacious hold on Adderbury.
The estate was partly freehold and partly held by lease on lives from the
Bishop of Winchester. The Dowager Countess, to whom it was bequeathed
by Rochester's father on his death in 1658, used the proceeds of the sale of
Wilmot House, Scotland Yard, to renew the Adderbury leases, securing

now resolv'd against ever moving from hence) puts mee upon some thoughts wch were allmost quite out of my head; but you may bee sure I shall determine nothing that does not tend as much to your reall happiness as lies in my power. I have therefore sent you this letter to prepare you for a remove first hither, & afterwards as fate shall direct which is (I find) the true disposer of things whatever wee attribute to wisdome or providence, bee therefore in a readiness upon the first notice from mee to put that in execution wch I shall first informe you particularly of—let me have an answar & dispatch this messenger quickly.

God bless you
yours
Rochester

These for the C. of R.

Rochester to his wife   ?1674

I will be with you shortly, & if my mother pleases, I will take the trouble of you & yours upon mee & thinke my selfe a very happy man, in the meane time, have but soe much discretion to

them after the deaths of Rochester in 1680 and his son in 1681 for her eldest grandson by her first marriage, Edward Lee, later Earl of Lichfield. In view of the fortunes coming to Rochester's daughters from their mother's family these arrangements were equitable, but the Dowager Countess's immovability clearly added to the friction between her and her son and daughter-in-law, and may have given Rochester an additional motive for pursuing the Rangership of Woodstock Park, a Court appointment carrying with it a house at Woodstock (the High Lodge). Rochester became Ranger in February, 1674. (L. F. Salzman, ed., *The Victoria History of the Counties of England: Oxford*, London, 1939–71, pp. ix, 15.)
some thoughts: perhaps of their both moving to Woodstock (see above).
hither: to Adderbury.

Source: MS. Harl. 7003, f. 264.
Date: ?1674 (see below).

dissemble a little & I will deliver you immediately; money you
shall have as soone as ever I come to you.

Rochester to his wife at Enmore   *1674-5*

Deare Wife I receiv'd y^r three pictures & am in a greate fright
least they should bee like you, by the biggnes of ye heade I
should apprehend you farr gone in ye Ricketts, by the severity of
the Count'nance, somwhat inclin'd to prayer & prophesy, yett
there is an alacrity in the plump cheeke, that seemes to signify
sack & sugar, & the sharp sighted nose has borrow'd quickness
from the sweete-smelling eye, I never saw a chin smile before, a
mouth frowne, & a forehead mump, truly ye Artist has done his
part, (god keep him humble) & a fine man hee is if his excel-
lencyes doe not puff him up like his pictures; the next impertinence I have to tell you is that I am coming down to you I
have gott horses but want a coach when that defect is supply'd
you shall quickly have the trouble of

Yr. humble servant

deliver you: ?from my mother. The letter seems to relate to the plans mentioned on p. 95. Perhaps Rochester had returned to London to push
through the Woodstock arrangements, with a view to moving his wife
and children to High Lodge.

Source: MS. Harl. 7003, f. 228.
Date: Summer 1674–Autumn 1675 (see *all the Babyes,* below).
y^r three pictures: the first part of the description could easily apply to Lely's
portrait of the Countess (see plate 4).
alacrity: liveliness.
sack & sugar: a reference to Falstaff ('If sack and sugar be a fault, God help
the wicked', *1 Henry IV* II. iv. 461, quoted again by Rochester in a letter
to Savile, p. 193.) In *Merry Wives* (III. v. 13) Falstaff admits to having 'a
kind of alacrity in sinking', which may have suggested the previous phrase
to Rochester. And, of course, when Falstaff died, 'his nose was as sharp as
a pen' (*Henry V* II. iii. 17).
mump: grimace.

Present my duty to my Lady & my humble service to my Sister, my brother, & all the Babyes not forgetting Madam Iane.

my Lady: Lady Warre, Rochester's mother-in-law.
my Sister, my brother: if (as the reference to Lady Warre suggests) the letter was sent to Enmore, these are probably Elizabeth's step-brother Sir Francis Warre and his wife Anne.
all the Babyes: presumably Anne, Charles and Elizabeth who, if the letter was written within the year after Elizabeth's birth around June, 1674, would have been aged about five, three, and a few months, respectively. An earlier date is made unlikely by 'all' (though of course there may have been other babies among the guests at Enmore); a later one would make 'Babyes' seem odd, and be hard to reconcile with the letter's buoyant tone.
Madam Iane: unidentified—the children's nurse?

1675
Dear Madam

Rochester to Elizabeth Barry   ?1675

Dear Madam,
You are stark mad, and therefore the fitter for me to love; and
that is the reason I think I can never leave to be

                               Your humble servant

Rochester to Elizabeth Barry   ?1675

Madam,
Your letter so transports me that I know not how to answer it.
The expressions are so soft and seem to be so sincere, that I
were the unreasonablest creature on earth could I but seem to
distrust my being the happier, and the best contrivance I can
think of for conveying a letter to me is making a porter bring it
my footman wherever I am, whether at St James's, Whitehall or
home. They are at present pulling down some part of my
lodging, which will not permit me to see you there, but I will
wait on you at any other place, what time you please.

Source: FL ii, p. 6.
Date: ?1675. For the approximate dates of Rochester's affair with Elizabeth
   Barry, see Introduction, pp. 29f.

Source: FL ii, p. 39.
Date: ?1675 (see p. 29).
St James's: the Duke of York's palace.
Whitehall: the King's palace.
my lodging: ? in Lincoln's Inn Field—see p. 58.

Rochester to Elizabeth Barry   *?1675*

Madam,
So much wit and beauty as you have should think of nothing
less than doing miracles, and there cannot be a greater than to
continue to love me. Affecting everything is mean, as loving
pleasure and being fond where you find merit; but to pick out
the wildest and most fantastical odd man alive, and to place your
kindness there, is an act so brave and daring as will show the
greatness of your spirit and distinguish you in love, as you are in
all things else, from womankind. Whether I have made a good
argument for myself I leave you to judge, and beg you to believe
me whenever I tell you what Mrs B. is, since I give you so
sincere an account of her humblest servant. Remember the hour
of a strict account, when both hearts are to be open and we
obliged to speak freely, as you ordered it yesterday (for so I must
ever call the day I saw you last, since all time between that and
the next visit is no part of my life, or at least like a long fit of the
falling sickness wherein I am dead to all joy and happiness).
Here's a damned impertinent fool bolted in that hinders me from
ending my letter. The plague of —— take him and any man or
woman alive that take my thoughts off of you. But in the evening
I will see you and be happy, in spite of all the fools in the
world.

Source: FL ii, p. 1.
Date: ?1675 (see p. 29).
Mrs B.: FL ii's 'Mrs R' is presumably a misprint.
when both hearts are to be open: cf. the Collect in the Anglican Ante-Com-
    munion, 'Almighty God, unto whom all hearts be open, all desires
    known, and from whom no secrets are hid. . . .'
falling-sickness: epilepsy.

Rochester at Adderbury to his wife at Enmore   *?1675*

Madam,

I am at last come to Adderbury, where I find none but the
housekeeper, the butler and rats who squeak mightily and are
all in good health. Your daughter our next-door neighbour is
well; I gave her your present which she received handsomely.
Your maids for good husbandry and equipage sake I would
have sent you from tithing to tithing, as the law of England

Source: The Museum, xxxi, May 23, 1747, p. 158.

Date: ?1675. Rochester seems to refer to two daughters: 'your daughter our
next-door neighbour' who is not in Somerset with Elizabeth, and 'the
little girl whom my soul loveth', who is. It is tempting to suggest that the
postscript refers to the news of Elizabeth's pregnancy with their third
daughter, Malet, who was baptized on January 6, 1676. Their second,
Elizabeth, had been baptized on July 13, 1674.

your daughter our next-door neighbour: perhaps Anne, their first daughter, had
gone to stay with her cousins at Ditchley Park. Ditchley is about 12 miles
from Adderbury but only four or five from Woodstock (see below).
Fielding remarks in *Tom Jones* (IV, xii) that 'Persons who live two or
three miles distance in the country are considered as next door neighbours.'

from tithing to tithing: for a number of practical purposes, including administration of the poor laws, the ancient tithing was still an important
geographical unit in Rochester's time. Under an old tradition reinforced
and extended by an Act of 1662, a poor person not belonging to a parish
could, on complaint by the churchwardens or overseers of the parish, be
sent back from place to place to where he was last 'legally settled either as
a native householder, sojourner, apprentice, or servant'. I have not been
able to identify the maid in question but if, as seems likely, she was
brought by Elizabeth from Enmore when she married Rochester, this is
the point of the joke. Cf. Sterne, *Tristam Shandy* (published, like *The
Museum*, by Dodsley) I, xviii:

> Was I an absolute prince . . . I would appoint able judges at every
> avenue of my metropolis, who should take cognizance of every fool's
> business who came there;—and if, upon a fair and candid hearing, it
> appeared not of weight sufficient to leave his own home, and come up,
> bag and baggage, with his wife and children, farmer's sons, etc. etc.,
> at his backside, they should be all sent back, from constable to
> constable, like vagrants as they were, to the place of their legal
> settlements.

allows, but Florence was gentle and penitent and deserves
something better. I have given her counsel for one end and
a soft pillion for the other, upon which she ambles to Somersetshire, where I am glad to hear your ladyship is, I hope in good
health, at this present writing. Your other maid is a very
eloquent person and I have paid her wages. Tomorrow I intend
for Woodstock and from thence to London, where I hope to
receive your commands. Present my humble duty to my Lady
Warre, whose favours will ever be in my grateful memory; my
humble service to Lady La Warre, to cousin Betty, sweet honey,
Mrs Windham, the sprite, and the little girl whom my soul
loveth. I hope my brother is well, but it is not usual to present
our service to men in ladies' letters, so like a well-bred
gentleman I rest,

> Madam,
> Your humble servant,
> Rochester.

If you are pleased, I am pleased; were my mother pleased, all
were pleased, which God be pleased to grant.

> Rochester.

(See S. and B. Webb, *English Local Government from the Revolution to the
Municipal Corporation Act*, 1906, i, p. 10; W. S. Holdsworth, *A History
of English Law*, 1903–24, vi, 351–2.)

Florence: unidentified.

my Lady Warre: Rochester's mother-in-law. The repetition of her name is
presumably a mistake.

cousin Betty: Elizabeth Hawley, eldest daughter of the Countess's uncle and
aunt, Francis and Gertrude Hawley.

Mrs Windham: Perhaps a relation of John Wyndham, killed at Rochester's
side in the Battle of Bergen (see pp. 43f). Rochester's account of the
incident to his mother seems to suggest that the families knew one
another.

the little girl, etc.: perhaps their daughter Elizabeth (see note on the date of
the letter, above).

my brother: Elizabeth's step-brother, Sir Francis Warre.

If you are pleased, etc.: see note on the date of the letter, above.

8

Rochester to Elizabeth Barry   ?1675

Madam,

There is now no minute of my life that does not afford me some
new argument how much I love you. The little joy I take in
everything wherein you are not concerned, the pleasing perplexity of endless thought which I fall into wherever you are
brought to my remembrance; and lastly, the continual disquiet
I am in during your absence, convince me sufficiently that I do
you justice in loving you so as woman was never loved before.

Rochester to Elizabeth Barry   ?1675

Madam,

Nothing can ever be so dear to me as you are, and I am so
convinced of this that I dare undertake to love you whilst I live.
Believe all I say, for that is the kindest thing imaginable, and
when you can devise any way that may make me appear so to
you, instruct me in it, for I need a better understanding than my
own to show my love without wrong to it.

Source: FL ii, p. 9.
Date: ?1675
the pleasing perplexity of endless thought, etc.: cf. Rochester's poem about
    absent lovers, 'The Mistress', especially the last stanza:

> Kind jealous doubts, tormenting fears,
>   And anxious cares, when past,
> Prove our hearts' treasure fixed and dear,
>   And make us blest at last.

Source: FL ii, p. 10.
Date: ?1675 (see p. 29).

Rochester to Elizabeth Barry   *?1675*

Madam,
You are the most afflicting fair creature in the world and however
you would persuade me to the contrary, I cannot but believe the
fault you pretend to excuse is the only one I could ever be
guilty of to you. When you think of receiving an answer with
common sense in it, you must write letters that give less confusion than your last. I will wait on you, and be revenged by
continuing to love you when you grow weariest of it.

Rochester to Elizabeth Barry   *?1675*

Madam,
Believe me, dearest of all pleasures, that those I can receive from
anything but you are so extremely dull they hardly deserve the
name. If you distrust me and all my professions upon the score
of truth and honour, at least let 'em have credit on another, upon
which my greatest enemies will not deny it me, and that is its
being notorious that I mind nothing but my own satisfaction.
You may be sure I cannot choose but love you above the world,
whatever becomes of the King, Court, or mankind and all their
impertinent business. I will come to you this afternoon.

Source: FL ii, p. 12.
Date: ?1675 (see p. 29).
however you would persuade me to the contrary, etc.: the context is difficult to
   reconstruct, but perhaps she has written to him saying she is not 'the most
   afflicting fair creature in the world' (a view which portraits and contemporary comment support) and apologizing for being in love with him.
   Being in love, he replies, is the only fault he could ever be guilty of in his
   relationship with her.

Source: FL ii, p. 29.
Date: ?1675 (see p. 29).
those: those pleasures.

Rochester to Elizabeth Barry *?Summer, 1675*

Madam,

I was just beginning to write you word that I am the most unlucky creature in the world, when your letter came in and made me more certain, for you tempt me by desiring me to do the thing upon earth I have the most fondness of at this time—that is, going with you to Windsor. But the Devil has laid a block in my way and I must not for my life stir out of town these ten days. You will scarce believe me in this particular as you should do, but I will convince you of the truth when I wait on you. In the meantime, to show the reality of my intentions, there is a coach ready hired for tomorrow which, if not true, you may disprove me by making use of it.

Rochester to Elizabeth Barry *?Summer, 1675*

Madam,

My faults are such as among reasonable people will ever find excuse, but to you I will make none, you are so very full of mystery. I believe you make your court with good success—at least I wish it, and as the kindest thing I can say, do assure

Source: FL ii, p. 28.

Date: ?Summer 1675, when the Court was at Windsor from July 7 until September 10. In 1676 it was only there briefly in February, when Rochester was still in disgrace in the country. There is no record in *CSPD* of the Court's having gone to Windsor at all in 1677, which was almost certainly the last year of their affair: see Introduction, p. 30 (*CSPD*, 1675-8, passim.)

Source: FL ii, p. 21.

Date: ?Summer, 1675. See below, and previous letter.

make your court: ?at Windsor (see p. 104). Elizabeth Barry certainly had influential friends at Court by the time her child was born. (See Savile's letter of December 17, 1677, p. 174.)

you, you shall never be my pattern either in good nature or friendship, for I will be after my own rate, not yours.

Your humble servant.

———

pattern: model, exemplar.

1675–76
Run Down by a Company of Rogues

Rochester in the country to Savile in London   August–September, 1675

Harry,

That night I received by yours the surprising account of my lady Duchess's more than ordinary indignation against me, I was newly brought in dead of a fall from my horse, of which I still remain bruised and bed-rid, and can now scarce think it a happiness that I saved my neck. What ill star reigns over me, that I'm still marked out for ingratitude, and only used barbarously by those I am obliged to? Had I been troublesome to her in pinning the dependence of my fortune upon her solicitations to the King, or her unmerited recommendations of me to some great man, it would not have moved my wonder much if she had sought any occasion to be rid of a useless trouble. But a

Source: FL i, p. 43.

Date: August–September, 1675. This is Rochester's first reference to having fallen out with the Duchess of Portsmouth. The cause of his quarrel with her is not known. He had offended her early in 1674 with an obscene poem about her relationship with the King, beginning 'I' th' isle of Britain, long since famous grown' (see *Complete Poems*, p. 60, where Vieth corrects his previous dating of the poem in *PQ*, xxxvii, 1958, pp. 424–32), but there is no record of a more recent attack. Rochester clearly felt he had been wronged, and he would not have lied to Savile. All the same, his position at Court had been jeopardized in June, when he smashed the King's new glass sundial at Whitehall, and it would not have been difficult for his enemies to put him further out of favour by attributing another anti-Portsmouth satire to him.

my lady Duchess: the Duchess of Portsmouth, see above, and p. 27.

by those: FL i 'to those'.

creature who had already received of her all the obligations he ever could pretend to, except the continuance of her good opinion, for the which he resolved and did direct every step of his life in duty and service to her and all who were concerned in her; why should she take the advantage of a false, idle story to hate such a man, as if it were an inconveniency to her to be harmless, or a pain to continue just? By that God that made me, I have no more offended her in thought, word or deed, no more imagined or uttered the least thought to her contempt or prejudice, than I have plotted treason, concealed arms, trained regiments for a rebellion.

If there be upon earth a man of common honesty who will justify a tittle of her accusation, I am contented never to see her. After this she need not forbid me to come to her; I have little pride or pleasure in showing myself where I am accused of a meanness I were not capable of even for her service, which would prove a shrewder trial of my honesty than any ambition I ever had to make my court to. I thought the Duchess of P. more an angel than I find her a woman, and as this is the first, it shall be the most malicious thing I will ever say of her. For her generous resolution of not hurting me to the King, I thank her; but she must think a man much obliged, after the calling of him knave, to say she will do him no farther prejudice. For the Countess of P——, whatever she has heard me say, or anybody else, of her, I'll stand the test of any impartial judge, 'twas neither injurious nor unmannerly, and how severe soever she pleases to be I have always been her humble servant and will continue so.

I do not know how to assure myself the D. will spare me to the King, who would not to you. I'm sure she can't say I ever injured you to her, nor am I at all afraid she can hurt me with you. I dare swear you don't think I have dealt so indiscreetly in

in thought, word or deed: a quotation from the General Confession in the Anglican Holy Communion service.

the Countess of P——: probably, as Wilson suggests (p. 83), the Duchess's sister Henrietta, who married the Earl of Pembroke in December 1674.

my service to her as to doubt me in the friendship I profess to you. And to show you I rely upon yours, let me beg of you to talk once more with her, and desire her to give me the fair hearing she would afford any footman of hers who had been complained of to her by a less worthy creature (for such a one I assure myself my accuser is), unless it be for her service to wrong the most faithful of her servants, and then I shall be proud of mine. I would not be run down by a company of rogues, and this looks like an endeavour towards it. Therefore, dear Harry, send me word how I am with other folks. If you visit my Lord Treasurer, name the calamity of this matter to him and tell me sincerely how he takes it. And if you hear the King mention me, do the office of a friend to

Your humble servant,
Rochester.

Rochester in the country to Savile in London   August–September, 1675

Dear Savile,
If it were the sign of an honest man to be happy in his friends, sure I were marked out for the worst of men, since no-one e'er lost so many as I have done or knew how to make so few. The severity you say the D. of P—— shows to me is a proof that 'tis not in my power to deserve well of anybody, since (I call truth to witness) I have never been guilty of an error that I know to her. And this may be a warning to you that remain in the mistake of being kind to me, never to expect a grateful return, since I am so utterly ignorant how to make it. To value you in

my Lord Treasurer: Thomas Osborne, Earl of Danby, Lord Treasurer, 1673–1679.

Source: FL i, p. 33.
Date: late August–early September, 1675. Halifax's daughter Elizabeth, referred to in the last sentence, was born on August 28 and baptized on September 4. (Wilson, 83–4.)

my thoughts, to prefer you in my wishes, to serve you in my words, to observe, study and obey you in all my actions is too little, since I have performed all this to her without so much as an offensive accident, and yet she thinks it just to use me ill. If I were not malicious enough to hope she were in the wrong, I must have a very melancholy opinion of myself. I wish your interest might prevail with her, as a friend of hers, not mine, to tell how I have deserved it of her, since she has ne'er accused me of any crime but of being cunning; and I told her, somebody had been cunninger than I to persuade her so. I can as well support the hatred of the whole world as anybody, not being generally fond of it. Those whom I have obliged may use me with ingratitude and not afflict me much; but to be injured by those who have obliged me, and to whose service I am ever bound, is such a curse as I can only wish on them who wrong me to the Duchess.

I hope you have not forgot what G—y and you have promised me, but within some time you will come and fetch me to London. I shall scarce think of coming till you call me, as not having many prevalent motives to draw me to the Court, if it be so that my master has no need of my service, nor my friends of my company.

Mr Shepherd is a man of a fluent style and coherent thought if, as I suspect, he writ your postscript.

I wish my Lord Halifax joy of everything, and of his daughter to boot.

Rochester.

G—y: Henry Guy. See p. 93.

Mr Shepherd: Sir Fleetwood Shepherd (1634–98), 'a debauchee and atheist, a grand companion with Charles Lord Buckhurst . . . Henry Savile, and others' (Wood, *Athenae Oxonienses*, iv, 627), was the author of a number of topical verses. Rochester named him among the friends whose literary judgement he valued, at the end of *An Allusion to Horace*, written around this time.

my Lord Halifax: Savile's brother George, Marquess of Halifax. His newly-born daughter Elizabeth (see note on the date of the letter, above) was to be the object of his famous *Advice to a Daughter*, 1688.

Rochester in the country to Elizabeth Barry in London   Autumn, 1675

Madam,

To convince you how just I must ever be to you, I have sent this
on purpose that you may know you are not a moment out of
my thoughts; and since so much merit as you have and such
convincing charms (to me at least) need not wish a greater
advantage over any, to forget you is the only reprieve possible
for a man so much your creature and servant as I am; which I
am so far from wishing, that I conjure you by all the assurances
of kindness you have ever made me proud and happy with,
that not two days can pass without some letter from you to me.
You must leave 'em, etc. —— to be sent to me with speed. And,
till the blessed hour wherein I shall see you again, may happiness
of all kinds be as far from me as I do, both in love and jealousy,
pray mankind may be from you.

*To Rochester from Sir Joseph Williamson   October 29, 1675
in London*

Whitehall Friday yᵉ 29. Oct. 1675

My Lord
To morrow being yᵉ Day appointed by my Lord Keeper for yᵉ
heareing yᵉ matter in difference between my Lady Lindsey &

Source: FL ii, p. 7.
Date: ?Autumn, 1675, when Rochester was in exile in the country.

Source: P.R.O., MS. S.P. Dom. Entry Book 43, p. 59.
Date: as heading, October 29, 1675.
Sir Joseph Williamson: see p. 65.
my Lord Keeper: Sir Heneage Finch, Keeper of the Seal.
yᵉ matter in difference: Elizabeth, Countess of Lindsey, had formerly been
married to Rochester's step-brother Sir Francis Lee, who died in 1667.
By him she had a son, Edward, who was 'married' as a child of four to
Lady Charlotte Fitzroy, an illegitimate daughter of the King by the

your Lo^(rp) concerning Woodstock, And y^t appointment haveing been made, as my Lady sayes, with your Lo^(rp's) knowledge, his Ma^(ty) commands me to signify to your Lo^(rp), that you doe take Order that some person, whoever your Lo^(rp) shall think fitt to choose, be there to heare it jointly with my Lord Keeper, according to ye Reference formerly made upon it.

I am w^(th) respect,

My Lord,

your Lo^(rp's)

most &c.

JW.

Ea. Rochester

To Rochester in the country from   *November 4, 1675*
Anthony Carey, Viscount Falkland in Paris

Paris Nov. 14

My Lord   1675
Sometimes when I have a mind to sporte with ill fortune, I fancy my selfe one of the troope of Lincoln's Inne fields, where

---

Duchess of Cleveland. On their marriage, Edward was created Earl of Lichfield. Three weeks before Williamson's letter, despite a previous protest by Rochester, the King signed a warrant granting the reversion of the Rangership of Woodstock Park, after the determination of Rochester's estate, to Lord Lichfield's guardian, Sir Walter St John (Rochester's uncle) to be held during the lives of the Earl and Countess of Lichfield. The move did not affect Rochester's own situation, but he must have valued the salaried position and its house for the security they offered his heirs. Everyone knew how keenly he had pursued the office, granted him eighteen months previously (see p. 94), and the slight shows how badly he had fallen out of favour. He mentions it wryly in his letter to Savile of February 29, 1676, p. 114. (*CSPD*, September 27; October 9 and 29, 1675.)

Source: MS. Harl. 7003, f. 186.
Date: as heading, November 14, 1675, new style: i.e. November 4 in England.
Anthony Carey, Viscount Falkland: (1656–1694), grandson of the cavalier poet Lucius Carey. Whether or not he was really poor (he had a royal

I have had my standing so long, that now I begin to know the humour of all my Masters that passe by: Some looke too busy to heare; and these are not unkind, for though they give nothing they spare my lungs; Others looke oblidgingly to provoke my prayers and Reverences, and at last bid me hope at the next Returne; One perhaps of a thousand is of a modest compassion and prevents my asking with an almes. It must be acknowledged, My Lord, that this Idea does too much resemble the truth of my Condition; I have been long a Beggar, and tedious attendance, and fruitless applications, and defeated hopes have been the Sting of my necessity: but the Generous Treatment that I have found at your Lordship's hands, hath Reconciled me to my wants, and almost made me pleased with them, since they gave occasion for Y^r lordship to espouse mee; For I can without feining averre that it would be a more gratefull Reflection to mee to have been assisted by Y^r Lordship's Freindship, then not to have wanted. And now y^r Lordship well knowes what a Beggar's thankes amounts to: 'tis only an addresse for farther bounty; and it is this, My Lord, I humbly desire of you, that you would be pleas'd to continue the Kindnesse that you have begun in solliciting his Majesty the only life of my Fortunes. And since I cannot hope for lesse then this from so much humanity as you have already exprest, I cannot but fixe this for my perpetuall stile

My Lord,

Y^r Lordship's

most obliged Servant

& Creature

Falkland.

---

pension of £300 p.a. at this time, in addition to his inherited income), Falkland had not yet married the wealthy Rebecca Chapman or acquired any of the remunerative public positions he later filled. But he may have been simply greedy: he was imprisoned in 1694 on a charge of embezzling public funds. (*GEC*, Falkland; *CTB*, passim.) His request to Rochester to speak to the King on his behalf could not have been worse timed.

had my standing: i.e. as a petitioner.

For the Right Honble John Earle of Rochester These

A letter from the Ld Falkland

Rochester in the country to Savile in London   *?Autumn, 1675*

Harry,

You are the only man of England that keep wit with your
wisdom, and I am happy in a friend that excels in both. Were
your good nature the least of your good qualities I durst not
presume upon it as I have done, but I know you are so sincerely
concerned in serving your friends truly that I need not make an
apology for the trouble I have given you in this affair. I daily
expect more considerable effects of your friendship, and have the
vanity to think I shall be the better for your growing poorer. In
the meantime, when you please to distinguish from Progers and
Windham and comply with Rogers and Bull, not forgetting
John Stevens, you shall find me

Your most ready and most obedient servant,

Rochester.

[A letter from the Ld Falkland: *added in Rochester's hand.*]

Source: FL i, p. 49.
Date: ?Autumn, 1675. The 'affair' is probably the quarrel with the Duchess
   of Portsmouth.
your growing poorer: Savile has presumably been engaged to bribe potential
   allies of Rochester, but the letter is not clear in detail.
distinguish from: ?'separate [yourself] from' (*OED, Distinguish, v.,* 1).
Progers: [FLi 'Prosers'.] Edward Progers was a Groom of the King's
   Bedchamber. (*CTB, passim.*)
Windham: Thomas Windham, Groom of the Bedchamber from October,
   1673. (*CTB, passim.*)
comply with: make yourself agreeable to (*OED, Comply, v.,* 3).
Rogers: [FLi 'Rosers'.] Francis Rogers was a Page of the King's Bedchamber.
   (*CTB, passim.*)
Bull: Arundel Bull, another Page of the Bedchamber. (*CTB, passim.*)
John Stevens: three people of this name are mentioned in *CSPD* in connection
   with Court affairs, but it is not possible to identify the one in question.

From Rochester at Adderbury to Savile in London   February 29, 1676

Dear Savile,

This day I received the unhappy news of my own death and burial. But hearing what heirs and successors were decreed me in my place, and chiefly in my lodgings, it was no small joy to me that those tidings prove untrue. My passion for living is so increased that I omit no care of myself, which, before, I never thought life worth the trouble of taking. The King, who knows me to be a very ill-natured man, will not think it an easy matter for me to die now I live chiefly out of spite. Dear Mr Savile, afford me some news from your land of the living; and though I have little curiosity to hear who's well, yet I would be glad my few friends are so, of whom you are no more the least than the leanest. I have better compliments for you, but that may not look so sincere as I would have you believe I am when I profess myself,

Your faithful, affectionate, humble servant,
Rochester.

Adderbury, near Banbury, February *ult*.
My service to my Lord Middlesex.

Source: FL i, p. 7.

Date: as letter, February 29 [1676], a leap-year. The postscript refers to their friend Charles Sackville, Lord Buckhurst, who succeeded to the Earldom of Middlesex on April 4, 1675. By August 27, 1677, he was Earl of Dorset, and the possibility of the letter's belonging to that year is removed by its connection with Howard's to Rochester, following.

my own death and burial: the rumour in London that Rochester had died, perhaps started by the King's actions over the Rangership of Woodstock Park (see p. 111), is mentioned again by Sir Robert Howard, in the following letter.

in my place: the Rangership.

Lord Middlesex: see note on the date of the letter, above.

To Rochester at Adderbury from   *April 7, 1676*
Sir Robert Howard in London

Though this towne is apt enough to like an ill entertainment
better than A good one, yet I Cannot beleeue them soe stupid
as to be ins[ens]ible what they shoud haue lost by your death,
and I am soe well pleased with your health that I am troubled
I Cannot assure you that I owe such an abundance of satisfaction
to my freindship only, but must allow some share to the pleasure
I promise my selfe by enioyinge such things as the Doctor was
pleased to declaime against; but like an angry Impeacher;
(nature beinge that great monarch for whose fauours there is soe
many Riualls;) the Doctor drew up his Charge against her
Cheife minister. The next satisfaction to your health; your
Company will giue mee; and shall bee oblidged to know when I
may expect you in this modest towne; where the worst men and
women censure the best; and the silent knaue is sheltered under
the Charracter of A sober person. The Criticks on men's Actions,
are like the ill natured ones of the stage, most busie where there
is greatest Ingenuity; beinge Commonly more provokt by there

Source: MS. Harl. 7003, f. 291.

Date: as letter, April 7, [1676]. (See note on 'your death' below.) Prinz's odd
    mis-transcription 'Juill: 7th', followed by all subsequent editors and
    biographers, has produced some confusion.

Sir Robert Howard: see p. 44.

your death: Rochester was rumoured dead in February 1676 (see his previous
    letter to Savile). The possibility that the year in question is 1677 is removed
    by this letter to Howard, since Rochester was in London in April 1677, but
    almost certainly at Adderbury the previous spring. (See J. Treglown,
    'The Date of Rochester's "Scaen",' *RES*, N.S. xxx, 1979, pp. 434-6.)

an angry Impeacher . . . : the conceit is that Rochester's doctor has criticized
    ('impeached') him for his way of life, instead of blaming nature for making
    him ill; similarly, politicians are blamed for the monarch's errors by
    courtiers who want to stay in favour.

the Criticks . . . : Howard was satirized often, both as a politician and as a
    writer (see for example *The Session of the Poets*, Yale *POAS*, i, 327f.; *On
    the Prorogation*, ibid., 1. 179f.), so was in a position to sympathize with
    Rochester.

enuie then there iudgment; but I forgett how ill I entertaine though upon A good subiect; and am sure I shall be better by you though upon an ill one; I meane by the sceen you are pleased to write; nor shall I repine to see how far you Can exceed me; noe more then I doe to see others that haue more wealth then I liue by mee with A greater plenty; I haue tooke pleasure that you exceed all that can excell mee; and those aduantages of my Lord Rochester must need's bee pleasinge to me that is soe perfectly his

most and faithfull and humble
seruant
R. Howard

Aprill: 7th.

For the Earle of Rochester at adderbury neare Banbury in Oxfordshire.
[*Two words in another hand are illegible—perhaps the messenger's name.*]

Rochester in the country to Savile in London   *?Spring, 1676*

Dear Savile,
'Tis not that I am the idlest creature living, and only choose to

the sceen you are pleased to write: Rochester's scene for *The Conquest of China*, printed in Pinto's edition, pp. 61–9. Within weeks of this letter, Howard became embroiled in Danby's investigation into the organization and conduct of the Exchequer. The enquiries lasted about a year and a half, and Howard never completed his play. (See J. Treglown, art. cit., above.)

Source: FL i, p. 22.
Date: ?Spring, 1676. The disillusioned tone of the letter suggests a date after 1675, supported by Rochester's enquiries about a sitting of parliament, prorogued for 15 months from November, 1675. A *terminus ante quem* is supplied by the reference to Lord Lisle, who became Earl of Leicester on November 2, 1677. The reference to 'a season of tribulation' may imply Lent.

employ my thoughts rather upon my friends than to languish all the day in the tediousness of doing nothing, that I write to you; but owning that though you excel most men in friendship and good nature, you are not quite exempt from all human frailty, I send this to hinder you from forgetting a man who loves you very heartily. The world, ever since I can remember, has been still so insupportably the same that 'twere vain to hope there were any alterations, and therefore I can have no curiosity for news. Only I would be glad to know if the parliament be like to sit any time, for the peers of England being grown of late years very considerable in the Government, I would make one at the session. Livy and sickness has a little inclined me to policy. When I come to town I make no question but to change that folly for some less, whether wine or women I know not, according as my constitution serves me. Till when, dear Harry, farewell! When you dine at my Lord Lisle's let me be remembered.

Kings and princes are only as incomprehensible as what they pretend to represent, but apparently as frail as those they govern. This is a season of tribulation, and I piously beg of Almighty God that the strict severity shown to one scandalous sin amongst us may expiate for all grievous calamities—so help them God whom it concerns!

the peers of England, etc.: Charles became increasingly dependent on the support of the House of Lords as Whig opposition gained strength in the second half of the decade.

Livy: the Roman historian.

Lord Lisle: Philip Sidney, Lord Lisle (1619–1698), who succeeded as Earl of Leicester on November 2, 1677. An active parliamentarian under Cromwell, Lisle took little part in public life after the Restoration, but in his late years became a patron of literature and used to entertain the Court wits at his house at Sheen. (*DNB.*)

a season of tribulation: perhaps Lent.

the strict severity shown to one scandalous sin, etc.: perhaps, as Wilson suggests, a reference to venereal disease.

9

Rochester to Elizabeth Barry   *?Spring, 1676*

Madam,

If there be yet alive within you the least memory of me (which I can hope only because [all] of the life that remains with me is the dear remembrance of you, and methinks your kindness, as the younger, should outlive mine), give me leave to assure you I will meet it very shortly with such a share on my side as will justify me to you from all ingratitude, though your favours are to me the greatest bliss this world, or womankind—which I think Heaven—can bestow, but the hopes of it. If there can be any addition to one of the highest misfortunes, my absence from you has found the way to give it me, in not affording me the least occasion of doing you any service since I left you. It seems, till I am capable of greater merit, you resolve to keep me from the vanity of pretending any at all. Pray consider, when you give another leave to serve you more than I, how much injustice you run the hazard of committing, when it will not be in your power to reward that more deserving man with half so much happiness as you have thrown away upon my worthless self.

Your restless servant,

———

Source: FL ii, p. 3.
Date: Plate Spring, 1676, when Rochester came out of exile.
the younger: Elizabeth Barry, born about 1658, was eleven years younger than Rochester.
I will meet it: i.e., I will match your kindness.
justify me to you for all ingratitude: i.e., defend me against any charge of ingratitude.
but the hopes of it: the sense seems to be: 'your kindness gives me the greatest happiness that either this world or women, who are my version of the *next* world, can offer, except the anticipation of that happiness (which, because it is purely imaginary, is more perfect)'. Cf. Rochester's poem 'The Fall', with its reference to pleasures which 'lessen still as they draw near'.

Rochester in the country to Savile in London   *Spring, 1676*

Harry,

You cannot shake off the statesman entirely, for I perceive you have no opinion of a letter that is not almost a gazette. Now, to me, who think the world as giddy as myself, I care not which way it turns and am fond of no news but the prosperity of my friends and the continuance of their kindness to me, which is the only error I wish to continue in 'em. For my own part, I am not at all stung with my Lord M——'s mean ambition, but I aspire to Lord L——'s generous philosophy. They who would be great in our little government seem as ridiculous to me as schoolboys who with much endeavour and some danger climb a crab-tree, venturing their necks for fruit which solid pigs would disdain if they were not starving. These reflections, how idle soever they seem to the busy, if taken into consideration would save you many a weary step in the day and help G—y to many an hour's sleep which he wants in the night; but G—y would be rich, and by my troth there is some sense in that. Pray remember me to him and tell him I wish him many millions, that his soul may find rest. You write me word that I'm out of favour with a certain poet whom I have ever admired for the dis-

Source: *FL* i, p. 4.

Date: probably some time in the spring of 1676, when Savile went around insulting a number of important people at Court. He was dismissed in March for being rude to the Duke of York. (See p. 23.) See also *the declining D——ss*, below.

shake off the statesman: see above.

my Lord M——: probably Rochester's enemy the Earl of Mulgrave, who in April, 1676, was reported as having curried favour with the Duke of York by declaring himself a Catholic. (*HMC*, Seventh Report, p. 467a.)

my Lord L——: perhaps Lisle, see p. 117. According to the *Memoirs of Thomas, Earl of Ailesbury*, 'he loved to be at ease and not to talk of anything that related to State affairs and politics'. (*GEC*, Leicester; *DNB*.)

crab-tree: crab-apple tree.

G—y: the greedy Henry Guy, see p. 93.

a certain poet: Rochester's former protégé Dryden, who had been annoyed by Rochester's well-aimed criticisms of him and of his work in *An Allusion*

proportion of him and his attributes. He is a rarity which I
cannot but be fond of, as one would be of a hog that could
fiddle, or a singing owl. If he falls upon me at the blunt, which is
his very good weapon in wit, I will forgive him if you please and
leave the repartee to Black Will with a cudgel. And now. dear
Harry, if it may agree with your affairs to show yourself in the
country this summer, contrive such a crew together as may not
be ashamed of passing by Woodstock. And if you can debauch
Alderman G——y, we will make a shift to delight his gravity.
I am sorry for the declining D——ss and would have you
generous to her at this time, for that is true pride and I delight
in it.

Rochester.

to Horace. It has been widely debated whether this letter proves Rochester's
complicity in the Rose Alley attack on Dryden three years later, in
December, 1679. Wilson argues that the time-gap disproves the connection
(*RES*, xv, 1939, 294–301), but the quarrel between the two poets continued throughout the period, gaining in intensity, and many scholars
believe Rochester is likely to have been behind it. (See his letter nearer the
time of the attack, p. 232, and Yale *POAS*, i, 396f., and Pierre Legouis,
'Rochester et sa réputation', *Etudes Anglaises*, i, 1937, pp. 53–69.)
admired: wondered at.
attributes: reputation.
at the blunt: a pun, of course, but the literal meaning is 'at fencing'. A blunt
was a foil. (*OED, Blunt, sb.,* 1.)
debauch: entice (into coming to Woodstock). (*OED, Debauch, v.,* 1.)
Alderman G——y: Charles II dubbed the Duke of Buckingham 'Alderman
George' in 1675. (Arthur Bryant, *King Charles II*, revised edn, 1955, p.
193.) The reference to his gravity is ironic.
the declining D——ss: ousted as the King's mistress by the Duchess of
Mazarin, Portsmouth became increasingly miserable and ill. She had a
miscarriage in March, 1676, and retired to Bath that June. (Jeanine
Delpech, *The Life and Times of the Duchess of Portsmouth*, 1953, pp. 102–4.)

Rochester in London to Elizabeth Barry   *?May, 1676*

I came to town late last night, though time enough to receive
news from the King very surprising, you being chiefly concerned in't. I must beg that I may speak with you this morning
at ten o'clock. I will not fail to be at your door. The affair is
unhappy, and to me on many scores but on none more than that
it has disturbed the heaven of thought I was in to think, after so
long an absence, I had lived to be again blessed with seeing my
dearest dear, Mrs ——.

Source: FL ii, p. 23.

Date: ?May, 1676, when Rochester seems to have returned to London.

news from the King: the details are not known. Perhaps Barry had been having
  an affair during Rochester's absence, and this was the piece of news
  which dismayed him on his return. But many other explanations are
  possible.

1676–77
Much Business

Rochester to Elizabeth Barry   ?

Madam,

Though upon the score of love, which is immediately my
concern, I find aptness enough to be jealous, yet upon that of
your safety, which is the only thing in the world weighs more
with me than my love, I apprehend much more. I know by
woeful experience what comes of dealing with knaves; such I
am sure you have at this time to do with. Therefore look well
about you and take it for granted that unless you can deceive
them, they will certainly cozen you. If I am not so wise as they
and therefore less fit to advise you, I am at least more concerned
for you and for that reason the likelier to prove honest and the
rather to be trusted. Whether you will come to the Duke's Playhouse today, or at least let me come to you when the play is done,
I leave to your choice. Let me know, if you please, by the bearer.

Rochester to Elizabeth Barry   ?

Madam,

Now, as I love you, I think I have reason to be jealous. Your
neighbour came in last night with all the marks and behaviour of

Source: FL ii, p. 15.
Date: uncertain.
Duke's Playhouse: in Lincoln's Inn Fields, near Rochester's lodgings.

Source: FL ii, p. 11.
Date: uncertain.
   The letter is mysterious, but the gist seems to be that Rochester thinks a

a spy; every word and look implied that she came to solicit your love or constancy. May her endeavours prove as vain as I wish my fears. May no man share the blessings I enjoy without my curses. And if they fall on him alone without touching you, I am happy, though he deserves 'em not; but should you be concerned, they'll all fly back upon myself, for he whom you are kind to is so blessed, he may safely stand the curses of all the world without repining; at least if, like me, he be sensible of nothing but what comes from Mrs ——.

Rochester to Elizabeth Barry   ?

Madam,
I know not well who has the worst on't: you, who love but a little, or I who dote to an extravagance. Sure, to be half kind is as bad as to be half-witted; and madness, both in love and reason, bears a better character than a moderate state of either. Would I could bring you to my opinion in this point. I would then confidently pretend you had too just exceptions either

neighbour of Barry's has been soliciting her on behalf of some man. Any rival of Rochester's will, he says, earn his curses, though he is not to be blamed for trying, and Rochester cannot bring himself to curse Barry. But if she is 'concerned'—that is, perhaps, if she is herself responsible for attracting the man's attention—he will be impervious to any curse, because (according to the elegant conceit of the conclusion) he will, if he is like Rochester, take no notice of anything felt by anyone other than her.

jealous: perhaps simply 'suspicious', here (*OED, Jealous, a.,* 4.)
concerned: implicated (*OED, Concern, v.,* 11b)—see above.

Source: FL ii, p. 5.
Date: uncertain.
pretend: assert (without the modern implication of falsehood). The sense seems to be: 'If only you agreed with me that it is better to be madly in love than lukewarmly so, I would have no hesitation in asserting that the allegations of sexual extravagance made against me by all men and a couple of unattractive women are completely just. It is best to love in this way, and that is how I love you.'

against me or my passion, the flesh and the devil; I mean, all the fools of my own sex, and that fat with the other lean one of yours whose prudent advice is daily concerning you, how dangerous it is to be kind to the man upon earth who loves you best. I, who still persuade myself by all the arguments I can bring that I am happy, find this none of the least, that you are too unlike these people every way to agree with them in any particular. This is writ between sleeping and waking, and I will not answer for its being sense; but I, dreaming you were at Mrs N——'s with five or six fools and the lean lady, waked in one of your horrors, and in amaze, fright and confusion send this to beg a kind one from you, that may remove my fears and make me as happy as I am faithful.

To Rochester in London from Henry Bulkeley   *?May–June, 1676*

My deare Lord,
Though there is noe man living more faithfully concern'd y^{en} I am at any good or ill that can happen to you, yet I doen't wonder you fall into such persecutions, as ye last, since you live

my passion, the flesh and the devil: cf. 'the world, the flesh and the devil' (see
  p. 60).
Mrs N——: perhaps Nell Gwynn.
in one of your horrors: 'in a jealous state like one of yours'?

Source: MS. Harl. 7003, f. 287.
Date: ?May–June, 1676. Rochester's 'persecutions'—see below—continued
  until the spring of 1676, but he was probably back in London in May and
  June. He was involved in the Epsom brawl on June 17 (see p. 28), but
  there is no reference to it in this letter, which was presumably sent to him
  in London some time before then.
Henry Bulkeley: (1638–98) Master of the Household and a Groom of the
  Bedchamber.
such persecutions, as ye last: presumably Rochester's quarrel with the Duchess of
  Portsmouth, and subsequent exile.

in an Age when fooles are ye most powerfull Enemyes, & the
few Wise wee have either cannott or will not befreind vs, since
ye Fop is the only fine Gentlman of the Times, & a committee of
those able Statesmen assemble dayly to talke of nothing but
fighting & fucking at Locketts, & will never be reconciled to
men who speake sense & Reason at ye Beare or Coven garden.
It is thay are the hopeful spriggs of ye Nation whose knowledge
lyes in their light Periwiggs & trimed shoes, who herd wth one
another not because thay love y^{em}selves, but understand noe
body else, whose Honour, Honesty & Freindship is like the
consent of Hounds, who knowe not why thay runn together,
but y^t thay hunt ye same sent, fellowes that woud make y^e
World believe they are not afraid of dying, & yet are out of
heart if the Wind disorders their Hair or ruffles their Cravatts; &
yet these Raskalls fancy y^t since Cromwel sold the English

Locketts: Adam Locket's tavern in Charing Cross. One of the statesmen
reputed to have fought there is the then Lord Steward of the Household,
Sir Stephen Fox, identified by Pope as the subject of some lines in the
anonymous *Satyr Unmuzzled,* 1680:

> One play'd at dice all night at Locket's door,
> Quarrel'd and cuff'd till he was blood all o'er.
> Next day he sat at the wise Green Cloth Board.
>   (Yale *POAS,* ii, p. 210.)

(The Green Cloth Board was a department of the Royal Household.)
ye Beare: a tavern at the Southwark end of old London Bridge, often
mentioned by Pepys.
Coven garden: both Kate's Tavern and Will's Coffee House, favourite meeting
places of the Court group, were in Covent Garden. Bulkeley's sense of
superiority to the Court 'Raskalls' recalls Rochester's approving reference
to him in *An Allusion to Horace:* ll. 110–14:

> I've no ambition on that idle score,
> But say with Betty Morris heretofore,
> When a Court lady called her Buckley's whore,
> 'I please one man of wit, am proud on't too:
> Let all the coxcombs dance to bed to you!'

y^{em}selves: i.e. 'each other'.
Cromwel sold the English Timber to ye Dutch: 'timber' is presumably used in
the sense of 'shipping', here (see *OED, Timber, sb.,* 6b). Cromwell in fact

Timber to yᵉ Dutch, Fortun has reprised vs with noe other
defence then what may be hop't from their fashionable Blockheads & Embroidered Belts. These are Men I'me sure soe
inconsiderable that thay are fitter to provoke ones spleen yᵉⁿ his
rage, but that I doen't know how this damn'd Allay is preferred
before yᵉ true Ore, & yᵉ Genius yᵗ Governs now seems to stand
at arms length wᵗʰ men of sense & Vnderstanding, but embraces
yᵉ dull Image & yᵉ formal Coxcomb. I coud therefor when
ever I leave London (wᶜʰ is a sort of dying) bequeath my body
to any man of witt or skill to dissect into as many Jests as I have
veines, & pardon all y ill things that are soe said of me, &
rather because I'me sure thay who talke well will find noe
creditt, but to be dirtily stab'd by yᵉ stay'd young Gentlman &
yᵉ civil lyar, is as bad as heretofor being accus'd by my Ladys

made strong efforts, notably in the Treaty of Westminster (1654), to
prevent the Dutch from gaining favourable terms of trade which would
damage English maritime interests, but Dutch successes in general were
often blamed on what was seen as his over-conciliatory posture. See
M. Ashley, *Oliver Cromwell, the Conservative Dictator*, 1937, pp. 318–19, and
C. Jenkinson, *A Collection of all the Treaties of Peace, Alliance, and Commerce, between Great-Britain and other Powers*, 1785, i, pp. 48f.

reprised: compensated (*OED*, *Reprise*, *v.*, 5).

spleen: in the sense of 'amusement', here (*OED*, *Spleen*, *sb.* 3, 8).

Allay: = alloy.

Image: presumably in the sense of 'copy' or 'imitation'.

all yᵉ ill things that are soe said of me: I have not been able to trace the particular criticisms, but Bulkeley figures in some contemporary satires and,
as the style of this letter suggests, was an aggressive man, quick both to
give and take offence. He killed his opponent in a duel in 1668 and was
wounded in a fight in 1673. In 1675 he was imprisoned twice, both times
in connection with duels. The first occasion was when he challenged
James Butler, Earl of Ossory, whom he suspected, probably rightly, of
having an affair with his wife Sophia. Bulkeley was sent to the Tower on
January 30, 1675, and released after begging the King's pardon on
February 24. He was in again on June 3 after carrying a challenge to an
unnamed peer on behalf of Thomas Felton, Groom of the Bedchamber,
and was released two days later. The Ossory quarrel was still going on in
1677, when Bulkeley fought him again. (*Court Satires*, pp. 230–1; *CSPD*,
1675, passim; *HMC*, 24, *Rutland*, ii, p. 42.)

Chaplain, whose clean nightcap & reverent Cassock has of late (God be thanked) yealde up ye care of family Duty to flanting Pantaloon & bushy Wigg. My Lord all I can say is that since wee who reverence bottle & bold Truth are contemned, these Creatures have Interest enough to invade o^r Ease & o^r reputation, may thay who beleeve a man y^t is extravagant when he has nothing else to doe, cannott be serious when he is employ'd, purchase their conviction at as dear a rate as y^r Lordp:s mercy and mine would adiudge them to.

I hope it wont now be long befor I shall be soe happy as to wayte vpon your Lord:p for I have rec:d ye Kings Comands to march wth my company to London. In order to it I shall I beleeve embark wth in a fortnight for Chester & soe on, where if I may live in ye same felicity I enioyd last Summer in ye Honour of being neere you, I may have my greatest aime, for I am wth all ye unreservedness in ye world

My Lord

Yr most faithfull humble

serv:^{t}

H. Bulkeley.

This For the right hon^{ble} the Earle of Rochester at the Arbor house in Portugal row in Lincolns Inn field, London.

Rochester in London to his wife at Adderbury   ?

The stile of y^r La^{sps} last though kinder than I deserve, is nott

my Ladys Chaplain: Lady Sophia Bulkeley's chaplain, whom I have not identified. The rest of the sentence is either about her affair with Ossory (see above), or about Post-Restoration changes in clerical dress.

to march wth my company . . . : Bulkeley was a captain in the King's Guards, who spent some of their time stationed in Ireland, and would have passed through Chester on the way from there to London. (See *Court Wits*, pp. 54f., 208.)

Source: MS. Harl. 7003, f. 225.
Date: uncertain.

without some alloy from y[r] late conversations wth those whom I should extreamly honour, if they would doe mee the right and you the justice never to come neare you. when I am really as well wth you as I wish & you pretend I shall att least obtaine that favour in the meane time I will excercise my usuall tallent of patience & submission; I would bee very glad to imploy my selfe in those affaires you have to be done here, had I the least hopes of doing them to y[r] satisfaction, but despairing of that happiness pray send y[r] Cosin & my freind to towne, & lett her please you better, I know not who has perswaded you that you want five pounds to pay a servants wages, but next weeke Blancourt is going in to the West, att whose returne you may expect an Account of y[r] intire revenue, w[ch] I will bee bould to say has hitherto, & shall (as long as I can gett bread without itt) bee[n] wholly imploy'd for the use of y[r] self & those who depend on you, if I prouve an ill steward, att least you never had a better, w[ch] is some kind of satisfaction to

your humble servant

To Rochester in London from his wife   ?

If I could haue bin troubled att any thing when I had the happyness of resceiuing a letter from you I should be soe because you did not name a time when I might hope to see you: the uncertainty of which very much aflicts me whether this ode kind of proceeding be to try my patience or obedyence I cannot guesse but I will neuer faile of e[i]ther when my duty to you requier

y[r] Cosin & my freind: perhaps one of the three Hawley sisters, daughters of Elizabeth's uncle Francis Hawley.
Blancourt: a servant of Rochester's family's (see pp. 65, 249).
the West: i.e. to Elizabeth's family estates in Somerset.

_____

Source: MS. Harl. 7003, f. 261.
Date: after January 1671 ('Children').

them. I doe not think you design staying att bath now that it is
like to be soe full and God knows when you will find in your
hart to leaue the place you are in: pray consider with your selfe
wheather this be a reasonable way of proceeding and be pleased
to lett me know what I am to expect for thear being soe short a
time betwixt this and the sitting of Parlemant I am confident you
will find soe much bussine[ss] as will not allow you to come into
the country thearfore pray lay your commands upon me what
I am to doe and though it be to forgett my children and the long
hopes I haue liued in of seeing you, yett I will endeauour to
obey you or in the memory only torment my selfe with out
giuing you the trouble of puting you in the mind thear liues such
a creature as your faithfull humble

Rochester to Elizabeth Barry   *?Early summer, 1676*

Madam,
I assure you I am not half so faulty as unfortunate in serving
you. I will not tell you my endeavours nor excuse my breach of
promise, but leave it to you to find the cause of my doing so ill
to one I wish so well to. But I hope to give you a better account
shortly. The complaint you spoke to me, concerning Miss, I

the place you are in: London. (Rochester has said he intends to go and stay in
    Bath, but has not yet left.)

Source: FL ii, p. 32.
Date: ?Early summer, 1676. See *my endeavours*, below.
my endeavours: perhaps to get her a part in a play (see Introduction, p. 29).
the complaint you spoke to me: Elizabeth Barry almost certainly had plenty of
    rivals, but the only person named as having been specifically in con-
    tention with her over Rochester is another actress, Elizabeth Bowtell, who
    had created the role of Margery Pinchwife in Wycherley's *The Country
    Wife* in January 1675. Curll tells a story about their performing opposite
    each other much later in *Alexander the Great, or the Rival Queens,* and
    acting on one occasion with 'such Vivacity' that

know nothing of, for she is as great a stranger to me as she can be to you. So, thou pretty creature, farewell.

Your humble servant,

———

Rochester to Elizabeth Barry   *?Early summer, 1676*

Madam,

That I do not see you is not that I would not, for that the devil take me if I would not do every day of my life, but for these reasons you shall know hereafter. In the meantime I can give you no account of your business as yet but of my own part, which I am sure will not be agreeable without others who I am confident will give full satisfaction in a very short time to all your desires. When 'tis done I will tell you something that perhaps may make you think that I am, Mrs ———,

Your humble servant,

Sunday.   ———

Statira on hearing the King was nigh, begs the Gods to help her for that Moment; on which *Roxana* [Elizabeth Barry] hastening the designed Blow, struck with such Force, that tho' the Point of the Dagger was blunted, it made way through Mrs. *Boutel*'s Stayes, and entered about a Quarter of an Inch in the Flesh . . . some affirmed, Mrs. *Barry* was jealous of Mrs. *Boutel* and Lord *Rochester*, which made them suppose she did it with Design to destroy her.

Curll sides with the others, who attributed the quarrel to an off-stage dispute over a piece of costume. Whatever the cause, the two actresses did not perform together in the play until after the amalgamation of their respective companies in 1682–3, two years after Rochester's death. (T. Betterton, *The History of the English Stage*, 1741, pp. 21–2; W. van Lennep, ed., *The London Stage, 1660–1800*, i, pp. 227, 225–6.)

Source: FL ii, p. 30.
Date: ?Early summer, 1676. (See below.)
your business: perhaps the business of getting her a part in *Abdelazar*: see p. 129 and Introduction, p. 29.

Rochester to Elizabeth Barry   **?**

Madam,

Dearest of all that ever was dearest to me, if I love anything in the world like you, or wish it in my power to do it, may I ever be as unlucky and as hateful as when I saw you last. I who have no way to express my kindness to you but letters, which cannot speak it half, whether shall I think myself more unfortunate who cannot tell you how much I love, or you, who can never know how well you are beloved? I would fain bring it about, if it were possible, to wait upon you today, for besides that I never am without the passionate desire of being with you, at this time I have something to tell you that is for your service and will not be unpleasant news. But here I am in chains and must seek out some device to break 'em for a quarter of an hour.

Rochester to Elizabeth Barry   **?**

Madam,

Till I have mended my manners I am ashamed to look you in the face, but seeing you is as necessary to my life as breathing, so that I must see you or be yours no more, for that's the image I have of dying. The sight of you, then, being my life, I cannot

Source: FL ii, p. 18.
Date: uncertain.
whether: which of the two. The construction is awkward; Rochester presumably meant to write 'Whether shall I think more unfortunate: myself . . . or you?'
something to tell you: conceivably relating to the 'business' mentioned in the previous letter.
here: presumably at Court.

Source: FL ii, p. 31.
Date: uncertain.
For the mock-religious style of the letter, see p. 24.

but confess with an humble and sincere repentance that I have hitherto lived very ill. Receive my confession and let the promise of my future zeal and devotion obtain my pardon for last night's blasphemy against you, my heaven. So shall I hope hereafter to be made partaker of such joys in your arms as meeting tongues but faintly can express. Amen.

Rochester to Elizabeth Barry   ?

Madam,

Though not for real kindness' sake, at least to make your own words good (which is a point of honour proper for a woman), endeavour to give me some undeniable proofs that you love me. If there be any in my power which I have yet neither given nor offered, you must explain yourself. I am perhaps very dull, but withal very sincere. I could wish for your sake and my own that your failings were such. But be they what they will, since I must love you, allow me the liberty of telling you sometimes unmannerly truths when my zeal for your service causes, and your own interest requires it. These inconveniences you must bear with from those that love you with greater regard to you than themselves. Such a one I pretend to be, and I hope if you do not yet believe it, you will in time find it.

You have said something that has made me fancy tomorrow will prove a happy day to me. However, pray let me see you before you speak with any other man. There are reasons for it, dearest of all my desires. I expect your commands.

An hour after I left you.

Source: FL ii, p. 26.
Date: uncertain.
were such: 'were the same as mine' (i.e. dullness and sincerity).
pretend: claim.

1 Rochester, by an unknown artist
The Earl Bathurst

2 Rochester and his monkey, after Huysmans
National Portrait Gallery

3 Anne, Dowager Countess of Rochester,
by Wissing after Lely
National Portrait Gallery

4 La Triste Héritière, probably
Elizabeth Malet, engraved from a painting
by Lely *Courtauld Institute*

5 Elizabeth, Countess of Rochester,
by Mytens or possibly Lely
Dr and Mrs James Johnston

6 Charles, Lord Wilmot, by T. Hawker
The Hon. Victor Montagu

7 Lady Anne Wilmot and
Lady Elizabeth Wilmot, by Wissing
Courtauld Institute

8 Elizabeth Barry, after Kneller
The Garrick Club

9 Louise de Kéroualle,
Duchess of Portsmouth, by Gascar
Courtauld Institute

10 Rochester's coffin plate (*above*) and Elizabeth, Countess of Rochester's coffin plate (*below*) from the vaults of Spelsbury Parish Church
The Vicar and Churchwardens of Spelsbury

11 Adderbury House today
Photograph by Redmond O'Hanlon

Rochester to Elizabeth Barry ?

Madam,
I have not sinned so much as to live two whole days without
seeing of you. From your justice and good nature therefore I
will presume you will give me leave to wait on you at night, and
for your sake use not that power (which you find you have
absolute over me) so unmercifully as you did last time, to divert
and keep me off from convincing you by all the reasons imaginable how necessary 'tis to preserve you faultless and make me
happy, and also that you believe and use me like the most
faithful of all your servants, etc.

Rochester in London to his wife at Adderbury ?

It is now some weekes since I writt you word that there was
money return'd out of Somerts. for y^r use, wch I desir'd you to
send for by what summes your self pleas'd; by this time I believe
I have spent itt half however you must bee supplied if you
thinke fitt to order itt; shortly I intend to give you the trouble
of a visitt, 'tis all I have to begg y^r pardon for att present, unless
you take itt for a fault that I still pretend to bee
y^r humble servant
Roch:

I doe not know if my mother bee att Ricott or Adderbury, if att
home present my duty to her.

Source: FL ii, p. 17.
Date: uncertain.

Source: MS. Harl. 7003, f. 208.
Date: uncertain.
Somerts.: Elizabeth's family estates in Somerset.
Ricott: Rycote Park, near Thame, Oxfordshire, home of the Dowager
  Countess's granddaughter Eleanor Lee after her marriage to Lord
  Norreys in February, 1672.

To Rochester in the country from Savile in London   August 15, 1676

Whitehall. Aug. 15. 76

Though it was not good manners to interrupt your L^P upon
your first returne to your Family, it would seem want of
Kindnesse to delay any Longer asking your good honour how
the Country air agrees with you, and if a hansome mixture of
the sobriety of Adderbury and the debauchery of Woodstock
bee yet putt into such a method that it can countervale the noble
variety of this towne, which stands just where it did, is full as
foolish, and full as wise, full as formall, and full as impertinent
as you left it, there is noe one condradiction you left in it but
you will find again at your returne, noething changing in it but
some few mortall lives, as for example this last weake has
bereaved us of poor Harry Bayly who through much sweating
in this hott [weather fell] into a feavour which carryed him
fro[m this earthly] beare garden to that of Eden; God s[end the
poor] man rest there, for truly to outward app[earances he] had
but an unquiet though an active l[ife here.] And tothers death
spares noe place, nor g[reatness, it] has seized upon my Lord
John Butler [himself,] who was latedly called Earle of Gowran,
[and now being] dead is pittyed as a man of parts, I suppose as
all who are hanged are called proper men, it is unimaginable
how absence, a new name, and dyeing at last, will change a

Source: MS. Harl. 7003, f. 300.

Date: as heading, August 15, 1676.

poor Harry Bayly: a murderous courtier in the train of Sir Philip Howard.
   (*CTB*, February 5, 1674.)

weather fell: for this and most of the other substitutions where the MS. is
   torn I have followed Wilson.

beare garden: on Bankside. Bear Gardens is still the name of a road running
   parallel with Rose Alley, near Southwark Bridge on the South Bank.

Lord John Butler: (1643–76) seventh son of the Duke of Ormonde. Ten
   years before, he had been one of Elizabeth Malet's suitors. Soon after his
   marriage in January 1676 to the daughter of the Earl of Donegal, he had
   been created Baron Aghrim, Viscount Clonmore and Earl of Gowran.
   He died of consumption in Paris that August. (*GEC*, Gowran.)

absence, a new name: see previous note.

mans character, for wee that knew the paire wee must needs
laugh to see the flattering idle world call Etheridge Yarmouth,
and Darby Macchiavell, things soe commonly practised, that it is
not more ordinary to heare my fatt Scotch neighbour make an
ill jest, or to smell a statesmans breath stinke. There is a very
warme report that my Lord Mordaunt has maryed Mall Kirke at

call *Etheridge Yarmouth, Darby Macchiavell:* Etherege is the dramatist, and the
contrast is between his reputation for idleness (complained of by the
author of 'A Session of the Poets', who may have been Rochester—see
Pinto, ed., *Rochester*, p. 104) and the rapacious self-advancement of
Robert Paston, Viscount (later Earl of) Yarmouth, who in this period
gained the Viscountcy, was appointed High Steward of Great Yarmouth
and Lord Lieutenant and Vice-Admiral of Norfolk, and entertained the
King at his country home. Any resemblance suggested between him and
Etherege was presumably a matter of Etherege's rapid rise to Court
favour from humble origins—he was an articled clerk, the son of a captain
living on a small estate in Maidenhead. He became a Gentleman of the
Privy Chamber in Ordinary in 1668, and by 1676 was probably pursuing
the knighthood conferred on him between 1677 and 1679 which, according
to contemporary gossip, he bought in order to marry his 'rich old widow'
Mary Sheppard Arnold. (See F. Bracher, ed., *Letters of Sir George Etherege*,
California, 1974, p. xvi.)

Derby is William Stanley, Earl of Derby, not a conspicuously devious or
politically minded person. Perhaps his detractors were jealous of his
appointment that May, at the age of 21, as Lieutenant of Cheshire and
Lancashire and of the city of Chester (*CSPD*, May 3, 1676).

Lord Mordaunt: Charles Mordaunt (*c.* 1658–1735), later third Earl of Peter-
borough, one of the Court circle. The report of his marriage was false.
Mordaunt secretly married Cary Frazier, a Maid of Honour to Queen
Catherine and a daughter of the King's physician, making the marriage
public in 1681. (*DNB; Court Satires*, p. 267.)

Mall Kirke: daughter of George Kirke, Groom of the Bedchamber to
Charles I. She was Maid of Honour to the Duchess of York from around
1673 until 1675, and mistress of the Duke of York, the Duke of Monmouth and the Earl of Mulgrave, more or less concurrently. In June 1675
she gave birth to a child who died a few hours later. She was turned out
of St James's Palace and went to live at first with her mother in Whitehall,
then (from August 30) in a convent in France. She was in France when
this rumour reached Savile. The following year she married Sir Thomas
Vernon of Hodnet, Shropshire. (*Savile Correspondence*, p. 57; *Court Satires*,
pp. 257–9).

Paris, Mrs Kirke hopes it is false for shee dos not look upon him
as a good match, this may looke like a jest but is as true as that
shee has said shee feares her sonn Piercy's wife will dishonour
her family, our friend Bridges beeing soe busy about her that
Mrs Smith has sent her husband word of it, as I am credibly
informed; would not such doeings make Carbery himselfe write
satyre, semper ego Auditor tantum nunquam reponam vexatus
toties? were I not too old [and much to]o fatt for poetry surely
all this stuffe should [inspire me] but beeing soe full of naturall
impediments [I gladly sen]d all these matters to your L^p, whose
Genius [is able to] shew the world theire follyes as your leasure
[serves you to] shew your abilities, for Gods sake, my most
[dear Lord, make] this use of your retreat, or returne as [soon as
you c]an to towne this beeing the criticall time [for you to
ta]ke your fortune, for Monsr Rabell is soe [much the fau]ourite
of his Maj^{ty} and your L^p of Monsr Rabell, that I doe not see you
can ever have a better opportunity of doeing your businesse;
now, your Chymicall Knowledge will give you entrance to a

Mrs Kirke: Mall's mother Mary, daughter of the poet Aurelian Townshend.
her sonn Piercy's wife: Percy Kirke (c. 1646-91) had married Lady Mary
   Howard, daughter of George Howard, fourth Earl of Suffolk. (*DNB.*)
Bridges: George Rodney Bridges, who the following year married the
   Countess of Shrewsbury, former mistress of the Duke of Buckingham. He
   was one of the group involved with Rochester in the Epsom murder two
   months earlier (see p. 28).
Mrs Smith: unidentified.
Carbery: Richard Vaughan, second Earl of Carbery (c. 1600-86), had been
   removed from office as Lord Lieutenant of Wales in 1672 for oppressing
   his tenants, some of whom had had their ears cut off and one of whom had
   lost his tongue. (*DNB.*)
semper ego, etc.: 'semper ego auditor tantum? nunquamne reponam/vexatus
   toties rauci Theseide Codri?' ('Am I always to be a mere listener? Shall I
   never retaliate, though so often tormented by the *Theseis* of a hoarse
   Codrus?')—the opening lines of Juvenal's first *Satire.*
Monsr Rabell: an apothecary to the King. (*HMC,* 22, *Leeds,* p. 12.) Charles
   was interested in chemistry, and spent much of his spare time that summer
   making experiments. (See Arthur Bryant, *King Charles II,* revised edn,
   1955, p. 199.)
your Chymicall Knowledge: perhaps a reference to the Bendo episode (see p. 33).

place where Manchester himselfe is kept out for his ignorance, which hitherto has carryed him through all, in a word the dayes of learning are comeing upon us, and under a receipt for the wormes noe man will be admitted soe far as the privy chamber, pray for your friends my most deare Lord in this day of tryall, and if I come in danger, send me a ♃ for a purge or upon my expulsion hence prepare to receave mee for a lead lap [or woollen] which I thinke in a little time will bee [the likelier] of the two, and soe health wealth and hap[piness to] your good L^p.

My duty to my Ld Lovelace if hee bee in Oxfordshire
To the R^t Honble the Earle of Rochester att Adderbury humble
   present
To bee left wth ye Postm^r of Banbury In Oxfordshire

Manchester: Robert Montagu, third Earl of Manchester (1634–83), Gentleman of the Bedchamber from 1666 to 1681. (*GEC*, Manchester.)
under: for less than: 'unless he has a prescription for the worms, he won't be welcome to the King.'
receipt: prescription.
♃ for a purge: 'This is the astrological symbol for Jupiter and the alchemical symbol for tin. Since Savile has mentioned a "receipt for the wormes" he may be using the symbol here to stand for muriate of tin—"Salt of Jove"— which was highly valued as a vermifuge (cf. A. C. Wootton, *Chronicles of Pharmacy*, 1910, II, 311). On the other hand, since Roman times the symbol appears to have been used interchangeably with the conventional Rx to prefix the formula in a prescription (cf. C. J. S. Thompson, *The Mystery and Art of the Apothecary*, 1929, p. 159). Savile, I believe, is ending his letter with a characteristic, if rather forced, jest. Pretending to fear expulsion from Court, he asks his medically inclined friend for a *new* "receipt for the wormes," to gain him access to the privy chamber.' (Wilson, p. 90.)
lead lap [or woollen]: i.e. a coffin or a poor man's shroud. 'Or woollen' is Wilson's conjecture, and has the support of Savile's general worries about money, particularly noticeable in his letters to his brother.
Lovelace: John, third Baron Lovelace of Hurley (1638–93), M.P. for Berkshire 1661–70, was at Wadham around the same time as Rochester. They took their M.A. degree on the same day, September 9, 1661. Lovelace lost the Rangership of Woodstock Park to Rochester, see p. 94, and *CSPD*, February 27, May 2, 1674.

Rochester in Oxford to Savile in Paris   *September 5, 1676*

Dear Savile,

Whether love or the politics have the greater interest in your
journey to France, because it is argued among wiser men I will
not conclude upon; but hoping so much from your friendship
that without reserve you will trust me with the time of your stay
in Paris, I have writ this to assure you, if it can continue a month
I will not fail to wait on you there. My resolutions are to employ
this winter for the improvement of my parts in foreign countries,
and if the temptation of seeing you be added to the desires I
have already, the sin is so sweet that I am resolved to embrace it
and leave out of my prayers 'Libera nos a malo'—for thine is my
kingdom, power and glory, for ever and ever.

                                        Rochester.
Oxford, September 5.

Rochester in the country to Elizabeth Barry   *October 6, 1676*
in London

Madam,

It is impossible for me to neglect what I love, as it would be
impertinent to profess love where I had none; but I take the

Source: FL i, p. 29.
Date: as letter, September 5, [1676]. Savile had left for Paris on August 31
   to consult with the Duchess of Cleveland, one of whose lovers he may
   have been. (*CSPD*, August 31 and November 25, 1676.)
love or the politics: see above.
Libera nos a malo: 'deliver us from evil'.

Source: FL ii, p. 19.
Date: as letter, October 6, [1676]. Rochester talks of returning to London,
   which he could not have done in 1675, when he was in disgrace, and did
   not do in 1677, when he was very ill (see p. 33). By 1678 their affair had
   probably ended (see Introduction, p. 30).

vanity to assure myself you cannot conclude so severely both of
my truth and reason as to suspect me for either of those faults.
If there has been a misfortune in the miscarriage of my letters, I
beseech you not to add to it by an uncharitable censure, but
do me the right to believe the last thing possible in the world
is the least omission of either kindness or service to you. I wish
the whole world was as entirely yours as I am; you would then
have no reason to complain of anybody. At least it would be
your own fault if they were not what you pleased. Those
wretches you speak of in your letter are so little valuable that
you will easily forget their malice and rather look upon the more
considerable part of the world, who will ever find it in their
interest, and make it their vanity, to serve you. And now to let
you know how soon I propose to be out of pain, two days hence
I leave this place in order to my journey towards London, and
may I then be but as happy as your kindness can make me, I
shall have but very little room either for envy or ambition.

October 6th. This morning your messenger came.

Rochester in London to his wife at Adderbury   *?Autumn, 1676*

Since my coming to towne, my head has bin perpetually
turn'd round, but I doe nott find itt makes me giddy; this is all

I take the vanity: the construction seems to be a conflation of the French
prendre vanité, which would not have taken an infinitive though it was
current in the Seventeenth Century preceding a noun, and *prendre la
liberté*, common at the time with an infinitive.
Those wretches: it is not clear what is referred to, except that some women,
possible servants, have spoken maliciously to Elizabeth Barry about
Rochester, perhaps (see p. 140) about his past affairs with them.
in order to: for the purpose of.

Source: MS. Harl. 7003, f. 198.
Date: ?Autumn, 1676: after the birth of Malet (see below). The oats and coal
suggest autumn.

the witt you shall receive in my first Letter, hereafter you may
expect more God willing; pray bid John Tredway purchase my
Oates, as soone as possible, & what-ever Coale you order I shall
returne money for upon notice; ready Cash I have but little, 'tis
hard to come by, but when Mr Cary comes downe hee shall
furnish you wth as much as I can procure, when you have more
commands I am ready to receive 'em being most extreamely

y^r humble servant
Rochester

Pray bidd my daughter Betty present my duty to my daughter
Mallett.

For the Countess of Rochester
att Adderbury neare
Banbury; Oxfordshire

Rochester to Elizabeth Barry   *?October, 1676*

Madam,
You shall not fail of —— on Saturday, and for your wretches, as
you call 'em, 'tis usually my custom when I wrong such as they
to make 'em amends, though your maid has aggravated that
matter more to my prejudice than I expected from one who
belonged to you, and for your own share, if I thought you a

John Tredway: unidentified.
Mr Cary: John Cary, agent and friend of the Rochesters.
Betty: their second daughter, Elizabeth.
Mallett: their third daughter, born in the winter of 1675–6.

Source: FL ii, p. 14.
Date: ?October, 1676 (see p. 139, on the 'wretches' who have been
  maligning Rochester).
your wretches: see p. 139.

woman of forms, you should receive all the reparations imaginable. But it is so unquestionable that I am thoroughly your
humble servant, that all the world must know I cannot offend
you without being sorry for it.

Rochester to Elizabeth Barry   ?

Madam,
I found you in a chiding humour today, and so I left you.
Tomorrow I hope for better luck, till when neither you nor any
you can employ shall know whether I am under or above
ground. Therefore lie still and satisfy yourself that you are not,
nor can be, half so kind to Mrs —— as I am.

                                              Good night.

Rochester to his wife   ?

[This letter was one of a number printed in Stephen Collet's
Relics of Literature, 1823 (p. 50), where it appeared under the
heading 'The Countess of Rochester to the Earl', an attribution
followed by Prinz and (by omission) Hayward. Unknown to
both editors, though not to Collet, the letter had previously
been published in *The Museum* (see p. 84) as Rochester's. It
survives in Rochester's holograph in the British Library and
there is no reason except the form of address ('y^r honour') for

of forms: i.e. very formal in etiquette.

Source: FL ii, p. 20.
Date: uncertain.
Mrs —— : presumably Mrs Barry herself.

Source: MS. Harl. 7003, f. 220.
Date: uncertain.

thinking it could be from Elizabeth. In fact it was a recurring joke of Rochester's to talk about her as if she were a domineering husband. In a verse epistle also printed in *The Museum*, 'I am, by fate, slave to your will' (see *Complete Poems*, p. 23), for example, he says he will write her a poem expressing his duty and

> With low-made legs and sugared speeches,
> Yielding to your fair bum the breeches,
> I'll show myself, in all I can,
> Your faithful, humble servant,
>
> John.

It seems very unlikely that the letter, which is full of corrections, is a copy; and the hand is unmistakably Rochester's (the slope erratic, the characters spiky and often unconnected, the loops of the descenders uncompleted) and not Elizabeth's, which is more even, rounded, and flowing.]

The last letter I received from y^r honour, was somthing scandalous, soe that I knew not well how to answer it, 'twas my designe to have writ to my Lady Anne willmot to intercede for mee, but now wth joy I find my selfe againe in y^r favour, it shall bee my endeavours to continue soe; In order to wch very shortly I will be wth you; in the meane time my Mother may bee pleas'd to dispose of my children, & my chimists, and my little doggs and whatever is myne as shee will, only if I may have nothing about mee that I like, it will bee the cause of making the felicity of waiting on her, befall mee very seldome, thus I remaine wth my duty to her, my service to you and all those things ——

somthing scandalous: it was Elizabeth who was scandalized, clearly.
Lady Anne willmot: their eldest daughter.
my chimists: As Burnet points out (p. 27), pharmacology was a study 'which the ill state of health he was fallen into, made more necessary to himself.'
my little doggs: cf. p. 84.

Rochester to his son Charles, Lord Wilmot   *?1676-8*

I hope Charles when you receive this, and know that I have sent this gentleman to bee y^r tutour, you will bee very gladd to see I take such care of you, and bee very gratefull, wch is best showne in being obedient & dilligent, you are now grown bigg enough to bee a man if you can bee wise enough; & the way to bee truly wise is to serve god, learne y^r booke & observe the instructions of y^r Parents first and next y^r Tutour, to whom I have intirely resign'd you for this seven yeare, and according as you imploy that time you are to bee happy or unhappy for ever. but I have soe good an opinion of you y^t I am glad to thinke you will never deceive mee, deare Child. Learne y^r Booke, & bee obedient, & you shall see what a father I will bee to you[;] you shall want noe pleasure while you are good, & that you may be soe are my constant Prayers

Rochester

For my Ld Willmott

Rochester to Arthur Capel, Earl of Essex   *April 22, 1677*

My Lord   Apr: 22 ——
The bearer of this being to present y^r Excellence with a reference

Source: MS. Harl. 7003, f. 249.
Date: uncertain—presumably 1676-8, when Charles was 5-7 years old.
this gentleman: Charles's tutor may have been Thomas Alcock, Rochester's accomplice in the Bendo exploit, who was probably the children's writing master. (*The Famous Pathologist*, p. 9.)

Source: British Library, MS. Stowe 211, f. 330.
Date: April 22, 1677. (See C. E. Pike, ed., *Selections from the Correspondence of Arthur Capel Earl of Essex*, 1913, p. 123.)
Arthur Capel, Earl of Essex: (1631-83). He was just completing his five-year tour of duty as Lord Lieutenant of Ireland.

from ye King, wherein my name is to appeare, it becomes my
duty to Lett you know that I am made use of only as a Trustee
for Mrs Nelly & that by a perticular direction y^r favour is humbly
begg'd, and much rely'd upon by her in this Affayre. & my part
is noe more but to advise her (as I would all I wish well to,) by
any meanes to bee oblidg'd to y^r Excellence if they can, since there
is noe where to bee found a better freind or worthyer Patron,
how sincerely this is my opinion You would not doubt my Lord,
could I make appeare to you, wth how much zeale & faithfull-
ness, I am, & wish ever to continue

Y^r humble servant
Rochester

a Trustee for Mrs Nelly: Nell Gwynn had been granted a warrant for certain
disputed lands in Ireland and, with Rochester acting as her trustee,
submitted her claim to the Lord Lieutenant. The issue was delayed for
several months and she made efforts through Henry Coventry to persuade
the King to intervene. Although he made a public show of refusing, he
seems to have used Rochester as the go-between for a bribe to the Lord
Lieutenant. The matter is mentioned in a note among the Essex Papers,
enclosed with a letter from Coventry to Essex dated June 12, 1677:

> Whereas the King hath referred a Pencon in Lord Rochester's name
> to the Lord Lieutenant of Ireland for granting certain lands . . . to the
> use of Mrs Gwyn these lands are likely to be disposed of otherwise
> then the King intends by the Court of claymes. It is therefore humbly
> desired his Ma^{ty} will be pleased to order Mr Secretary to write to the
> Lieutenant to take private order with the comm^{nrs} of the Court of
> Claymes that the hearing of all causes concerning the said lands
> named in the schedule may be deferred and that the other causes may
> be finished before these be meddled with.

(Essex Correspondence, ed. cit., p. 145.)

The properties were eventually granted to her in November, 'farmed' for
her benefit by Buckhurst and Thomas Felton, and brought her an
additional income of £800 a year. (J. H. Wilson, *Nell Gwyn, Royal Mistress*
1952, p. 163.)

Rochester to Elizabeth Barry   *?*

Madam,

I have a very just quarrel to business, upon a thousand faults, and will now continue it whilst I live since it takes me some hours of your company. Till two in the afternoon I cannot come to you. Pity my ill fortune and send me word where I shall then find you.

To Rochester from Buckingham   *April–May, 1677*

My Lord   Fryday
I haue sent your Lordship the Petition signed, and doe beg of

---

Source: FL ii, p. 27.
Date: uncertain.

Source: MS. Harl. 7003, f. 280.
Date: April–May, 1677: see *the Petition*, below.
the Petition: in February, 1677, on parliament's return from a 15-month prorogation, Buckingham had raised the question whether it had not in fact been dissolved by being prorogued, citing two unrepealed statutes of Edward III. He was supported by Shaftesbury, Wharton and Salisbury, but the motion was rejected and the House ordered the lords to ask pardon. They refused, and on February 16 were sent to the Tower. Buckhurst, then Earl of Middlesex, organized a petition to secure Buckingham's release, and it was delivered on May 8 (see *Savile Correspondence* for that date). Every obstacle was put in his way, and Buckingham's first release was a temporary parole granted him amidst frustrating delays late in June, to go and inspect the building work in progress on his house at Cliveden. This occasion is also described by Savile, in a letter of Sunday, June 24:

> On Thursday night late, too late to deliver it, a warrant was sign'd for leave for the Duke of Buckingham to go yesterday to Cliveden to view his building, and return this night to the Tower; but betwixt my Lord Northampton and Sᵗ Jo. Robinson it was so order'd that he stir'd not out of the Tower till six of clock last night, then lay at his house in the city, and is gone this morning about viewing Cliveden, and returns this night according to the former orders . . .; it is fifty-two miles forward and backward.
>   (*Savile Correspondence*, p. 62.)

you to loose noe time in making use of the Kings good nature
and kindnes to mee, becawse of some certaine well natured
persons who (your Lordship knowes) are apt to make speeches,
though not much better then that orator Higgen made to My
Lord Plimouth about Lawrells bands and feathers. I am entirely

My Lord

Your Lordships

Most humble and

Most obedient seru[ant]

Buckingham

For the Earle of Rochester.

To Rochester in London from Buckingham   *July, 1677*

My Lorde.
I can truly assure your Lordship as my Lord of Bristol did the

> Buckingham was released again in July for a month, and this time his
> freedom was made permanent after intercession by 'Nelly, Middlesex,
> Rochester and the merry gang'. (*HMC*, 29, *Portland*, iii, p. 355.)
>
> *persons . . . apt to make speeches:* the original House of Lords debate provoked
> by Buckingham's stand lasted for some five hours.
>
> *orator Higgen:* perhaps Sir Thomas Higgons (1624–91), Member of Parlia-
> ment for New Windsor and later Ambassador to Venice. He published a
> panegyric to Charles II in 1660, and a parliamentary speech in 1661, but
> the precise point of Buckingham's reference is not known.
>
> *My Lord Plimouth:* Charles Fitzcharles (1657?–80), an illegitimate son of
> Charles II, became Earl of Plymouth in July, 1675. (*GEC*, Plymouth.)

Source: MS. Harl. 7003, f. 282.

Date: July, 1677 (see note on *Mrs Nellis Commands*).

my Lord of Bristol: George Digby (1622–77), 2nd Earl of Bristol, a
prominent courtier. Clarendon says that in conversation he had 'a very
luxurious style, unlimited by any rules of truth or modesty'. Buckingham
had some reason to enjoy this particular blunder by the Earl, who had
seconded the Shrewsbury family's petition against him in the Lords in
1674. (*JHL*, vol. XII, p. 597; and see Dorothea Townshend, *George Digby,
2nd Earl of Bristol*, 1924, p. 213.)

Duches of Richmond, that I haue not contaminated my body
with any person below my quality since I saw you. which I hope
may serue to vindicate mee from any uniust suspicion about the
busines of sarding. I am now very busy drinking your Lordships
health and shall very shortly haue the honour to receiue your
and Mrs Nellis Commands. in the meane time I haue sent you
two of the ciuillest Carpes that euer I had to doe with. and if they
could speake they would infallibly (according to Mr boyls way
of morrall reflections) assure your Lordship that I am more
then any man liuing

My Lord
Your Lordships
Most humble
and faithfull
Seruant
Buckingham.

the Duches of Richmond: the beautiful Frances Stuart, maid of honour to
Queen Catherine, married the twice-widowed Duke of Richmond in 1667.
He died in 1672. She had been pursued by Charles II in the early 1660s
with the assistance of a group led by Buckingham, who soon began to act
on his own behalf as well as the King's. Both men were rebuffed. Richmond remained an object of fascination and wild rumour throughout the
reign. (*GEC* Richmond; C. H. Hartmann, *La Belle Stuart,* 1924, *passim;*
Court Satires, passim.)

sarding: thus, very clearly, in the MS. (*pace* Prinz, p. 279, who gives *carding*).
It was an obsolete word for practical joking, surviving in proverbial
phrases (see *OED, Sard*); but it may have had a code meaning at the
Court.

your and Mrs Nellis Commands: Rochester and Nell Gwynn were instrumental
in ensuring that Buckingham's temporary release from the Tower in
July 1677 was made permanent—see p. 146.

Carpes: see p. 153.

Mr boyls way of morrall reflections: the reference may be to Robert Boyle's
Occasional Reflections upon Several Subjects, 1665 (parodied by Swift in
Meditation upon a Broomstick). Boyle's philosophical ruminations are
prompted by the most commonplace observations, including (particularly
in Section IV, 'Which treats of Angling Improv'd To Spiritual Uses')
ones about fish.

Rochester to Elizabeth Barry   *?*

Madam,

Might I be so happy to receive such proofs of your kindness as I
myself would choose, one of the greatest I could think of were
that all my actions, however they appeared at first, might be
interpreted as meant for your service. Since nothing is so agreeable to my nature as seeking my own satisfaction, and since you
are the best object of that I can find in the world, how can you
entertain a jealousy or fear? You have the strongest security our
frail and daily changing frame can give, that I can live to no
end so much as that of pleasing and serving you.

To Rochester from Buckingham   *August, 1677*

My Deare Lorde

Whither my busines is done or noe, I thinke my selfe soe much
oblidged to you for your care in it, that I assure you as long as I
liue you shall finde mee hartily and entirely your seruant. I doe

Source: FL ii, p. 16.
Date: uncertain.
our frail and daily changing frame: the idea that inconstancy is an unavoidable
   fact of the human condition, found in Montaigne, understandably
   fascinated Rochester and his contemporaries. See for example Rochester's
   song 'Love and Life', and Etherege's poem beginning 'Chloris, it is not in
   our power/To say how long our love will last'.

Source: MS. Harl. 7003, f. 285.
Date: August, 1677 (see below).
my busines: despite the events of the previous months Buckingham began to
   pursue the position of Lord Steward as soon as he was released from the
   Tower. (Winifred, Lady Burghclere, *George Villiers, Second Duke of
   Buckingham, 1626–1687*, p. 330.) He was unsuccessful—see below.

not like this aduising with the Cabinet Cowncell, but if it does succeed notwithstanding, I shall begin to hope better for all the Kings affaires. it being my opinion that till hee can distinguish that his interest is different from the interest of some about him; hee will neuer bee soe happy as hee is wished to bee both by your Lordship and

> Your Lordships
> Most humble and most
> faithfull seruant
> Buckingham.

Fryday night.

Rochester to Elizabeth Barry ?

Madam,
I could say a great deal to you but will conceal it till I have merit, so these shall be only to beg your pardon for desiring your excuse till Monday, and then you shall find me an honest man and one of my word. So Mrs ——

> Your servant,

——

this aduising with the Cabinet Cowncell: while occupied with the 'business' of the Stewardship, Buckingham, according to Marvell, 'layd constantly in Whitehall at my L: Rochester's logings leading the usuall life'. A number of ministers, including Danby and the Dukes of York and Monmouth, 'remonstrated to the King that this was to leap over all rules of decency and to suffer his authority to be trampled on'. Buckingham was accordingly warned to leave Whitehall, which he did. (*Poems and Letters of Andrew Marvell*, ed. cit., ii, p. 355.) Buckingham's general point, the increasing influence of the cabinet during Charles's reign, is a historical fact widely noted at the time. (See W. R. Anson, 'The Cabinet in the Seventeenth and Eighteenth Centuries', *English Historical Review*, xxix, 1914, pp. 56–78.)

Source: FL ii, p. 34.
Date: uncertain.

II

Rochester to Elizabeth Barry   ?

Madam,

My visit yesterday was intended to tell you I had not dined in
company of women, which, though for a certain reason I could
not very well express with words, was however sufficiently made
appear, since you could not be so very ill-natured to make
severe reflections upon me when I was gone. Were men without
frailties, how would you bring it about to make 'em love you so
blindly as they do? I cannot yet imagine what fault you could
find in my love-letter. Certainly 'twas full of kindness and duty
to you, and whilst these two points are kept inviolable, 'tis very
hard when you take anything ill. I fear staying at home so much
gives you the spleen, for I am loath to believe 'tis I. I have
therefore sent you the two plays that are acted this afternoon—
if that diversion could put you into so good a humour as to make
you able to endure me again, I should be very much obliged to
the stage. However, if your anger continue, show yourself at the
play that I may look upon you and go mad. Your revenge is in
your own eyes and if I must suffer, I would choose that way.

Source: FL ii, p. 25.
Date: uncertain.
staying at home so much: in her pregnancy? See p. 30.

1677

Pissing of Blood

To Rochester at Woodstock from Buckingham   *August 11, 1677*
in London

My Deare Lord
After the obligations I haue to you I showld not bee soe unmannerly as to desire your Lordship to neglect any of your
owne occasions for my sake but my noble friends at cowrt
haue now resolued as the most politick notion they can goe
upon, to ly most abominably of your Lordship and mee. in
order to which they haue brought in a new Treasonable lampoone
of which your Lordship is to bee the Author. for this and for
seuerall other reasons there will bee a necessity of your Lordships being heeere when the King comes to Towne. but Mr
Sheapheard and I will entertaine you more upon this subiect
before it bee long. for wee are resolued to wayte upon you

Source: MS Harl. 7003, f. 283.
Date: as heading, August 11, 1677.
the obligations I haue to you: see Buckingham's previous letters, pp. 145f.
a new Treasonable lampoone: perhaps a violent satire beginning 'Preserv'd by
    wonder in the oak, O Charles', attacking Charles for his promiscuity. It is
    dated 1677 in one manuscript and was ascribed to Rochester in early
    printed texts, though the author was probably John Lacy. (See Yale
    POAS, i, pp. 425f.)
when the King comes to Towne: he had gone to sea on August 7 and was
    expected back the day before Buckingham's letter, but was delayed by
    contrary winds and did not return until August 21. (*CSPD.*
Mr Sheapheard: Sir Fleetwood Shepherd, see p. 109.

at Woodstock: where I shall assure your Lordship of my being
unalterably

> My Lord
> Your Lordships
> Most humble and most obedient seruant.
> Buckingham.

August the iith 1677.

For the Earle of Rochester.

To Rochester at Woodstock from Buckingham   *August 19, 1677*
at Cliveden

> Clifden.
> August: 19
> Sunday.

My Lorde
Your kinde letter has giuen mee more sattisfaction then I am
able to expresse, for I doe assure your Lordship that I hartily
loue you, and shall doe soe till the last minute of my life: and
nothing is truer then what is elegantly expressed in a frensh
song: Le plaisir est extresme, daymer et destre aymé, quand on
ayme. I am sorry I did not aske Mr Pouies opinion abowt this
Song who came hither the other day to see my building, and

Source: Harl. 7003, f. 272.
Date: as heading, August 19, [1677]. (See previous letter.)
Clifden: Buckingham's country seat—see *my building,* below.
a frensh song: unidentified. The lines are so vacuous ('It is an intense pleasure
   to love and be loved when one is in love') that they could almost be a
   parody.
Mr Pouie: Thomas Povey, a Master of Requests, described by Evelyn as 'a
   nice contriver of all Elegancies, & exceedingly formall' (*Diary,* February
   29, 1676). His house in Lincoln's Inn Fields was regarded as a model of
   taste. (*DNB.*)

giue mee some instructions about the breeding of Carpes, which
I shall acquaint your Lordship with when I haue the honour to
see you. the circumstances of the matter are somthing long, but
this in short is the summe of it. That you must bee sure to
Cleanse your pond very well, and lett noe fish bee in it whatsoeuer but only two Carpes, a Male, and a female; and then that
the next yeare you must take them out of that pond, and put
them into another, for feare of theyre being eaten by Pykes.
this hee says will make them breed infinitly, and grow very fatt,
though hee has not as yet beene pleas'd to tell mee what they are
to bee fed with. I wish with all my hart that hee and our grand
Politicians were always to goe together in couples; for it is a
very great pitty that persons of such extraordinary parts showld
euer bee parted. hee is as angry against Lampoons as they, and
as much affrayed of them, though he does not deserue them soe
well. for hee is a foole that only makes one laugh, the others
make one cry too. which, that it may come to bee theyre turnes
to doe in Gods propper time is the harty wishes of

My Lord

Your Lordships

Most humble and

Most obedient seruant

Buckingham.

my building: Cliveden House, Buckinghamshire, was built by the Duke during
the period 1665 to 1680. The architect was William Winde. John Evelyn
described it in 1679:

> I went to *Clifden* that stupendious natural Rock, Wood, & Prospect
> of the Duke of *Buckinghams*, & building of extraordinary Expense. . . .
> The house stands somewhat like *Frascati* as to its front, & on the
> platforme is a circular View to the uttmost verge of the Horison,
> which with the serpenting of the *Thames* is admirably surprising: The
> Staire Case, is for its materials, singular: The *Cloisters*, Descents,
> Gardens, & avenue through the wood august & stately . . .
>
> (*Diary*, July 23, 1679.)

Buckingham's creditors were still fighting in 1711 over whether out-
standing building debts of more than £50,000 should have a prior claim
on his estate (*HMC*, 17, *House of Lords*, ix, p. 89).

Since my wayting upon your Lordship will bee noe trouble to
you I shall sende for Sheaphard tomorrow, and as soone as I
can appoint a day when wee can certainly bee at Woodstock, I
shall send your Lordship word of it. heere is noe newes at all of
the Kings comming back.

To Rochester at Woodstock from Buckingham   October 8, 1677
at Cliveden

My Lorde,
As persons inclined to corroborate the intentions of other men,
are euer more incumbent to a voluminous ubiquity, then any
way condecending to the notions of a iust medium, soe all true
louers of art, doe naturally preferr the cimetry of reuolutions,
before the corruscation, of any concatinations whatsoeuer. and
the reason of this is plaine, becawse else all vocall determinations
would bee frustrated, and then (as Aristotle obserues very well)
noe man cowld propperly say consummatum est. The meaning
of this simile is, that if your Lordship will giue mee leaue, I shall
imediatly wayte upon you, with the best pack of Hownds that
euer ran upon English grownd. I had done it sooner but that I

Sheaphard: Sir Fleetwood Shepherd, see pp. 109, 151.
the Kings comming back: see previous letter.

Source: MS. Harl. 7003, f. 274.
Date: as letter, October 8, 1677.
As persons inclined to corroborate . . .: for the mock-elevated style of this
    nonsensical passage, see Introduction, p. 24.
consummatum est: it is completed; cf. John 19:30.
wayte upon you: at Woodstock. Buckingham stayed there from about October
    20 to November 5 (see p. 21).
the best pack of Hownds: Buckingham was an enthusiastic huntsman with a
    famous pack of hounds. His death in 1687 was caused by a chill caught
    while he was out hunting. (See Winifred, Lady Burghclere, George Villiers,
    Second Duke of Buckingham, 1626–1687, 1903, pp. 393f.)

stayed for my Lord Dorsets and Mr Sheaphards company. but they hauing both failed mee, and not knowing how long your occasions will giue you leaue to stay in the Cowntry, I thought fitt to know of your Lordship by this bearer whither it would not bee inconuenient to you at this time to receiue a visit from

My Lord
Your Lordships
Most humble and most obedient seruant
Buckingham

Clifden. October 8. 1677

For The Earle of Rochester.

Rochester at Woodstock to his wife at Adderbury   *?October, 1677*

Deare Wife
I have dispatch't yᵉ messenger away to night to save you the trouble of rising early, hoping you have noe concerne to comunicate to mee of yᵉ owne, the D[uke] of B[uckingham] came hither to night & stay's two dayes, I must Lend him my Coach half way back therfore pray send itt mee; my Condition of health alters I hope for the better, though various accidents succeed, my paines are pritty well over, & my Rheumatisme begins to turne to an honest gout, my pissing of blood Doctor

Dorset: Buckhurst, see p. 114.
Sheaphard: Sir Fleetwood Shepherd, see p. 109.
how long your occasions will giue you leaue . . .: Rochester was in fact still in the country in December (see his letter to the Earl of Lichfield of December 22).

Source: MS. Harl. 7003, f. 211.
Date: October, 1677, when Buckingham stayed at Woodstock (see previous letter) and Rochester was very ill (see following letter).

Wetherly say's is nothing My eyes are almost out but that hee says will nott doe mee much Harme, in short he make[s] mee eate flesh & drinke dyett-drink—

God bless you

my duty to my mother, thanke her for my cordialls.

Rochester to Elizabeth Barry   *?October, 1677*

Madam,
This is the first service my hand has done me since my being a cripple, and I would not employ it in a lie so soon; therefore, pray believe me sincere when I assure you that you are very dear to me; and as long as I live, I will be kind to you.

P.S. This is all my hand would write, but my heart thinks a great deal more.

To Rochester at Woodstock from Savile   *October 16, 1677*
in London

Whitehall. Octob. 16. 77.
I will have vanity enough my deare Lord to beleeve you have

Doctor Wetherly: one of the King's physicians, who attended Rochester in his last illness and is a signatory to his will.
dyett-drink: medicinal drink.

Source: FL ii, p. 10.
Date: ?October, 1677 (Rochester's being 'a cripple'—see previous letter).

Source: MS. Harl. 7003, f. 298.
Date: as heading, October 16, 1677.

allready concluded my silence could proceed from noething but
my absence from hence for betwixt the North & Newmarkett I
have made a three monthes progresse and this is the first post-
day since my returne; I should out of naturall inclination have
taken this first opportunity of writing to you, but I am induced
to make more haste by the scurvy report of your being very ill of
which I desire to know the truth from yourselfe who alone doe
speake true concerning yourselfe, all the rest of the worlde not
beeing onely apt to beleeve but very ready to make lyes concerning you and if your friends were like them there has been
such a story made concerning your last adventure as would
perswade us grave men that you had stripd yourselfe of all your
prudence as well as of your breeches which you will give a man
leave to thinke impossible who knowes & admires your talents
as much as I doe. After all if you have not caught cold and made
yourselfe sick with your race, it is not one pinn matter for all the
other circumstances of it though the same advantages have been
taken of it heer that use to bee on any unseasonable pranke
performed by your L^p who have had experience enough upon
the like occasion to know that the best way is to make your
personall appearance heer which has never fayled you, and if this
bee not argument enough to bring you to towne I will add that
of the honour of your Country for without you the towne is soe

---

betwixt the North & Newmarkett: Savile went to Nottingham late in July,
and then on to stay with his brother at Rufford, Nottinghamshire, his
family home, presumably staying there until the King went to the races in
late September. (*Savile Correspondence*, pp. 65–6.)

such a story: Rochester's version appears in his reply, following. The incident
became legendary. Thomas Hearne, for example, wrote: 'This Lord . . .
used sometimes with others of his companions to run naked, and particularly they did so once in Woodstocke park, upon a Sunday in the
afternoon, expecting that several of the female sex would have been
spectators, but not one appeared. The man that stript them, and pulled off
their shirts, kept the shirts, and did not deliver them any more, going off
with them before they finish'd the race.' (J. Prinz, ed., *Rochesteriana*,
Leipzig, 1926, p. 15.)

dull that the Dutch men thinke themselves in Holland and goe Yawning about as if they were att home, for Gods sake come & helpe to entertain them for I am quite spent and can not hope to have my Spirits ever revived but by your L^{ps} Kindnesse and company of which I esteem one & love the other above all the happinesses I have ever enjoyed, and begg the continuance of both with the most earnest conjurations imaginable which I shall endeavour to deserve by beeing with all truth and sincerity most faithfully y^r L^{ps} servant whilst I am

Hen: Savile

For the R^t Honble the Earl of Rochester att Woodstocke

Rochester at Woodstock to Savile in London   *October, 1677*

Dear Savile,

Though I am almost blind, utterly lame, and scarce within the reasonable hopes of ever seeing London again, I am not yet so wholly mortified and dead to the taste of all happiness not to be extremely revived at the receipt of a kind letter from an old friend who in all probability might have laid me aside in his thoughts, if not quite forgot me by this time. I ever thought you an extraordinary man and must now think you such a friend who, being a courtier as you are, can love a man whom it is the great mode to hate. Catch Sir G.H. or Sir Carr at such an ill-bred

the Dutch men: William of Orange came to England with his entourage on October 9, after lengthy negotiations concerning his marriage to Princess Mary, announced on October 21.

Source: FL ii, 1697 edn, p. 39. (The letter is omitted from the 1699 edn.)

Date: October, 1677. The letter is a reply to Savile's of October 16, and is in turn replied to on November 1.

Sir G.H.: Sir George Hewitt (1652–89), a famous courtier and fop, traditionally the model for Etherege's Sir Fopling Flutter in *The Man of Mode.* (*Court Satires,* pp. 250–51.)

Sir Carr: Sir Carr Scroop (1649–80), minor poet attacked by Rochester in several satires and burlesqued in the song 'I swive as well as others do.'

proceeding and I am mistaken. For the hideous deportment which you have heard of concerning running naked, so much is true: that we went into the river somewhat late in the year and had a frisk for forty yards in the meadow to dry ourselves. I will appeal to the King and the Duke if they had not done as much; nay, my Lord Chancellor and the Archbishops both, when they were schoolboys—and at these years I have heard the one declaimed like Cicero, the others preached like St Austin. Prudenter persons I conclude they were, even in hanging sleeves, than any of the flashy fry (of which I must own myself the most unsolid) can hope to appear even in their ripest manhood.

And now Mr Savile, since you are pleased to quote yourself for a grave man of the number of the scandalized, be pleased to call to mind the year 1676, when two large fat nudities led the coranto round Rosamund's fair fountain while the poor violated nymph wept to behold the strange decay of manly parts since the days of her dear Harry the Second. P[rick], 'tis confessed, you showed but little of, but for a[rse] and b[uttocks] (a filthier ostentation, God wot!) you exposed more of that nastiness in your two folio volumes than we all together in our six quartos. 'Pluck therefore the beam out of thine own eye', etc. And now

the hideous deportment: see previous letter.

the Duke: of York.

my Lord Chancellor: Heneage Finch, Lord Finch of Daventry, later Earl of Nottingham.

the Archbishops both: Gilbert Sheldon (Canterbury) and Richard Sterne (York). Sheldon died on November 9, that year.

St Austin: St Augustine.

in hanging sleeves: i.e. as children, who wore clothes with loose open sleeves.

fry: crowd.

Rosamund's fair fountain: Rosamund's Well in Woodstock Park.

Harry the Second: Rosamund's lover, King Henry II. (According to the legend, his queen, Eleanor, bled her to death at Woodstock.)

Pluck therefore ....: 'how canst thou say to thy brother, Brother, let me pull out the mote that is in thine eye, when thou thyself beholdest not the beam that is in thine own eye? Thou hypocrite, cast out first the beam out of thine own eye, and then thou shalt see clearly to pull out the mote that is in thy brother's eye'. (Luke 6, 41.)

'tis time to thank you for your kind inviting me to London to make Dutchmen merry, a thing I would avoid like killing punaises, the filthy savour of Dutch mirth being more terrible. If God in mercy has made 'em hush and melancholy, do not you rouse their sleeping mirth to make the town mourn. The Prince of Orange is exalted above 'em and I could wish myself in town to serve him in some refined pleasures which I fear you are too much a Dutchman to think of.

The best present I can make at this time is the bearer, whom I beg you to take care of that the King may hear his tunes when he is easy and private, because I am sure they will divert him extremely. And may be ever have harmony in his mind, as this fellow will pour it into his ears. May he dream pleasantly, wake joyfully, love safely and tenderly, live long and happily, ever prays, dear Savile, un bougre lasse qui era toute sa foutue reste de vie votre fidèle ami et très humble serviteur,

                                        Rochester.

To Rochester in the country from Savile   *November 1, 1677*
in London

                        Whitehall. Nov^{er} 1st 77.
If y^r L^p was as ill as you told mee in your letter either you are a

---

Dutchmen: see previous letter.
punaises: bed-bugs.
Prince of Orange: see previous letter.
the bearer: James Paisible (1656?–1721), the fashionable French musician, who was in England by February, 1675. (*The London Stage*, ed. cit., i, p. 228; *DNB*.)
un bougre lasse . . . .: 'a tired bugger who all the rest of his wretched life will be your faithful friend and most humble servant.'

Source: Bath MS., Portland Papers, ii, f. 215.
Date: as heading, November 1, 1677.

greater Philospher in bearing of pain, or a greater Hypocrite in making it more then it is then wee can ordinarily meet with in these parts, however the case stands, I was mighty glad to find a man both lame and blind could bee soe merry; I thaught there could bee but one lame thing upon earth in perfect happinesse & that is Fanshaw for his having a daughter, a Princesse who yet remaines in Paganisme for want of Baptisme which the fond Father delayes to take some prudent resolution concerning the Godfathers, hee thinkes the King ought to bee kept for a sonn, and the Duke of Monmouth dos not yet owne the alliance enough to hold his Neece att the font, & therefore I beleeve that honour will att last fall upon his Grace of Buckingham. Mrs Nelly who is his great friend and faithfull Councellour advised him not to lay out all his stock upon the christning but to reserve a little to buy him new shooes that hee might not dirty her roomes, and a new periwigg that shee might not smell him stinke two storeys high when hee knocks att the outward door, what influence this wholsome advice may have in processe of time I doe not know, but noe longer agoe then yesterday hee was out att heeles and stunke most grieviously, and putt mee very much in mind of a Predecessour of his of our English

Fanshaw . . . a Princesse: a member of the Court circle, William Fanshaw is a good example of its incestuousness. Among his affairs was one with Lucy Walter, mistress and reputed wife of Charles II. Fanshaw later married Lucy's daughter Mary, whose father was supposedly Nicholas, Viscount Taafe, though the possibility of the King's paternity may have been the reason for his giving her a pension of £600 a year. At any rate, she liked to boast of her kinship with James, Duke of Monmouth (Charles II's son by her mother), was nicknamed 'the princess', was said to have cured someone of the King's Evil, and was herself rumoured to have slept with the King. Around 1670 she married William Sarsfield, and a year after Sarsfield's death in 1675 married Fanshaw, then one of the King's Masters of Requests. (*Court Satires*, pp. 58, 236-7.) For his lameness, see p. 184.
Duke of Monmouth: see below.
Mrs Nelly: Nell Gwynn.

Royall blood (as I take it a Duke of Excester) that was soe poor in Flanders (if you will beleeve Phillip de Comines) that hee had noe shoos att all.

Since the P. of Orange has declared his love to matrimony, that sacrament growes soe modish in the Court that Mr Roper has most happily consummated with Mrs Walker, how many times the first night is as yet knowne to none but the Queens Majesty.

Harry Killegrew has been a Widdower these two dayes and laments his condition that fortune has made it possible for him to play the fool again, considering what use hee is wont to make of the power of committing errours, besides human frailty in generall.

My Lord Manchester has to the astonishment of all his acquaintance a new suit, but it is black, and therefore fowly suspected it was left him by his sister Irwyn for mourning, else his Maj^{ty} concludes that ceremony had been performed in the auntient Russett his L^P use to weare upon the like occasions.

Notwithstanding all the demonstrations of Joy both in the Court and Citty for this great marriage I doe not heare of any of

Duke of Excester: 'Savile refers to the *Memoirs* of Philippe de Commynes (1447–1511): ". . . car j'ay veu un duc de Cestre all a pied san chausses, apres le train dudict duc, purchessant sa vie de maison en maison, sans se nommer" (*Memoirs*, ed. Joseph Calmette, Paris, 1924, 3 vols, I, 191–2).' (Wilson, p. 94.)

P. of Orange: see p. 158. The marriage took place on November 4.

Mr Roper: Francis Roper, a Groom of the Bedchamber, married Anne Walker, a Maid of Honour to the Queen. (*CTB*, May 28, 1678.)

how many times, etc.: omitted by *HMC.*

Harry Killegrew: the son of the dramatist Thomas Killigrew. He was a friend of Savile's and a Groom of the Bedchamber, and various of his exploits are described by Pepys. His wife has not been identified.

Lord Manchester: Robert Montagu, third Earl of Manchester (1634–83). His step-mother Margaret, the old Earl's fifth wife, had died the previous November. (*GEC,* Manchester.)

this great marriage: see note on the Prince of Orange, above.

the sweet singers except the old Bard Waller that has taken
notice of it, I have not yet seen his verses but am promised them
before I seale this letter and then yourselfe shall bee judge
whether the old Gentleman stinke in the sockett, or blaze a
little yett; and now I am upon Poetry I must tell you the whole
tribe are alarumd att a libell against them lately sent by the Post

the old Bard Waller: Edmund Waller (1606–87) wrote two poems on the
marriage, 'To the Prince of Orange, 1677', welcoming the Prince and
wishing him well in his suit, and an epithalamion, 'Of the Lady Mary
Princess of Orange'. (G. Thorn-Drury, ed., *The Poems of Edmund Waller*,
[1905], ii, pp. 80, 82.)

stinke in the sockett: i.e. like a burned-out old torch.

a libell: see p. 167, where Rochester implies he is not the author. Wilson
(p. 94) rightly discounts Hayward's suggestion that the poem referred to
is *A Satyr upon the Poets*, which was written after 1681, and contradicts
Pinto, who identified it as *A Trial of the Poets for the Bays*, which was
written before March 1677 and would therefore not have been sufficiently
topical for Savile's reference. Wilson's own candidate is 'Advice to Apollo,
1678', a mild and slight literary satire in the first volume of *Poems on
Affairs of State*, unfavourable to Scroop, Dryden and Mulgrave but
praising Dorset and Rochester. But this poem can hardly be described as a
libel, and there is no actual evidence for dating it earlier than its title-year
(which in Old Style means at least four months after Savile's letter).
Wilson's suggestion cannot be treated as more than a guess.

In the absence of firmer evidence any suggestion is bound to be
similarly speculative, but a poem which caused a fuss in the Court circle
and is dated 1677 in two MSS. is Scroop's *In Defence of Satyr* (Yale,
POAS, i, p. 364), a fierce attack on a large number of contemporary
figures including Rochester, who is condemned for the Epsom Downs
murder the year before. Savile's question whether the libel he refers to
might have been composed at Woodstock (i.e. by Rochester and the guests
he had staying with him there) does not conflict with this suggestion, since
he had not seen the poem; and there is no reason why *In Defence of Satyr*
could not have been 'commended' in his hearing, whether on personal
grounds (the poem attacks enemies of the Court wits, as well as friends) or
literary ones. As an imitation of Horace's fourth satire it was in the most
up-to-date literary fashion. Suggestions that the poem must have been
written immediately after the Epsom Downs fight (June 17, 1676) do not
add up to much, since the poem contains references to other less immediately topical matters, the allusion in l. 90f. to the Duke of Monmouth's war-games, for example, being prompted by an incident as far
back as August 1674.

to Will's coffe house, I am not happy enough to have seen it but I heare it commended and therefore the more probably thaught to be composed at Woodstock, espeacially considering what an assembly either is yet or att least has been there, to whom my most humble service, if they are yett with you.

It were worth your while to see how the old Ladyes and the young beggerly bitches are sueing for places about the Princesse of Orange (who is to bee the next week) my Lady Arabella Macarty and my Lady Elizabeth Dalaval take it monstrous ill not to bee Ladyes of her bedchamber, which they say is like to bee disposed of to my Lady Inchequin and Benticks wife when hee has one, and hee dos endeavour that Mad^elle Beverwest

---

Will's coffe house: famous meeting place of the Court wits and other literary groups in the Seventeenth and Eighteenth Centuries. It was at No. 1, Bow Street, Covent Garden.

Lady Arabella Macarty: wife of Justin Maccarty, later Viscount Mountcashell. She was a daughter of Thomas Wentworth, Earl of Strafford. (*GEC*, Mountcashell.)

Lady Elizabeth Dalaval: Wilson (p. 95) suggests the wife of Sir Ralph Delavall, a naval officer who came to prominence under William III.

Lady Inchequin: not, as Wilson suggests (p. 95), the ageing Elizabeth, Lady Inchiquin, but her daughter-in-law Margaret, wife of William O'Brien, Earl of Inchiquin. She was the younger daughter of the Earl and Countess of Orrery and went to The Hague as Lady-in-Waiting to Princess Mary, no doubt partly because her mother-in-law, the Dowager Countess, was half Dutch. (*GEC*, Inchiquin.)

Benticks wife: Hans Willem Bentinck, Nobleman of the Chamber to the Prince of Orange, had accompanied him on an earlier visit to England and been his chief envoy in the marriage negotiations. When William succeeded to the throne, Bentinck acquired various titles, including that of Earl of Portland. In February 1678 he did in fact marry one of the Princess's maids of honour, Anne Villiers. (*DNB*.)

Mad^elle Beverwest: perhaps one of the daughters of Lodewyk, Lord of Beverwaert or Beverweerd, a natural son of Maurice, Prince of Orange. In 1659, Beverwaert's eldest daughter, Lady Amilia Nassau, had married a Royalist hero, Thomas, Earl of Ossory (not, as Wilson says, Earl of Arlington), and the third daughter was to become a Lady of the Bedchamber to Queen Anne. (*GEC*, Ormond.)

should bee that happy weoman. A daughter of Ned Villiers now in France and another of S⁏ Charles Wheeler's are to bee maydes of honour, & England affording noe more beautyes I heare they have sent into Holland for two to bee ready against the returne of the Prince thither which must bee before the end of this month, I did propose a detachement from the Dutchesse of Mrs Clarke & Mrs Mannock but I had not interest enough to bee heard; S⁏ Gabriel Sylvius is to bee chiefe Major Domo, and would fain carry Mrs Howard over with him but I heare this new preferment adds noething to her inclinations to him. I obeyed y⁏ commands to his Maj⁏ who has heard with very great delight Paisible's new compositions, and was not lesse pleased at all the complements you bestowd upon him, but I would not have you thinke hee takes soe much pleasure in your good wishes as in your good company which is soe necessary heer to dispel the clowdes of dullnesse the Dutchmen have made that you can not bee thaught otherwise then a Trayteur to King & Country, and a most unmercifull monster to a[ll] your acquaintance if you come not quickly to towne, though upon croutches.

A daughter of Ned Villiers: Colonel Edward and Lady Frances Villiers were in charge of the York household at Richmond from the Restoration, and the family was well represented in Princess Mary's entourage. Lady Inchiquin (see above) was a niece of Lady Frances's; the couple's eldest son Edward, eldest daughter Elizabeth, and younger daughter Anne (later married to Bentinck, see above), all attended the Princess. Elizabeth Villiers became William's mistress. (N. M. Waterson, *Mary II Queen of England*, 1928; Hester W. Chapman, *Mary II Queen of England*, 1953.)

S⁏ Charles Wheeler: M.P. for Cambridge, and a close associate of Danby.

Mrs Clarke and Mrs Mannock: Possibly, as Wilson suggests (p. 95), ladies-in-waiting to the Duchess of York, though they are not named in J. R. Henslowe's account of the retinue in her *Anne Hyde Duchess of York*, 1915.

interest: influence (*OED, Interest, sb.*, 6).

S⁏ Gabriel Sylvius: Savile was wrong. Sylvius, an ambassador for the Duke of York on several occasions, married Anne Howard, a maid of honour to the Queen, on November 13, 1677. (*CTB*, 1677–8, passim.)

Paisible: see p. 160.

12

Rochester in the country to Savile in London   *November, 1677*

Harry,

You who have known me these ten years the grievance of all prudent persons, the byword of statesmen, the scorn of ugly ladies (which are very near all) and the irreconcilable aversion of fine gentlemen (who are the ornamental part of a nation), and yet found me seldom sad, even under these weighty oppressions; can you think that the having of lean arms, small legs, red eyes and nose (if you will consider that trifle too) can have the power to depress the natural alacrity of my careless soul? Especially upon receiving a fine letter from Mr Savile which never wants wit and good nature, two qualities able to transport my heart with joy though it were breaking! I wonder at M———r's flaunting it in Court with such fine clothes. Sure he is an altered person since I saw him, for, since I can remember, neither his own self nor any belonging to him were ever out of rags. His page alone was well clothed of all his family, and that but in appearance, for of late he has made no more of wearing second-hand c[un]ts than second-hand shoes, though I must confess, to his honour, he changed 'em oftener. I wish the King were soberly advised about a main advantage in this marriage which may possibly be omitted: I mean the ridding his kingdom of some old beauties and young deformities who swarm and are a grievance to his liege people. A foreign prince ought to behave himself like a kite, who is allowed to take one royal chick for his reward but then 'tis expected before he leaves the country his flock shall clear the whole parish of all the garbage and carrion

Source: FL i, p. 36.
Date: November, 1677. (Written in answer to Savile's of November 1.)
having of lean arms: FL i has 'loving', which Wilson (p. 96) suggests is a misprint for 'having'. The remark is in reply to Savile's joke that he was 'glad to find a man both lame and blind could be so merry' (p. 161).
M———r's: the Earl of Manchester's, see p. 162.
this marriage: see p. 158.
kite: scavenging bird, a member of the falcon family.

many miles about. The King had never such an opportunity, for
the Dutch are very foul feeders, and what they leave he must
never hope to be rid of, unless he set up an intrigue with the
Tartars or Cossacks. For the libel you speak of upon that most
unwitty generation the present poets, I rejoice in it with all my
heart and shall take it for a favour if you will send me a copy.
He cannot want wit utterly that has a spleen to those rogues,
though never so dully expressed. And now dear Mr Savile,
forgive me if I do not wind up myself with an handsome period.

Rochester.

To Rochester at Woodstock from his wife at Adderbury   ?

Though I cannot flater my selfe soe much as to expect it yett
giue me leaue to wish that you would dine to morrow att
Cornbury where nesecity forces

Your faithfull humble Wife
E. Rochester.

if you send to command mee to woodstock when I am soe near
as cornbury I shall not be alitle rejoyced.

For The Earle of Rochester

the libel you speak of: see Savile's letter (pp. 163–4).

Source: Harl. 7003, f. 195.
Date: uncertain.
Cornbury: Cornbury Park, Clarendon's country seat near Charlbury, Oxford-
    shire. Clarendon's son Henry Hyde, Viscount Cornbury, lived there
    during his father's exile in France from 1667. The family were related to
    Rochester's mother.
to woodstock: Cornbury is three miles from Woodstock.

Rochester in the country to Elizabeth Barry   ?Autumn–Winter, 1677

Madam,

I am forced at last to own that 'tis very uneasy to me to live so long without hearing a word of you, especially when I reflect how ill-natured the world is to pretty women, and what occasion you may have for their service. Besides, I am unsatisfied yet why that inconsiderable service you gave me leave to do you, and which I left positive orders for when I came away, was left unperformed, and if the omission reflect upon my servant or myself, that I might punish the one and clear the other. I have often wished, I know not why, but I think for your sake more than my own, that Mrs —— might forget me quite, but I find it would trouble me of all things should she think ill of me or remember me to hate me. But whenever she would make me happy, if she can yet wish me so, let her command some real service and my obedience will prove the best reward my hopes can aim at.

To Rochester at Woodstock from Savile   *November 6, 1677*
in London

Whitehall. Nov^br 6. 77.

This is onely to enclose these last workes of Mr Waller which I promised you in my last, hee has found noe more applause from

Source: FL ii, p. 24.
Date: ?Autumn–Winter, 1677. (Barry's 'occasion' for the women's service being her confinement, perhaps: see p. 30.)
pretty women: presumably Rochester had sent some maids to attend her, and had had no news of their arrival.

Source: Bath MS., Portland Papers, ii, f. 217.
Date: as heading, November 6, 1677.
last workes of Mr Waller: see p. 163.

them then I doubt Mr Butler will from a third volume of
Hudubras hee has newly putt out, whereby it is humbly con-
ceived that a muse is apt to decay towards fourscore as well as
other mortalls; I wishe y^r L^p would take the opportunity as you
have formerly in your indispositions done, to shew us that five
and twenty is much a better age for Poetry, you must pay some
fine for your absence from towne and therefore pray doe not
thinke to come empty, if you doe, att least come quickly and
that will make amends for all

Sunday night

morning, but   *piece cut out of MS*

seldome troub[led]

most of that

then they can count. My L^d of Leycester is att last dead and our
friend just as proud of the Earldome faln to him as our other

Mr Butler . . . Hudubras: the third and last part of Samuel Butler's mock-epic
  Hudibras was published in 1677, when Butler was 65. Waller was then 72.
  As Savile predicts, it was less interesting than the previous parts, and sold
  comparatively poorly. Part One had been in the bookshops by December
  1662 (much earlier than Wilson suggests), and became an immediate
  best-seller, running to nine editions in a year. Part Three took three years
  to go into three editions. (J. Wilders, ed., *Hudibras*, Oxford, 1967, pp.
  xix–xx.)

five and twenty: as with 'towards fourscore', Savile stretches the facts.
  Rochester was 30.

My L^d of Leycester: Robert Sidney, Earl of Leicester, died at Penshurst on
  November 2, 1677, aged 81, and was succeeded by his son Philip, then 57.
  The new Earl's comment that his inheritance was 'all one' must, as Wilson
  points out (p. 97), be set beside his rapaciousness in administering it.
  Wilson quotes Cartwright's *Sacharissa*, p. 200: 'Lord Lisle refused to pay
  the legacies bequeathed to his brothers, and was so indignant at the
  injustice which he held his father to have done him, that he quarrelled
  with all his family, and for many years refused to see his brothers and
  sisters.' The brothers took him to court, and won. (*DNB*; *GEC*,
  Leicester.)

friend of Dorsett was. My Ld Sunderland who is an Executour
is not yet returned from Penshurst, soe that wee doe not yet
know whether H. Sidney's portion bee left soe large as to
disturbe my Ld Leycester's philosophy, but in the mean time hee
sais, Tis all one. Pray, my deare Lord, let's heare some good
newes of your recovery which would bee welcome newes to
many good people, though it may bee some dull ones had rather
heare of your funerall then of your returne hither, but may God
in his indignation strike all such blockheads dead, & leave none
living but such as have in some measure the same good wishes
and service for you which is written in the very bottome of the
soule of

> [My] Lord
> [Y^r L^{ps}] faithfull
> [& humble se]rvant
> Hen: Savile.

For the R^t Honble the
Earle of Rochester
att
Woodstock

Rochester to his wife at Adderbury   *November 20, [?1677]*

Nov: the 20th

My most neglected Wife, till you are a much respected Widdow,
I find you will scarce bee a contented woman, and to say noe

our . . . friend of Dorset: Charles Sackville, Lord Buckhurst, had succeeded to
the Earldom of Dorset on August 27, 1677.
Ld Sunderland: Savile's friend Robert Spencer, Earl of Sunderland, a
Gentleman of the Bedchamber, see p. 22.

Source: MS. Harl. 7003, f. 245.
Date: as heading, November 20 [?1677]. (Rochester's illness—see previous
letters. His conviction that he would soon be dead increased throughout
the following year.)

more than the plaine truth, I doe endeavour soe fairly to doe you that last good service, that none but the most impatient would refuse to rest satisfy'd; what evill Angell Enimy to my repose does inspire my Lady Warr to visitt you once a yeare & leave you bewitch'd for elev'n months after? I thanke my god that I have the Torments of the stone upon mee (wch are noe small ones) rather than that unspeakable one of being an eye wittness to y^r uneasinesses; Doe but propose to mee any reasonable thing upon Earth I can doe to sett you at quiett, but it is like a madd woman to lye roaring out of paine and never confess in what part it is; these three yeares have I heard you continually complain nor has itt ever bin in my power to ob[tain] the knowledge of any considerable cause [to be] confident I shall nott have the like affliction three yeares hence, but that repose I owe to a surer freind than you; when [that] time comes you will grow wiser, though I feare nott much Happyer

For the Countess of Rochester att Adderbury neare Banbury Oxfordshire
[*One illegible word in a different hand.*]

Rochester to Elizabeth Barry   December, 1677

Madam,
Your safe delivery has delivered me too from fears for your sake,

my Lady Warr: Elizabeth's mother.
the stone: see Introduction, p. 34.
these three yeares: if my dating is correct, the years of his affair with Elizabeth Barry.
a surer freind: death.

Source: FL ii, p. 9.
Date: December, 1677. Elizabeth Barry gave birth to a daughter, Elizabeth, around the middle of the month. (See Savile's letter, following.)
Your safe delivery: see above.

which were, I'll promise you, as burthensome to me as your great-belly could be to you. Everything has fallen out to my wish, for you are out of danger and the child is of the soft sex I love. Shortly, my hopes are to see you, and in a little while to look on you with all your beauty about you. Pray let nobody but yourself open the box I sent you; I did not know but that in lying in you might have use of those trifles. Sick and in bed as I am, I could come at no more of 'em; but if you find 'em, or whatever is in my power, of use to your service, let me know it.

To Rochester in the country from Savile   *December 17, 1677*
in London

Whitehall. 10ᵇʳ17. 77.

Out of a quality common to most men of beleeving easily what they desire earnestly I have sufferd myselfe to bee silent longer not onely then kindnesse but even common manners would have suffered mee to bee, but the truth is the whole towne have soe confidently reported your Lᵖ would every day bee in towne, (nor was this contradicted by your own servants) that I have wearyed myselfe with that expectation and can noe longer hold out but I must aske your Lᵖ how you doe, your health beeing what I am most concerned for when I have not your company, which I valew soe much that as usually happens I preferr that both to your health and my owne. There is not one sinner in England now out of London but yourselfe, George Porter has

---

great-belly: specifically in the sense of pregnancy. See *OED, Great,* 22.

Source: Bath MS., Portland Papers, ii, f. 219.
Date: as heading, December 17, 1677. (10ᵇʳ = (Latin) *Decem*ber.)
George Porter: eldest son of Endymion Porter, and a Groom of the Bedchamber. About 1673 he left his wife and retired to Berkshire, making occasional forays into town to see his mistress (the actress Jane Long, see below), and his riotous son 'Nobbs'. (*Court Satires,* pp. 275–6.)

been heer a fortnight and is allready three surfeits before you, one of spratts, one of tripes, and the third of Newarke ale, the rogue is grown soe ravenous that now hee surfeits of every thing hee sees but Mrs Long and his sonn Nobbs which hee can never have enough on, Jack Hervey is really angry with him for committing all this filthynesse without him. Sheapherd has been overturned in a coach att Matt Clifford's funerall and broake his head, and a little before was runn with a sword under the eye endeavouring to part Buckly and Etheridge squabbling in a Taverne, soe that hee is absolutely become a man of blood and talkes of nothing but a regiment against the French, hee has

Mrs Long: Jane Long, a leading actress in the Duke's Company, notable for her performances in 'breeches' parts. Her last recorded appearance, as Betty Rash in Nevil Payne's *The Morning Ramble*, was in November 1672 (see *The London Stage*, ed. cit., i, passim), her theatrical retirement coinciding with the break-up of the Porters' marriage.

Nobbs: see note on George Porter, above.

Jack Hervey: John Harvey, Treasurer and Receiver General to the Queen and a close friend of Charles II. (H. Sidney, *Diary of the Times of Charles the Second*, ed. R. W. Blencowe, 1843, i, p. 252; *DNB*.) The sentence is omitted in *HMC*.

Sheapherd: Fleetwood Shepherd (see p. 54).

Matt Clifford's funerall: Martin Clifford, on the fringe of the Court circle, died on December 10, 1677, and was buried on December 13. (*CSPD*, December 12, 1677; Wilson, p. 97.)

Buckly and Etheridge: Henry Bulkely, Master of the Household to Charles II, and Sir George Etherege, the dramatist.

a regiment against the French: at the end of December 1677, as a result of intense political pressure on Charles II, a treaty was finally signed with the Dutch by which England contracted to help restore European peace on terms which the Kings of France and Spain were to be induced, by force if necessary, to accept. As part of the military preparations, a large English expeditionary force was to be sent to Ostend, and English warships were to be fitted out for the Mediterranean and the channel. Charles's intricate secret diplomacy with the French while all these plans were being made was well concealed, as Savile's letter shows, though in the event it was mainly Charles's procrastination which prevented their being carried out. Meanwhile, rumours of an Anglo-French war were inevitably widespread. Parliament was adjourned during the negotiations, from December 3, 1677, to January 15, 1678, and finally to January 28. (Ogg, ii, 546f.) See also p. 183.

allready alotted what estate hee will have in France and for a
house att Paris I doe not find hee will bee satisfyed under the
Palais Royall; this is a sorte of madnesse now soe common heer
that either to doubt of making warr with France or beating them
when it is made is an offence against the nation, and though the
Parlᵗ will occasion your comeing up within a month it were well
enough worthy a journey sooner to see how the stile of the
Court is altered in this point, and to see his Majᵗʸ soe merry
with the Confederates in the Queens withdrawing room whilst
poor Barillon stands by neglected. The greatest newes I can send
you from hence is what the King told mee last night, that your
Lᵖ has a daughter borne by the body of Mrs Barry of which I
give your honour joy, I doubt shee dos not lye in in much state,
for a friend and protectrice of hers in the Mall was much
lamenting her poverty very lately not without some gentle
reflexions on your Lᵖˢ want either of generosity or bowells
toward a lady who had not refused you the full enjoyment of all
her charmes. My Lady Portsmouth has been ill to the greatest
degree, the King imputes her cure to his dropps, but her
Confessour to the Virgin Mary to whom hee is said to have
promised in her name that in case of recovery shee should have
no more commerce with that known enemy to virginity &
chastity the Monarke of Great Brittain, but that shee should
return to a Cloyster in little Brittany and there end her dayes, I

the Confederates: the (Dutch) allies—see previous note.
Barillon: Paul de Barillon, French ambassador.
daughter: see pp. 29–30.
Portsmouth: the Duchess, who had fallen ill in 1676 when she was tem-
    porarily superseded as the King's mistress by the Duchess Mazarin (see
    p. 120), ailed again in December 1677. F. D. P. Senior says, with what
    evidence is not clear, that she took the opportunity to visit her native
    France, reaching Bourbonne-les-Bains in May 1678. (F. D. P. Senior, The
    King's Ladies, 1936, pp. 229f.) If she did go, she was back in July. (J.
    Delpech, The Duchess of Portsmouth, 1953, p. 122.)
a Cloyster in little Brittany: the Duchess of Portsmouth was Breton by birth,
    and had been taken from a convent school to be maid of honour to
    Charles II's sister, the Duchess of Orleans, in whose company he first

have not yet heard that her Grace has confirmed this bargain, but there are fooles who beleeve it and because the Physitians have concluded it necessary for her to goe to Bourbon and the tenth of March appointed for the day of her goeing, it is not hard to have wagers layd that shee will returne noe more. I had allmost forgott, for another argument to bring you to town that a French troop of Comœdians bound for Nimeguen were by adverse winds cast into this hospitable port and doe act at Whitehall soe very well that it is a thousand pittyes they should not stay especially a young wench of fifteen who has more beauty and sweetnesse then ever was seen upon the stage since a friend of ours left it, In good earnest you would bee delighted above all things with her, and it were a shame to the nation shee should carry away a maydenhead shee pretends to have brought and that noe body heer has either witt or addresse, or money enough to goe to the price of, the K. sighes and despaires, and sais noebody but Sʳ George Downing or my Lᵈ Ranelagh can possible purchase her. His Majᵗʸ has called to your house a new Peer or to speake more properly restored an old one, Sʳ Robert

met her in 1670. (Senior, op. cit., above, pp. 186f.) The joke is partly at the expense of Louis XIV's mistress, Louise de la Vallière, who entered a convent when she was superseded by Mme. de Montespan (see p. 85).

Bourbon: Bourbonne-les-Bains (see note on *Portsmouth*, above).

a French troop of Comœdians, etc.: the actress was Françoise Pitel, later famous as Mlle. Raisin (see W. J. Lawrence, 'Early French Players in England', *Elizabethan Playhouse and other Studies*, Stratford, 1912, 1st series, pp. 148–9).

a friend of ours: either Nell Gwynn, who had retired from the stage in 1671, or Elizabeth Barry (see above).

the K.: the King.

Sʳ George Downing: the wealthy soldier and politician. Earlier in 1677 he had been named in a pamphlet attributed to Marvell as having received at least £80,000 by the King's favour. (*A Seasonable Argument to Persuade all the Grand Juries in England to Petition for a New Parliament*, p. 14.) (*DNB*.)

Lᵈ Ranelagh: Richard Jones, Earl of Ranelagh. Rich, greedy and corrupt, he had already been accused of misappropriating crown revenues as governor of Athlone, a charge that was taken up by the attorney general in 1679. (*DNB*.)

your house: the House of Lords.

Sherly under the name of Lord Ferrers of Chartly which hee claimes in right of his Grandmother sister to the last Earle of Essex of yᵉ house of Devereux, And which is more extra-ordinary this is done meerly by his Majᵗʸ without any inter-position, or money given either to Mistresse or Minister. I will not thinke it soe essentiall to fill this fourth page as to aske pardon for the other three, but you know what your company is I could never leave it under severall houres, soe that in writing I can not leave you under severall pages, yᵉ Lᵖ will forgive my methods of this and many other kinds, they are most of them very unjustifiable, but if I am right in anything under the sunn it is in the most reall & unfeigned professions of beeing to you and yours a most faithfull humble servant.

[For] Lord Rochester

Rochester to his nephew, the Earl of Lichfield   *December 23, 1677*

My deare Lord, I would not have slipt this opportunity of

Sʳ *Robert Sherly:* Sir Robert Shirley, seventh Baronet (1650–1717). The succession was extremely complicated. Shirley's great-uncle, Robert Devereux, Earl of Essex and Baron Ferrers, died childless in 1646. The titles became extinct, and at the Restoration the Earldom was conferred on Arthur Capel. Devereux's coheirs were his childless elder sister Frances, and the son of his dead younger sister (Shirley's grandmother), an older Robert Shirley, the fourth Baronet. Frances survived until 1679, but the fourth Baronet died in 1656 and his son, Sir Seymour Shirley (fifth Baronet), died in 1667. Sir Seymour's only son and heir died childless in 1669, leaving the baronetcy to his uncle, Sir Seymour's brother, the Robert Shirley mentioned by Savile. This Sir Robert now in turn became coheir to the Devereux estate, on the strength of which he claimed the extinct Barony. It was granted him by a special writ of summons on December 14, 1677. *GEC* quotes Savile's letter as evidence of the contemporary reaction. (*GEC*, Essex.)

Source: MS. Harl. 7003, f. 254.

Date: as letter, December 23, 1677.

The Earl of Lichfield: Rochester's nephew Edward Lee who, though still a child, had married Charles II's illegitimate daughter by the Duchess of Cleveland earlier that year, and was now heir to the Woodstock Ranger-ship. See p. 110.

waiting upon you, but the change of the weather makes itt a dangerous journey for a man in noe better health than I am, neither would you condemne the care I take of my self, did you know how kind an Unckle & how faithfull a servant I preserve for you, the Character you have of mee from others may give you some reason to concider this noe farther than good Nature oblidges you, but If I am ever soe happy to live wher my inclinations to you may shew themselves, bee assur'd you shall not want very good proofes, how much the memory of y^r father, the favours of my Lady Lyndsey, (how long-soever past) & y^r owne merritt, can oblidge a very gratefull man to bee faithfully sincerely & eternally deare Nephew

Y^r most humble servant
Rochester

Dec: 23–77

For the Earle of Leitchfeild

Rochester at Woodstock to his wife at Adderbury   *December ?1677*

I have my deare wife sent you some Lamb about an ounce, I have sent to my Mother one Westphalia Ham, one joule of Sturgeon & on Christmas day I will send her a very fatt Doe. I feare I must see London shortly, & begin to repent I did not bring you wth mee for since these rakeHells are nott here to

Character: i.e. 'description of my character'.

y^r father: Sir Francis Lee, Rochester's step-brother, who had died earlier in the year.

my Lady Lyndsey: Sir Francis's widow Elizabeth.

Source: MS. Harl. 7003, f. 237.

Date: December ?1677, when Rochester was at Woodstock.

Westphalia: German province famous for its bacon.

joule: cut of fish consisting of the head and shoulders.

rakeHells: i.e. rakes (the abbreviated form), debauchees.

disturb us you myght have past y' devotions this Holy season as well in this place as att Adderbury, but deare Wife one of my Coach mares is dying, or I had sent my Coach instead of my Complement.

For My Wife.

in this place: Woodstock.

1678

Anger, Spleen, Revenge and Shame

Rochester to Elizabeth Barry   *?1678*

Madam,

Yesterday it was impossible to answer your letter, which I hope for that reason you will forgive me; though indeed you have been pleased to express yourself so extraordinarily that I know not what I have to answer to you. Give me some reason, upon your own account only, to be sorry I ever had the happiness to know you, since I find you repent the kindness you showed me, and undervalue the humble service I had for you, and that I might be no happier in your favours than you could be in my love, you have contrived it so well to make them equal to my hatred, since that could do no more than these pretend to—take away the quiet of my life. I tell this not to exempt myself from any service I can do you (for I can never forget how very happy I have been) but to convince you, the love that gives you

Source: FL ii, p. 13.

Date: ?1678 (see Introduction, p. 30).

Give me some reason: difficult to unravel, but the sense seems to be that she has written to Rochester saying she has heard that he hates her, and she regrets ever having shown any affection for him. Rochester asks in return for some first-hand evidence ('upon your own account only') that the relationship is not working. He says that by treating him in this way she has made the memory of her favours as painful to him as it would be for him to hate her: since his peace of mind has already gone, hatred would make little difference. As they are making one another so unhappy they should no longer try to keep the affair alive. 'The trouble of perceiving it' sounds blasé now, but the noun was used of real grief and affliction in Rochester's time.

the torment of repentance on your side, and me the trouble of perceiving it in the other, is equally unjust and cruel to us both, and ought therefore to die.

Rochester to Elizabeth Barry   *1678*

Dear Madam,
My omitting to write to you all this while were an unpardonable error had I been guilty of it through neglect towards you, which I value you too much ever to be capable of. But I have never been two days in a place since Mrs —— went away, which I ought to have given you notice of and have let you know that her crime was making her court to —— with stories of you, entertaining her continually with the shame she underwent to be seen in company of so horrid a body as yourself in order to me obtaining of her ——'s employment, and lastly that my —— was ten times prettier than that nasty B—— I was so fond of at London, which I had by you. This was the grateful acknowledgement she made you for all your favours, and this recompense for all the little services which upon your account she received from
                    Your humble servant, etc.

Rochester to Elizabeth Barry   *?*

Madam,
Anger, spleen, revenge and shame are not yet so powerful with me as to make me disown this great truth, that I love you above

Source: FL ii, p. 35.
Date: 1678 (after the birth of their daughter.)
Mrs ——: the names left out by the FL ii editor remain unknown.
know: FL ii 'known'.
B——: Betty, Rochester's daughter by Elizabeth Barry.

Source: FL ii, 36.
Date: uncertain.

all things in the world. But I thank God I can distinguish, I can see very woman in you, and from yourself am convinced I have never been in the wrong in my opinion of women. 'Tis impossible for me to curse you, but give me leave to pity myself, which is more than ever you will do for me. You have a character and you maintain it, but I am sorry you make me an example to prove it. It seems, as you excel in everything, you scorn to grow less in that noble quality of using your servants very hardly. You do well not to forget it, and rather practise upon me than lose the habit of being very severe, for you that choose rather to be wise than just or good-natured may freely dispose of all things in your power without regard to one or the other. As I admire you, I would be glad I could imitate you; it were but manners to endeavour it. Which since I am not able to perform, I confess you are in the right to call that rude which I call kind and so keep me in the wrong for ever (which you cannot choose but take great delight in). You need but continue to make it fit for me not to love you and you can never want something to upbraid me with.

Three o'clock in the morning.

To Rochester at Adderbury from Savile in London   *June 2, 1678*

June. 2. 78.

My deare Lord

Though wee have had some scurvy alarums since you left us concerning your health, yet the last time I saw my Lord

Source: Bath MS., Portland Papers, ii, f. 221.
Date: as heading, June 2, 1678.
since you left us: Wilson (p. 99) cites various other pieces of evidence suggesting that Rochester had been back in London at some time in the spring. See also Savile's letter of June 18.

Cornwallis hee assured mee you were upon the improving hand, of which if there bee a man living gladder then myselfe I am much mistaken; as for mee, you can not but have heard the misfortunes that have befallen both my body naturall and body politick, how I have been sacrificed to that filthy dogg Lauderdale, and how the returne of my venereall paines have throwne mee back to dry mutton & dyett drinke, and whether this latter does most afflict the pleasure of my body, or the former the pride of my soule it is hard to determine, but both togather doe for the present make mee unhappy enough; how soon his Maj^{ty} will deliver mee from the one and Mr Barton from the other lyes in the ones Royall breast and in the others sckill chirurgicall. I suppose ye L^p has heard that all the fine Gentlemen

Lord Cornwallis: Charles, third Baron Cornwallis of Eye, a young member of the Court group. He was married to Elizabeth Fox, one of 'The Women about Town' mentioned in Rochester's poem of that title. (*GEC*, Cornwallis; *Complete Poems*, p. 46.)

that filthy dogg Lauderdale: the Scottish High Commissioner, John Maitland, second Earl and first Duke of Lauderdale. A letter from Sir Andrew Forrester to Lauderdale, dated May 9, 1678, describes the King's reaction when Savile voted with the opposition against Lauderdale in the House of Commons over the matter of Charles's delays—blamed on Lauderdale—in taking measures against France:

> the King was mightily displeased against him, and to so high a degree, that when he was late that night goeing to bed, and Saville comeing in after his ordinary way, the King upon the first sight of him fell into such a passion, that his face & lipps became as pale (almost) as death, his cheeks & armes trembled, and then he sayd to Saville, You Villayne how dare you have the impudence to come into my presence when you are guilty of such basenes as you have showne this day? I doe now & from hence forth discharge you from my service, commanding you never to come any more into my presence nor to any place where I shall happen to be.
>
> (O. Airy, ed., *The Lauderdale Papers*, London, 1884–5, iii, p. 140.)

venereall: cut in *HMC.*

Mr Barton: evidently a doctor who specialized in treating venereal diseases.
    Cf. Savile's letter in July, p. 197, and Rochester's reply, p. 201.

chirurgicall: surgical.

who intended to conquer France are disappointed, and that this
noble Army is out of hand to bee disbanded, to the griefe I
thinke of none but those who are of it, and of them many have
layd out summes which will inconvenience them, soe that if
suffering bee part of the businesse of a souldier, diverse of them
have made a notable progresse for the time. On Monday there
goes a yacht into Holland to bring Ambassadour Hyde again
into England, the use of publick ministers abroad growinge
lesse necessary every day. Not knowing how strongly y^r L^{ps}
spirits are I will not venture to oppresse them too much and
therefore with tenne thousand most reall wishes for your L^{ps}
health I am most unfeignedly yours etc.

H.S.

For the Right Honble the
Earle of Rochester
   att Adderbury
Too bee left wth ye Postm^r of
   Banbury in Oxford for to be
   sent as above said

Franke.

To Rochester at Adderbury from Savile in London   *June 4, 1678*

June 4. 78.

Your L^p will find the inconvenience of having a friend in towne

the fine Gentlemen who intended to conquer France: see note to p. 173, *a regiment
against the French.* Despite his secret negotiations with Louis, Charles had
been obliged by the terms of the Anglo-Dutch treaty to send several
battalions to Ostend that spring. But by refusing either to declare war on
France or on the other hand to disband his troops, he successfully played
on parliamentary fears of a standing army, so that on June 4 the Commons
voted £200,000 towards disbandment. (Ogg, ii, p. 554.)

on Monday: June 3, 1678. Lawrence Hyde, Ambassador to The Hague, was
back in England by June 18, according to Savile's letter of that date.

Source: Bath MS., Portland Papers, ii, f. 223.
Date: as heading, June 4, 1678.

that keeps much att home, for betwixt kindnesse & idlenesse you will find yourselfe in danger every post day of beeing asked how you doe, Fanshaw, who has better intelligence of your health then enjoyment of his owne gives mee new assurances of your beeing recovered beyond all hazzard of a relapse, that is just the state your friends would see you in, for you have had soe many returnes of your disease that till you are growne to a considerable strength wee shall allwayes thinke you in some danger. And now I talke of poor Fanshaw hee is just returned from an expidition I suppose hee made y* L^p privy too, I was intrusted as beeing able to give him some instructions, I doe not find him otherwise altered by it but that his mouth stands quite awry (which hee onely calls a soare lipp) but it has taken noe thing from his lameness onely added to his leanenesse hee weares three flannell wastcoates & is slenderer than Churchill. The truth is of all men living I ought not to railly him, but as hee is the onely creature upon earth poorer and pockier then myself there is somewhat in the nature of mortall man, that though never soe miserable hee will look out something to trihumph over, now in this case poor Fanshaw is the onely trophy I have in this world.

For Parl^t affaires, tomorrow is appointed in your house for the

Fanshaw: see note to Savile's letter of November 1, 1677, p. 161. He visited Rochester when he was ill—see Introduction, p. 34.

an expidition: Wilson (p. 100) suggests that Fanshaw may have gone to Bath or Epsom 'for the curative (and laxative) values of the waters', though it is hard to see why this should have been a matter for such secrecy and gossip. Clearly he was suffering from venereal disease (see p. 198), and had been recommended to a sweatshop by Savile, who was an expert. Fanshaw's lameness was probably due to arthritis, a common result of gonorrhoea, and his mouth's standing 'quite awry' to gingivitis caused by mercury poisoning.

Churchill: John Churchill, first Duke of Marlborough.
railly: mock.
and pockier: omitted in *HMC.*
your house: the House of Lords.

utmost decision whether my Ld Purbeck bee a Viscount or noe.
Viscount Montaigue has brought in a petition against Viscount
Hereford, to prove that there can bee noe such title pretended to
by him who has it, & tis said it is like to bee made out soe that
you see all the businesse of the Lords is upon the Viscounts
bench where my Lords Viscounts Yarmouth & Newport make

Ld *Purbeck:* Robert Villiers, otherwise Danvers, was born about 1656 and
assumed the title Viscount Purbeck on his father's death in 1674. But the
father was apparently illegitimate. He was said to have been baptized
Robert Wright, and on the death of his mother's husband, the first
Viscount, in 1658, he disclaimed his peerage and took a seat in the House of
Commons, claiming the privilege of a member of the House of Commons
in 1660 when he was accused, among other charges, of speaking treason
against the King. At this stage the House of Lords considered him to be
Viscount Purbeck, and the King 'fined' him 'all his peerage dignities, in
possession and remainder, with a view to extinguishing the same'.

His son's claim to the title was referred by the King to the Lords on
April 22, 1675, where it was opposed both on the ground of this fine and
on that of his father's illegitimacy. When Villiers attained his majority in
1677 he tried again, but on July 9, 1678, the House (though now deciding
that the fine had been invalid) sustained the objection on the ground of
the illegitimacy. See also p. 196. (*GEC*, Purbeck; *JHL* April 30, 1675;
July 9, 1678.)

Viscount Montaigue: Francis Brown, fourth Viscount Montagu, petitioned the
King for inspection of records concerning the Viscountcy of Hereford,
arguing that it had been extinguished on the death without issue of
Robert, the fourth Viscount, in 1646. The petition was referred to the
Lords, who on May 30 agreed to postpone judgement until the then
Viscount, who was an infant, reached his majority.

Montagu's action was prompted by ancestral rivalry. The Hereford
Viscountcy, created in 1550, had suffered various interruptions, including
forfeiture of the title when the third Viscount was beheaded in 1601. The
title was restored by James I on his accession, however, and in 1643, with
the extinction of the Viscountcy of Fitzwalter (cr. 1525), became the
premier—i.e. senior—Viscountcy of England. This seniority would in
turn have devolved on the Montagu Viscountcy (cr. 1554) on the death of
the fourth Viscount Hereford in 1646, had the Hereford title not been
inherited by his cousin, a grandson of the first Viscount. (*GEC*, Essex,
Hereford, Montagu; *JHL*, May 30, 1678.)

Lords Viscounts Yarmouth and Newport: for Yarmouth, see note to Savile's
letter of August 15, 1676, p. 135. Francis Newport (1619–1708) became
Viscount Newport of Bradford, Shropshire in 1675. He was a Privy
Councillor and Treasurer of the Household. (*DNB*.)

noe small figures. Your Cosen her Grace of Cleaveland having (as shee thinkes) broak the match of her sonn Grafton & gott her sonn Northumberland made Duke prepares for her returne into France on monday next. Wee the poor Commons goe gently on towards disbanding the Army and discharging the Fleet, tomorrow is appointed to rayse money for the latter, & if you will fright your Neighbours with a land tax I beleeve wee shall make your wordes good before this sessions ends. As for court newes you know all prudent persons have ever been wary of writing, espacially since Mr Lane was once turned out about it, but since I am out allready I will venture att one small piece of intelligence, because one who is allways your friend and sometimes (espeacially now) mine, has a part in it that makes

Your Cosen her Grace: Rochester's maternal grandfather, Sir John St. John, was the brother of the Duchess of Cleveland's grandmother, Barbara, wife of Sir Edward Villiers. (Collins, vi, pp. 52–3.)

the match of . . . Grafton: Henry Fitzroy, the second of the Duchess of Cleveland's three sons by the King, was granted various titles on his 'marriage' in 1672, when he was nine, to Arlington's five-year-old daughter Isabella. He became first Duke of Grafton in 1675. By 1678, Arlington had fallen from power and the Duchess tried to break off the match, but they were remarried at the King's insistence in November, 1679. (*GEC,* Grafton; *DNB.*)

Northumberland: George Fitzroy, Earl of Northumberland, third son of the Duchess of Cleveland and Charles II, was eventually created Duke, but not until 1683. (*GEC,* Northumberland.)

disbanding the Army, etc.: see p. 183. Parliamentary fears of a standing army reached a solution on June 4, the day of Savile's letter, when the Commons voted £200,000 for the disbandment of the army, provided this was completed by the end of June—a time-limit subsequently extended. The costs were added to those of paying the expenses of the fleet (a further £200,000) and to the dowry of the Princess of Orange, and merged, as Savile predicts, into a consolidated act for raising £619,368 by a land-tax, which passed the Commons on July 8 and received the royal assent on July 15. (Ogg, ii, p. 554.)

Mr Lane: Richard Lane, a Groom of the Bedchamber. It is not known when he was 'turned out', but he was received back into favour some time in April 1676. (*HMC,* Seventh Report, p. 467.)

I am out allready: see p. 182.

your friend: Nell Gwynn.

her now laughed att and may one day turne to her infinite disadvantage. The case stands thus if I am rightly informed, my Lady Hervey who allwayes loves one civill plott more, is working body & soule to bring Mrs Jenny Middleton into play, how dangerous a new one is to all old ones I need not tell you, but her L^{ap} having little opportunity of seeing Charlemagne upon her owne account wheadles poor Mrs Nelly into supping twice or thrice a week at W.C. and carryeing her with her; soe that in good earnest this poor creature is betrayed by her L^{ap} to pimp against herselfe, for there her L^{ap} whispers and contrives all matters to her owne ends, as the other might easily percieve if shee were not too giddy to mistrust a false friend. This I thaught it good for you to know, for though y^r L^P and I have different friends in the Court yet the friendship betwixt us ought to make mee have an observing eye upon any accident that may wound any friend of yours as this may in the end possibly doe her, who is soe much your friend and who speakes obliging and charitable things of mee in my present disgrace. When all this is done I doe not see in y^r present condition how you can make her sensible of this, for to write to her were vain; but I fancy my

Lady Hervey: Ann Montagu, wife of Sir Daniel Hervey, was the sister of Ralph Montagu, the Ambassador to France. He was involved in an elaborate scheme to get himself made Secretary of State in place of Henry Coventry, who was about to retire. Because both of the King's influential mistresses (for different reasons) were opposed to him, he made moves to discredit the Duchess of Portsmouth and to put Nell Gwynn out of favour. This second plot involved persuading Lady Hervey, a close friend of Nell Gwynn, to introduce a possible new mistress, the sixteen-year-old Jenny Middleton. (With typical Restoration incestuousness, she was reputedly the daughter of Ralph Montagu himself.) For various reasons, the plot failed. (See the later account of Montagu's falling out of favour, p. 200, and also J. H. Wilson, Nell Gwynn, Royal Mistress, 1952, pp. 171–6.)

a new one: a new mistress.

Charlemagne: Charles II.

W.C.: William Chiffinch (1602–88), Page of the King's Bedchamber from 1668, and a well-known procurer.

Lady Southaske has soe much witt & cunning that you might give her some directions in this matter that might prevent any future ill accident, I leave all to y^r L^p to whom alone of all men living I would write with this freedome, where prudence would have advised silence, but my zeale for your service and my trust in your secrecy overcome all other thoughts or considerations in the breast of yrs most intirely.

For the R^t Honble the Earle of
    Rochester
           att
       Adderbury
To bee left wth ye Postm^r of
    Banbury

Rochester in the country to Savile in London   *June, 1678*

Harry,

Any kind of correspondence with such a friend as you is very agreeable, and therefore you will easily believe I am very ill when I lose the opportunity of writing to you. But Mr Povey comes into my mind and hinders farther compliment. In a plainer way I must tell you I pray for your happy restoration but

Lady Southaske: the promiscuous and influential Anne, Lady Southesk, daughter of William, Duke of Hamilton. She was a close friend of the Duchess of Cleveland and had been the Duke of York's mistress. (Anthony Hamilton, *Memoirs of the Comte de Gramont*, tr. P. Quennell, 1930, pp. 165–167. See also Philip Stanhope, Earl of Chesterfield, *Letters . . . to Several Celebrated Individuals*, 1829, pp. 88–9; and *GEC*, Southesk.)

Source: FL i, p. 20.
Date: June, 1678 (written in answer to Savile's letter of June 4).
Mr Povey: the elaborate Thomas Povey, see p. 152.

was not at all sorry for your glorious disgrace, which is an honour, considering the cause. I would say something to the serious part, as you were pleased to call it, of your former letter, but it will disgrace my politics to differ from yours, who have wrought now some time under the best and keenest statesmen our cabinet boasts of. But to confess the truth, my advice to the lady you wot of has ever been this: take your measures just contrary to your rivals; live in peace with all the world and easily with the King; never be so ill-natured to stir up his anger against others, but let him forget the use of a passion which is never to do you good; cherish his love wherever it inclines, and be assured you can't commit greater folly than pretending to be jealous; but on the contrary, with hand, body, head, heart and all the faculties you have, contribute to his pleasure all you can and comply with his desires throughout; and for new intrigues, so you be at one end 'tis no matter which; make sport when you can, at other times help it.—Thus I have given you an account how unfit I am to give the advice you proposed. Besides this, you may judge whether I was a good pimp or no. But some thought otherwise and so, truly, I have renounced business; let abler men try it. More a great deal I would say, but upon this subject and for this time I beg this may suffice, from

Your humble and most affectionate faithful servant,

Rochester.

your glorious disgrace: see Savile's letter of June 2, p. 181.
the serious part . . . of your former letter, etc.: if, as seems clear, this is a reference
   to Savile's news about Nell Gwynn (p. 186), the phrase must imply a
   letter from Savile, now missing, in which the remark Rochester attributes
   to him was made. The 'best and keenest statesmen', etc., are presumably
   Lady Hervey *et al.* (see p. 187).
the lady you wot of: Nell Gwynn, see p. 186.
take your measures: form your opinions (*OED*, *Measure, sb.*, 3a.)
pimp: for the King. The details are not known, unless his encouragement of
   Elizabeth Barry in 'making her court' (see p. 104) is a clue.

To Rochester in the country from Savile in London June 15, 1678

June 15, 78.

How pretious a letter from your L^p is at any time I doe not intend to bee soe complementall as to tell you, but to find your L^p soe well recovered that you can reach ye fourth side of a sheet of paper is soe good newes that I will not thinke you any longer in danger of any accident whatsoever to throw you back to your former weaknesse, now y^t you are in soe safe handes and not in this wicked place of temptation. As to your opinion in that state matter I mentioned to you I doe very much approve it, and have myselfe been of late soe battered in Politicks that if there bee a man alive who ought to retire from businesse and have noe more civile plotts it is myselfe, but what would you have? the lease of my house lasts above two yeares longer & the steame of Guy's wisdome dos soe fly into my head, that I can not but attempt notable undertakings, and wanting ballast to sayle steadily upon the least foule weather I am apt to oversett, this is matter of fact and as well the truth as the stile politicall, such a Collier as Manchester will ride safe upon the dogger banke when it may bee such a pretty pinke as your L^p shall bee in danger, & where such a dungboate as Lauderdale rides Admirall, what vessell of valew or worth can thinke it calme

Source: Bath MS., Portland Papers, ii, f. 225.
Date: as heading, June 15 (or possibly 19, but not, *pace HMC*, 18) 1678.
the fourth side: i.e. of a sheet of paper folded in two.
soe safe handes: the hands of his wife and mother.
that state matter: see the previous letters, concerning Nell Gwynn.
Guy's wisdome: for Henry Guy, see p. 93. 'Guy's wisdom' is a joke euphemism for greed.
Collier: Savile is following through his marine metaphor, in the 'stile politicall'. A collier was a coal-carrying ship but also, as Wilson points out (p. 103), a cheat.
Manchester: see p. 137.
pinke: a general term for most kinds of sailing boat.
Lauderdale: see p. 182.

weather; God send him in charons ferry boate to end this
melancholy seavoyage quickly. Duke Hamilton and all the great
Scotch Lords are returned into his power with a very unkind
reception heer, how hee will use his ennemyes when hee has
them in his mercy wee shall soon see, and doe allready pretty
well guesse by ye nature of the man for whom I suffer that
glorious disgrace (as y^r L^p is pleased I thinke rightly to call it)
and in which I have as yet had noe other consolation but a
perfect assurance from Coll. Machnochton that my health is
drunke all over Scotland. More Martyrs thicken upon us, and
Sr Robert Carr for voting in an election contrary to orders from
Whitehall is removed from the Councell table, the report yet
flyes that your Cosen Sr John Talbott shall have his place, by

charons ferry boate: in Greek mythology, Charon ferries the souls of the dead
over the rivers Styx and Acheron to Hades.
Hamilton: William Douglas, 3rd Duke of Hamilton (1635–94), leader of the
Scottish opposition to Lauderdale. Threatened with attack and imprisonment early in 1678, he led a deputation of Scottish noblemen and
gentry to London to protest against Lauderdale. The King at first refused
to see him and gave him such short shrift that he went back to Scotland
in despair. (*DNB*.)
his power: i.e. Lauderdale's.
Machnochton: As Wilson says (p. 103), this may be the Colonel Alexander
Macnachan whom Pepys (April 26, 1669) says he saw often at court, and
who appears in the *Secret Service Accounts*. He died in 1682.
Sr Robert Carr: a vigorous and controversial member of the Council, Carr
was dismissed because, despite the King's commands to the contrary, he
gave his support in the Commons to Sir William Ellis, who had petitioned
against the allegedly false return of Sir Robert Markham for the borough
of Grantham. Ellis had held Grantham until 1660, when he was excluded
for his republican opinions, and he was still regarded as being 'disaffected
to the government'. His petition was unsuccessful, despite Carr's support;
but he was returned for Boston, Lincolnshire, in February 1679. Meanwhile, Carr quickly returned to favour, and was on all the Council's
committees in 1680. (E. M. Thompson, ed., *Correspondence of the Family of
Hatton*, 1878, i, p. 166; *JHC*, March 16, May 23, 1678; *DNB*, Ellis; E. R.
Turner, *The Privy Council of England, 1603–1784*, Baltimore, 1927–8, ii,
p. 370.)
your Cosen Sr John Talbott: of Laycock Abbey, Wiltshire. His grandmother,
Elizabeth Talbot, daughter of Sir Thomas Leighton, was the sister of
Rochester's grandmother, Lady Anne St. John. (Collins, v, p. 231.)

which y^r L^p may have att least this comfort that though you have not your selfe talents for businesse, yet you may find them in your owne flesh & blood, & doubtlesse there may some prudent embers lye hidden in y^r L^p if you would racke them up which in time might bee of use to your King and Country, I begg of y^r L^p to take this time of your leasure a little paines to examine yourselfe in this point. My Lord of Ossory & Lory Hyde for the civile and the military are returned from Holland there beeing noe more businesse left theyr for any man in either of those capacityes. Coll. FitzGerald is lately dead, much lamented by [all] who loved good officers and good understandings, but hee owed his ende to his modesty which would not suffer him to discover a clapp till a gangreen made it publick to the world and mortal to himselfe. The house of Lords have not done anything Lately worthy record, & though wee seem more busy, this week has advanced us but little, by reason the accounts of ye navy were not ready, but this day a vote has passed that after Tuesday noe motions shall be made for further supply till after the next recesse. Mr Harry Bertie is voted duely elected at ye Comitte but it is not yet reported to ye House. I will not keep y^r L^p any Longer, especially when I beleeve myselfe the man of all y^r acquaintance who have given you the least

racke: rake.

Ossory: Thomas Butler, Earl of Ossory (1634–80), had gone to Holland in February 1678 as general of the British forces in the pay of the States. (*DNB*.)

Hyde: Laurence (Lory) Hyde (1641–1711), second son of Edward Hyde, Earl of Clarendon, had been involved in the Netherlands negotiations since January, 1677. (*DNB*.)

Coll. FitzGerald: Colonel John Fitzgerald, Governor of Tangier. He was a Catholic, whose promotion was attributed by some to the religious sympathies of the Court. He was the Duke of Monmouth's aide-de-camp against the Dutch in 1673. (*HMC*, 78, *Hastings*, ii, pp. 147, 164.)

but hee owed . . . .: the end of the sentence is omitted by *HMC*.

a vote has passed: See *JHC*, June 15, 1678.

Harry Bertie: a son of Montagu, second Earl of Lindsey. He was related to Rochester, the widow of whose step-brother Sir Francis Lee had subsequently married the third Earl of Lindsey. (*GEC*, Lindsey.)

quarter of this kind in your weake condition. Adieu my deare
Lord,

For the Rt. Honble the Earle of Rochester
att Adderbury.
To bee left wth ye Postm^r of Banbury

Rochester in the country to Savile in London   *June 18/25, 1678*

Harry,
'If sack and sugar be a sin, God help the wicked' was the saying
of a merry fat gentleman who lived in days of yore, loved a glass
of wine, would be merry with a friend and sometimes had an
unlucky fancy for a wench. Now, dear Mr Savile, forgive me if
I confess that upon several occasions you have put me in mind
of this fat person, and now more particularly for thinking upon
your present circumstances I cannot but say with myself, if
loving a pretty woman and hating Lautherdale bring banish-
ments and pox, the Lord have mercy upon poor thieves and
s[wiver]s! But by this time all your inconveniences (for to a man
of your very good sense no outward accidents are more) draw
very near their end. For my own part, I'm taking pains not to
die without knowing how to live on when I have brought it
about. But most human affairs are carried on at the same

Source: FL i, p. 24.
Date: between Savile's letters of June 18 and June 25, 1678.
If sack and sugar . . .: *1 Henry IV*, II, iv, 461. Falstaff actually says 'if sack
   and sugar be a fault.' (Cf. p. 96.)
a merry fat gentleman: Falstaff. See above.
this fat person: cf. other jokes about Savile's size, pp. 67, 159.
Lautherdale: John Maitland, Duke of Lauderdale, see p. 182.
I'm taking pains, etc.: the first hint of the theological reading and discussion
   which were to absorb Rochester increasingly between now and his death
   two years later.

nonsensical rate, which makes me (who am now grown super-
stitious) think it a fault to laugh at the monkey we have here
when I compare his condition with mankind. You will be very
good-natured if you keep your word and write to me sometimes.
And so good night, dear Mr Savile.

Rochester.

To Rochester at Adderbury from Savile   *June 25, 1678*

June 25ᵉ 78.

I am most infinitely obliged to your good Lᵖ for your kind
remembrance of me, and if the good Gentleman who loved Sack
and Shugar soe well was soe lucky as to bring mee into your
mind I wishe there were more of them, though mee-thinks since
the death of poor Sᵉ Simon Fanshaw that sorte of excellent
breed is almost extinguished, or att least soe farr decayed that
except an old Cavalier Corporall that I beleeve you have seen
begging in Sᵉ James's parke, there is noe more any such person
than a Phoenix to bee found in these parts, a true good fellow is
like a Kingfisher, can onely breed in calme weather[.] the

the monkey we have here: cf. the famous portrait of Rochester crowning his
monkey, attributed to Wissing. Rochester frequently alludes to the view
that animals are superior to men. (See the conclusion of *Tunbridge Wells*,
the beginning of *A Satyr against Reason and Mankind*, and the discussion in
J. Treglown, 'Rochester and Davenant', *Notes and Queries*, N.S. xxiii,
1976, pp. 554-9.)

Source: Bath MS., Portland Papers, ii, f. 227.
Date: as heading, June 25, 1678.
the good Gentleman: Falstaff—see previous letter.
Sᵉ Simon Fanshaw: knighted by Charles I, Sir Simon received a Royal Bounty
in 1677, after which there is no reference to him in the Treasury Books.
like a Kingfisher: kingfishers were identified with halcyons, mythologically
supposed to breed about the time of the winter solstice in a nest floating
on the sea, and to charm the wind and waves so that the water was
specially calm during the period. (*OED, Kingfisher, Halcyon.*)

continuall noyse of horse, foot, dragoons, cuirassiers, Granadiers, Guidons, Aid-de Camps, and a hundred such wordes repeated tenn thousand times a day in Whitehall Gallery have frighted away even the thaughts of the least indulgence to a man's pleasure, and whoever is not now in this hott season in a drap de Berry coate with gold galoon enough to load a Mule is not thaught affectionate to the government of the Army, which y^r house has voted shall stand a month longer then wee intended & if wee can come of soe and att the end of August say Cedant Arma Togae, wee Senatours shall be mugh lighter att heart then wee are att present how cheerfully soever wee may beare our apprehensions in our faces. I will not say how good a time this is to bee in the country, how good a time to bee sick, nay how good a time to dye in for feare you should either thinke mee neer my end or beleeve I thaught you soe: and were therefore gathering some philosophicall comfort out of Solomon or Seneca or any other who has treated de vanitate mundi; but this I will say that my taille beeing now liker Dick Newport's then my Lords, & I presume my Spiritts wasted with my flesh I am troubled with spleenetick vapours that make mee dislike the

cuirassiers: cavalry soldiers.

Guidons: regimental flags.

drap de Berry, etc.: drap de Berry was a kind of woollen cloth, gold galloon was gold braid. For all this military fervour see previous and following letters.

y^r house, etc.: see *JHL,* June 21, 1678.

Cedant Arma Togae: Cicero, *De Officiis,* i, 77. The whole line reads, 'cedant arma togae, concedat laurea laudi' ('Let arms yield to the citizen's cloak, the laurel of victory to civic praise'). Wilson's *to goe* for *togae* is a howler.

de vanitate mundi: 'concerning the futility of the world'. Solomon was thought to have been the author of the pessimistic books of Ecclesiastes and Job. Seneca is the stoic Roman philosopher and tragedian, author of *De brevitate vitae* ('concerning the brevity of life').

taille: penis (*OED,* Tail, *sb,* 5c.)

Dick Newport: Richard Newport (1644–1737), later second Earl of Bradford. Pepys mentions him among the 'rogues' whose 'mad bawdy talk' made his heart ache and who were 'ready to take hold of every woman that came by them.' (*Diary,* May 31, June 1, 1668.)

spleenetick vapours: depression.

world as much as ever I approved it; from the rising of the Sun to the setting thereof, I see noething that pleases my eyes, nor heare noething but what grates my eares, onely I am promised a moment's titillation by Mr Staggins who is come over with great credit and many new aires, his Maj^{ty} has allready constituted him Lord Paramount over all the musick, hee may raigne there like great turke and cutt whose catts-gutts hee please if the harmony bee not to his liking, with what moderation hee will use this absolute power, I leave it to fate & the immortall Gods to determine. George Porter about a fortnight since brought a little stock of Berkshire health to towne, which hee has since swilled away in Tavernes and now lyes soaking in bedd for more breath, hee had a great tryall on Saturday last att the Barr of the Lords where there was an appeale against him, but hee came of soe victorious that there was not a voice against him. The Purbeck will tis thought at last prove as errant a sonne of a whore as hee was allwayes taken for, hee carryed the difficulty of the fine in y^r house, but for the Bastardy, the Duke of Buckingham has leave to bring in a bill for the confirmation of it. Not beeing att court I can send you noe newes of Ladyes, it is none,

from the rising of the Sun, etc.: Malachi, 1.11.

Mr Staggins: Nicholas Staggins (1650–1700), Master of the King's Music. (See *CTB*, May 6, December 14, 1678.)

George Porter: see p. 172, note. Porter had fought a lengthy court action to redeem a mortgage given to one Abraham Hubert on the Manor of Alfarthing, Surrey. Hubert took the case to the Lords in March 1678. After several postponements his appeal was heard and dismissed on Saturday, June 22. (*JHL.*)

Purbeck: see p. 185.

the Duke of Buckingham, etc.: see p. 185. Buckingham moved on June 20 that 'the King shall be petitioned to give Leave that a Bill may be brought in to disable the Petitioner to claim the title of Viscount Purbeck'—a resolution which was approved, though it was protested against by a group of Lords on ten counts, particularly that such a bill implied that he had a right to the title in the first place, and that the object of the petition was 'to assist One Subject, *videlicet*, the Duke of *Buckingham*, against another, in Point of Right, wherein Judges ought to be indifferent and impartial.' (*JHL.*)

it is none, etc.: the ending is omitted in *HMC*.

that Ladyes are weomen, and that weomen are bitches whom
God confound & let every cripple say Amen.

For the R^t Honble the Earle of
    Rochester
        att Adderbury
To bee left wth ye Postm^r of
    Banbury.

To Rochester in the country from Savile in London   *July 2, 1678*

Leather Lane in Hatton Garden
July. 2. 78.

Y^r L^p will see by the date of this letter why I have not troubled
you these tenn dayes, the truth is this is a place from whence you
cannot expect much newes & yet some little you shall have
before I have done, but heer I have chosen a neate privacy to
sweat in and soe finish the last act of a long teddious course of
Physick which has entertained mee ever since December last,
and if it had then been putt to my choice whether I would have
undergone what I have sufferd, or have turnd Turke, notwithstanding all my Zeale for the true Protestant faith, I doubt my
whole stock of religion had runn a great hazzard; I confesse I

weomen are bitches, etc.: Savile was now suffering terribly from venereal disease
   —see his letter of July 2, following.

Source: Bath MS., Portland Papers, ii, f. 229.
Date: as heading, July 2, 1678.
Leather Lane: in Holborn. Savile was staying at a sweatshop (see below).
by the date of this letter: i.e. by the superscribed address.
the true Protestant faith: cf. p. 226.
I doubt: in the sense of 'I am afraid that'.

14

wonder att myselfe and that masse of Mercury that has gone
downe my throate in seven monthes, but should wonder yet
more were it not for Mrs Roberts, for behold a greater then I,
shee is in the same house and wee have mett heer from severall
corners as mad folkes doe in Bethlem, what shee has endured
would make a damd soule fall a laughing att his lesser paines it is
so farr beyond description or beleefe that till shee tells it you
herselfe I will not spoyle her story my making it worser, or by
making your hayre stand on end & hinder any thing else from
doeing soe for a month after soe tragicall a relation. The other
day Mr Fanshaw came and made a third with us, but will have
his worse pox then ours passe for the scurvy out of civility to
his lady, though the rogue bee a filthyer leaper then ever was
cured in the Gospell, and without another pool of Bethesda, or
another Saviour hee is the most incurable Animall that now
crawles upon the earth. On Saturday last was a generall
rendezvous of above 10000 men upon Hounslow heath where all
the bloody doeings was that one souldier killed another for

Mercury: the standard 'cure' for venereal disease. The effects of mercury
poisoning were often worse than those of the disease itself. (Cf. 'Oh,
destructive mercury!', 'The Ladies' March', 1. 14, *Court Satires*, p. 56.)

Mrs Roberts: Jane Roberts, one of the King's mistresses and, for a while,
one of Rochester's. She died the following year. (See Introduction,
p. 34.)

behold a greater then I, etc.: this sounds like a joking reference to Genesis 39,
8–9, where Joseph rejects Potiphar's wife's invitation 'Lie with me'.
Joseph points out that Potiphar, his master, has treated him well: 'Behold
... There is none greater in this house than I; neither hath he kept any thing
from me, but thee ... how then can I do this great wickedness ...?'

Bethlem: or Bedlam, the London lunatic hospital since the early fifteenth
century, rebuilt in Moorfields in 1675.

Mr Fanshaw: William Fanshaw, see pp. 161, 184.

pool of Bethesda: miraculous pool in Jerusalem, where Jesus cured a lame man
in a crowd of blind, lame and paralysed people (John, 5. 1–9).

Hounslow heath: in Middlesex. It was a frequent site for military camps and
exercises. The rendezvous in question was ordered on Thursday, June 27
and held, as Savile says, the following Saturday, in preparation for the
Flanders expedition (see below). (*CSPD.*) July 2, 1678, p. 271. June 27,
1678, p. 254.

waking him when hee was asleep, who is to bee hanged for his paines but by yᵉ assistance of the civill power, for as yet the Army is not soe great but that Kingston Assises is better then Martiall law. To shew military discipline, Sʳ Phillip Howard was suspended his employment for not obeying some orders the D. of Monmouth gave him in wᶜʰ though his Grace bee found in the wrong it is thaught fitt the other should suffer for examples sake to shew that orders must bee obeyed though never soe foolish; some thinke they will take this occasion to bee ridd of a man they never cared much for, but others beleeve the Queen will have credit enough to make up the businesse the dispute hapning for the place & station of her troop. There are foure of our Regiments more gone into Flanders upon a certain alarum

souldier . . . to bee hanged: the only clue I can find about this is a warrant issued on July 7 for the hanging on Hounslow Heath of one James Smith, a soldier in the Duke of Monmouth's regiment; but Smith was convicted of desertion, not murder. (*CSPD*, July 7, 1678, p. 279.)

Sʳ Phillip Howard: A letter from Edward Smith to Lord Roos dated June 9, 1678, explains the circumstances of Howard's dismissal in more detail:

> At Hounslow the Duke of Monmouth ordered my Lord of Oxford and his regiment to march first, which Sir Phillip Howard thinkeing belong'd to himself and as the senior officer tooke the first place, whereupon the Duke of Monmouth came to his regiment and bid them noe more observe Sir Phillip's commands, for he would deprive him of his commission. (*HMC*, 24, *Rutland*, ii, 51.)

Howard was replaced by Louis Duras, Earl of Feversham, who took command of the Flanders expedition late in August. (*CSPD*, July 2, 1678; *DNB*.)

foure of our Regiments more, etc.: despite Charles's efforts to avoid a confrontation with the French so as to earn Louis's promised subsidy, continued French hostilities in the Netherlands necessitated some further show of strength against him under the terms of the Anglo-Dutch treaty (see p. 173)—a gesture anyway encouraged by the strengthening parliamentary support for a war against France. 4,000 troops were accordingly ordered to Flanders on June 27, 1678 (*CSPD*), though English aggressiveness still conflicted with English fears of a standing army, and bills were simultaneously being passed for the army's disbandment. Louis's demand for the restoration of all the Swedish possessions captured by the Elector of Brandenburg was abandoned under combined English, Dutch and Swedish pressure, and peace was signed on July 31.

of warr, the K. of France refusing to deliver the townes till ye K. of Sweden have Stetin restored to him, and though it is really now very probable, the House of Commons are resolved not to beleeve a word of it, but goe on towards the disbanding the Army, the Lords doe disturbe us with little conferences to gain time till wee can bee convinced of the certainty of the warr, wee both adhere, and God knowes where the dispute will end, but as little sanguin as I have been in beleeving it I am now for the first time of opinion the warr is very certain as you will soon heare by some act of hostility from his most Christian Majesty. There are terrible doeings att Paris betwixt my Lady Cleaveland and her daughter Sussex, as I am a friend to the family till the story bee more compleate I will not venture at sending you the whole relation, but whilst ye Mother was in England the daughter was debauched by our Embass^dr Mr Montaigue who has lived with her in most open scandall to the wonder of the French court and the high displeasure of this, the K. being very angry with the Emb^dr and his friends & ennemyes now strugg-ling att Court to support or ruine him, the latter is I thinke the

wee both adhere: both houses stick to their own position.
his most Christian Majesty: Louis XIV.
terrible doeings att Paris: the affair is described fully by P. W. Sergeant in *My Lady Castlemaine*, 1912, pp. 216–34. It was more complicated than these first hints of it in Savile's letter suggest, and resulted in Montagu's replacement as ambassador by Lord Sunderland on July 12, and his suspension as Master of the Great Wardrobe on August 13. (*CSPD*.)

According to Sergeant, Montagu and the Duchess had been lovers since his arrival in Paris in 1669, and he had made a number of allegations about her to Charles in revenge for her affair with a young French courtier, the Marquis of Chatillon. In the spring of 1678, while the Duchess was in England, Montagu's relationship with her 17-year-old daughter Anne, Countess of Sussex (whose father was almost certainly Charles II) became the talk of Paris, and on her return in May Cleveland wrote Charles a long letter exposing this affair, excusing herself from the allegations against her, and further accusing Montagu of running down Charles in conversation, plotting against his friends, and other disloyalties. When Montagu rushed to London to defend himself, Charles refused to see him and Sunderland was sent to Paris as a temporary replacement, to be succeeded by Henry Savile. Montagu remained out of favour throughout the rest of the reign.

likelyest in every Court it beeing the easyest and the worst natured; as this matter comes more to light I shall tell you more, & of any thing else that happens worth your knowing least you should fall to the ordinary ignorance of a meer Country Gentleman. Were I att home I should find somewhat more to entertain you, but y^r L^p will be pleased to consider that though Leather Lane bee in London, yet it is as remote from noble Court notions as either Woodstock or Banbury, all I can say is qui bene latuit, bene vixit, & if I can add bene sudavit, I am happy as I can bee in any other circumstance of my life but that most essential one of beeing to the Earle of Rochester & the noble Lord Wilmott as faithfull an humble servant as is in ye world.

Rochester in the country to Savile in London   *July, 1678*

Dear Savile,
Were I as idle as ever, which I should not fail of being if health permitted, I would write a small romance, and make the sun with his dishevelled rays gild the tops of the palaces in Leather Lane. Then should those vile enchanters Barten and Ginman lead forth their illustrious captives in chains of quicksilver, and

qui bene latuit, bene vixit: Ovid, *Tristia*, III, iv, 25. ('He who has succeeded in living in seclusion has lived well.')
bene sudavit: 'has sweated well'—a reference to Savile's present circumstances.
Lord Wilmott: Rochester's son Charles.

Source: FL i, p. 12.
Date: early July, 1678 (in reply to Savile's of July 2).
a small romance: for the mock-romance passage which follows, see Introduction, p. 24.
Leather Lane: see p. 197.
Barten and Ginman: for Barton, see p. 182. His luridly named colleague remains unidentified.
quicksilver: mercury—see p. 197.

confining 'em by charms to the loathsome banks of a dead lake of
diet-drink, you, as my friend, should break the horrid silence and
speak the most passionate fine things that ever heroic lover
uttered, which, being softly and sweetly replied to by Mrs
Roberts, should rudely be interrupted by the envious F——.
Thus would I lead the mournful tale along, till the gentle reader
bathed with the tribute of his eyes the names of such unfortunate lovers—and this, I take it, would be a most excellent
way of celebrating the memories of my most pocky friends,
companions and mistresses. But it is a miraculous thing (as the
wise have it) when a man half in the grave cannot leave off
playing the fool and the buffoon. But so it falls out to my
comfort, for at this moment I am in a damned relapse brought by
a fever, the stone and some ten diseases more which have
deprived me of the power of crawling, which I happily enjoyed
some days ago. And now I fear I must fall, that it may be
fulfilled which was long since written for our instruction in a
good old ballad,

> But he who lives not wise and sober
> Falls with the leaf still in October.

a dead lake . . . break the horrid silence: cf. the burning lake on which Milton's
    Satan and his angels lie in *Paradise Lost*, Book I, from which Satan,
    'Breaking the horrid silence' (i. 84), addresses Beelzebub.
Mrs Roberts: Jane Roberts, see p. 34.
F——: Fanshaw, see pp. 161, 184.
the tribute of his eyes: a stock phrase in romances—cf. Sidney, *Arcadia*, II.
    xvii, 'the tribute-offer of my teares'.
the stone: see Introduction, p. 34.
that it may be fulfilled, etc.: common biblical formula, especially in the
    Gospels (e.g. Luke 21:22).
But he who lives: a wry adaptation of the famous ending of an optimistic
    drinking song in *Rollo, Duke of Normandy, or the Bloody Brother*, attributed
    to John Fletcher:

> Drinke to day and drowne all sorrow,
> You shall perhaps not doe it to morrow.
> Best while you have it use your breath,
> There is no drinking after death.

About which time, in all probability, there may be a period
added to the ridiculous being of

Your humble servant,
Rochester.

To Rochester at Adderbury from Savile in London   July 13, 1678

Whitehall. July. 13. 78.

Your L^P is soe well read, that you can not but have heard of an
old Romane Generall, who was recalled from banishment to
command the army, noe other man in the Commonwealth
beeing found soe fitt for it, I shall desire y^r L^P to let that old
Gentleman putt you in mind of mee as well as your old man of

> Wine works the heart up, wakes the wit,
> There is no cure gainst age but it.
> It helps the head-ach, cough and tissick,
> And is for all diseases Physick.
>
> Then let us swill boyes for our health,
> Who drinkes well loves the common wealth.
> And he that will to bed goe sober,
> Falls with the leafe still in October.
> (ed. J. D. Jump, 1948, II. ii. pp. 46f.)

Source: Bath MS, Portland Papers, ii, f. 237.

Date: as heading, July 13, 1678.

an old Romane Generall: Livy (III, xi–xix) tells the popular Roman story of
how Lucius Quinctius Cincinattus, who had been forced to pay a heavy
fine when his son absconded from bail in 461 B.C., 'was obliged to sell all
that he had and live for some time on the other side of the Tiber, like one
banished.' Civil disorder rapidly increased in Rome in the face of various
threatened attacks, and within a few months Cincinattus was recalled as
consul.

your old man of Verona: an allusion to Claudian's poem celebrating rural
retirement, *De sene Veronensi qui Suburbium numquam egressus est* ('Of an old
man of Verona who never left his home'), *Carmina Minora*, xx. Most of
the poem was translated by Cowley at the end of his essay, *The dangers of an
Honest man in much Company* (A. R. Waller, ed., *The English Writings of
Abraham Cowley*, Cambridge, 1906, i, p. 447), which influenced Rochester's
A Satyr against Reason and Mankind.

Verona, for there beeing an affaire of some difficulty to bee performed in France, his Maj^{ty} sends mee in all haste, I am to see him this afternoon, and goe poste to morrow morning along with my Ld Sunderland who goes Embassadour Extraordinary; my stay need not bee long and shall not bee above three weekes, unlesse I can heare that y^r L^p will take the advice which all yr friends would give you, viz. to goe into France, & then I would stay your comeing, doubtelesse My Lord a winter att Mompellier would doe you much more good then att Adderbury, & if you saw how Sr John Chicheley is returned from thence & had seen in what condition hee went y^r L^p would bee of my opinion, but this is to bee left to y^r L^{ps} owne prudence who doe very well comprehend that all domestick considerations must bee sacrifised to those of health.

My Lord Feaversham has carryed his cause in the house of Lords for 3,000.^l *p.* an, during his life out of my Lady Katherine Watson's estate. Mr Montaigue is putt out of the Councell and banished the Court for comeing from Paris without orders from hence, what further resentment will bee shewn for soe un-

an affaire of some difficulty: (see previous letter). Savile was sent to Paris 'to compose matters between the Duchess of Cleveland and the Countess of Sussex'. (*HMC*, 36, *Ormonde*, iv, p. 445.)

my Ld Sunderland: Robert Spencer (1640–1702), second Earl of Sunderland, see p. 200. Savile's brother George, Viscount (later Marquis of) Halifax, had married Sunderland's sister Dorothy. (*Savile Correspondence*, p. 1.)

Mompellier: Montpellier, in the south of France.

Sr John Chicheley: (d. 1691), a commissioner of the navy. (*DNB*.)

My Lord Feaversham: Louis Duras, 2nd Earl of Feversham (1641–1709) (see also p. 199). The earldom was created in 1676 under special terms by which it would be inherited by Duras, who was married to Mary Sandes, the first Earl's daughter. On the first Earl's death in 1677, Duras duly came into the title. But Lady Mary had already died, and all the Sandes estates and titles previous to the earldom devolved on her sister, Lady Catherine, wife of Lewis Watson. The first Earl had settled £3,000 a year on Duras on his marriage to Lady Mary, which the Watsons were unwilling to pay now she was dead. He fought them through Chancery (where the case was decided against him) to the Lords, who heard his appeal on July 6 and 8, 1678, and overthrew the Chancery judgement. (*GEC*, Feversham; *JHL*.)

Mr Montaigue: see previous letter.

justifiable a proceeding lyes yet in his Maj^{ts} breast, though the
towne will needs foretell that hee shall loose all his places. My
Lady Shrewsbury is brought to bedd of a chopping boy. S^r
Richard Powell dyed heer in towne yesterday, & is gone to day
into Berkshire to bee buryed. Your L^p will easily beleeve that
upon such a journey & soe short warning I am in too great a
hurry to give y^r L^p much trouble, I should bee wonderfully
pleased if I could receave any commands for your service where
I goe and att my returne I shall immediately renew these frequent
occasions of telling you how sincerely & affectionately I love &
honour y^r good L^p.

For the R^t Honble the Earle of Rochester att Adderbury

Too bee left with ye Postm^r of Banbury.

Lady Shrewsbury: Buckingham's mistress Anna Maria Brudenell, Countess of
  Shrewsbury. See also p. 136. (*Court Satires*, pp. 285–7.)
chopping: strong and healthy.
Sr Richard Powell: of Berkshire, knighted in 1661. Sir Richard Southwell
  wrote to the Duke of Ormonde on August 27, 1678, saying 'There has
  been a high contention in Berkshire about making a Knight of the Shire
  to succeed Sir Richard Powell'. (*HMC*, 36, *Ormonde*, iv, 448.)
such a journey: i.e. to France.

1678-79
Undigested Heap of Thoughts

To Rochester from Charles Blount   *December, 1678*

Ludgate Hill. December, 1678.

My Lord,

I humbly ask your Lordship's pardon for this presumption, but
when I last had the honour of waiting upon you, your Lordship's candour gave me the freedom of venting my own

Source: Charles Blount, *Miscellaneous Works*, 1695, pp. 158–68.

Date: as heading, December, 1678. The letter was published under the
heading: 'To the Right Honourable and most ingenious Strephon, *giving a
Political human account of the Subversion of* Judaism, *Foundations of* Christianity,
and Origination of the Millenaries.'

Charles Blount: (1654–93), admirer of Hobbes and author of a number of
sceptical theological and philosophical books including *Anima Mundi, or
historical relation of the ancients concerning man's soul after life, according to
unenlightened nature* (1679), the subject of which had become important to
Rochester (see p. 202). It seems possible that he had met Blount at Court
and discussed his ideas, perhaps reading the book in manuscript.

I have not attempted to annotate Blount's letters fully. He was a keen
plagiarist, cobbling together passages of Milton or Lord Herbert o
Cherbury and publishing them with new titles under his own name, and
to provide a full commentary would require both more space than seems
warranted in a book devoted to Rochester, rather than to Blount, and
more knowledge than I have of the history of theology. All the same,
Rochester clearly solicited Blount's views and was very much exercised in
the last years of his life by theological questions. However boring and
obscure the letters may seem to modern readers, they are relevant to
Rochester's discussions with Burnet, and are reproduced here in full, with
whatever annotation has seemed necessary to make them intelligible. The
copy-text's frequent errors in references to the sources of quotations have
been silently corrected, but quotations themselves are given exactly as
they appear.

thoughts; and then, as the subject of our discourse was about the great changes and revolutions that from time to time had happened in the universe, so I made bold to assert that in all mutations, as well ecclesiastical as civil, I would engage to make appear to your Lordship that a temporal interest was the great machine upon which all human actions moved, and that the common and general pretence of piety and religion was but like grace before a meal. Accordingly, I have presumed to trouble your Lordship with these ensuing remarks to justify the same assertion.

There was never any republic which dwindled into a monarchy, or kingdom altered into an aristocracy or common-wealth, without a series of preceding causes that principally contributed thereunto. Had not other circumstances concurred, never had Caesar established himself, nor Brutus erected a Senate. And if you enquire why the first Brutus expelled Tarquin and the second could not overthrow Augustus and Antony, or why Lycurgus, Solon and Numa could establish those govern-ments which others have since in vain attempted to settle in Genoa, Florence and other places, you will find it to arise from hence: that some, considering those antecedent causes which secretly and securely incline to a change, took advantage thereof, whilst others did only regard the speciousness or justice of their pretensions without any mature examination of what was principally to be observed. For nothing is more certain, than that in these cases, when the previous dispositions all intervene, but a very slight occasion, nay, oftentimes, a meer casualty, opportunely taken hold on and wisely pursued, will produce

the first Brutus, etc.: Livy (1–5) tells the story of how Lucius Junius Brutus, traditionally the founder of the Roman Republic, expelled the last King of Rome, Tarquinius Superbus. The second Brutus is the tyrannicide, defeated at the second battle of Philippi by Mark Antony and Caius Octavius Augustus.

Lycurgus: traditional founder of the Spartan constitution.

Solon: Athenian constitutional reformer in the sixth century B.C.

Numa: second King of Rome and, traditionally, the builder of its seat of authority, the Regia.

those revolutions which (otherwise) no human sagacity or courage could have accomplished.

I cannot find any authentic ground to believe that the sects among the Jews were more ancient than the days of the Maccabees, but arose after that Antiochus had subdued Jerusalem and reduced the generality of the Jews to paganism, when (the better to confirm his conquests) he erected therein an academy for the Pythagorean, Platonic and Epicurean philosophers. This, I conceive (and so do others), was the original of the Pharisees, Sadducees and Essenes; though afterwards, when the Maccabees had anathematized all that taught their children the Greek philosophy, one party did justify their tenets by entituling them to Sadoc and Baithos, and the other to a cabbala derived successively from Ezra and Moses. The introduction of those sects and of that cabbala occasioned that exposition of the prophecy of Jacob, viz. 'The sceptre shall not depart from Judah, nor a lawgiver from between his feet until Shiloh come, and unto him shall the gathering of the people be.' From whence they did (according to that fantastic cabbala) imagine that whensoever the sceptre should depart from Judah and the dominion thereof cease, that then there should arrive a Messiah. But as for his being of the line of David, this was no general opinion. For how then could any have imagined Herod the Great to have been the Messiah? Or how could Josephus fix that character upon Vespasian as him who should restore the empire and glory

the Maccabees: celebrated Jewish family whose genealogy was discussed by the historian Josephus (first century B.C.).
Antiochus: King of Syria in the second century B.C., whose subjugation of Jerusalem was ended by a revolt led by the Maccabees (see above), described in the Apocryphal books named after them.
one party: an attempt, presumably, to explain the non-canonical Fourth Book of the Maccabees, a Greek philosophical treatise addressed to the Jews on the supremacy of devout reason over the passions. (*ODCC*.)
entituling: ascribing.
cabbala: system of Jewish theology.
'*The sceptre shall not depart*', etc.: Genesis, 49: 10.
Josephus: see above.

of Israel to whom all nations should bow and submit unto his
sceptre? I do not read that the Jews harboured any such
exposition during their captivity under Nebuchadnezzar, albeit
that the sceptre was at that time so departed from the tribe of
Judah and the house of David that it never was resettled in it
more. After their return to Jerusalem no such thing is spoken of,
when Antiochus Epiphanes subdued them, prophaned their
temple, destroyed their laws and left them nothing of a sceptre
or lawgiver—during all which time, notwithstanding they had
the same prophecies and scriptures among them, there is no
news of any expected Messiah. But after the curiosity of the
Rabbis had involved them in the pursuance of mystical numbers
and pythagorically or cabbalistically to explain them according
to the Gematria, then was it first discovered that Shiloh and
Messiah consisted of letters which make up the same numerals,
and therefore that a mysterious promise of a Redeemer was
insinuated thereby. As also that the prophecy of Balaam concerning a star out of Jacob and a sceptre rising out of Israel,
with a multitude of other predictions (which the condition of
their nation made them otherwise to despair of) should be
accomplished under this Messiah. I name no other prophecies
because they are either general and indefinitely expressed as to
the time of their accomplishment, or inexplicable from their
obscurity, or uncertain as to their authority, such as are the
works of David, which book the Jews reckon among their
Hagiographa, or sacred but not canonical books.

This prophecy likewise had a contradictory one where 'tis
said of Coniah that no man of his seed shall prosper sitting upon
the throne of David, and ruling any more in Judah (Jer. 22: 30).
Also Ezek. 21: 26, 27: 'Thus saith the Lord God, remove the
diadem and take off the crown, this shall not be the same', etc.
Now the aforesaid obscure prophecy, which did not take effect
at first until the reign of David, and which suffered such a

Gematria: numerological method of interpretation used by the Rabbis to
extract hidden meanings from words. (*ODCC.*)

variety of interruptions, seemeth to have fallen under this interpretation in the days of Herod the Great, whom the Jews so hated for his usurpation over the Maccabees' Levitical family and for his general cruelties, that he was particularly detested by the cabbalistical Pharisees, who, to keep up the rancour against him and his lineage, as well as to alienate the people from him, I could easily imagine the exposition of this prophecy to have been for no other purpose. Neither perhaps was Herod much displeased with the said interpretation of the prophecy after the Herodians had accommodated it to him and made him the Messiah, who (after their conquest and ignominy under Pompey), having restored the Jews to a great reputation and strength and rebuilt their temple, found some who could deduce his pedigree from the thigh of Jacob as directly as David's and Solomon's were.

Now this construction of the prophecy being inculcated into the people, and into all those Jews, strangers or proselytes which resorted to Jerusalem at their great festivals (from Alexandria, Antioch, Babylon and all other parts where the Jews had any colonies), there arose an universal expectation of a Messiah to come (excepting amongst the Herodians, who thought Herod the Messiah) and afterwards possessed the Jews (for our Jews are but the remains of the Pharisees) to this very day. But their impatience for his appearance seems to have been less under Herod the Great than ever since the first inter- pretation of the prophecy (there being no mention of false Messiahs at that time), perhaps because the prophecy was not so clear and convincing whilst that Herod was King, since under him the sceptre and legislative power seemed to be still in Judah (though swayed by an Idumaean proselyte) the priesthood continued, the temple flourished and there was a Prince of the Sanhedrin, Rabbi Hillel, of the lineage of David. But ten years after the birth of Christ, when Archelaus was banished to Vienna,

---

the Herodians: this account of Herod's messianic claims is drawn from now- discredited patristic conjecture, particularly by Philaster. (Ibid.)

Idumaean: Herod came from an Idumaean (Edomite) family. (Ibid.)

and Judea reduced into the form of a province, the sceptre then seemed to be entirely departed from Judah. The kingdom was now become part of the government of Syria and ruled by a procurator, who taxed them severely. Then the sense of their miseries made the people more credulous, and whether they more easily believed what they so earnestly desired might happen, or whether the malcontents, taking the advantage of their afflictions, did then more diligently insinuate into the multitude that opinion, it so happened that there arose at that time sundry false Messiahs, and the world was big with expectation (raised in every country by the Jews, who had received the intelligence from their common metropolis Jerusalem), that the great Prince was coming who should re-establish the Jewish monarchy and bring peace and happiness to all the earth.

Now these circumstances made way for the reception of Christ and the miracles he did (for miracles were the only demonstrations to the Jews), convincing the people that he was the Messiah. They never stayed till he should declare himself to be so (for I think he never directly told any he was so, but the woman of Samaria), or evinced his genealogy from David. For though some mean persons called him the Son of David, and the mob by that title did cry Hosanna to him, yet did he acquiesce in terming himself the Son of Man, but esteemed him a prophet, Elias, Jeremiah and even the very Messiah. Also when he made his cavalcade upon an asinego, they extolled him as the descendant of King David. But his untimely apprehension and death, together with his neglect to improve the inclination of the people to make him king, did allay the affections of the Jews towards him, disappoint all their hopes, and so far exasperated them against him that they who had been part of his retinue at his entrance did now call for his execution and adjudge him by common suffrage to be crucified, insomuch that his disciples fly, the apostles distrust, and sufficiently testify their unbelief by not crediting his resurrection. But after that he was risen again, and

asinego: donkey.

they assured thereof, they reassume their hopes of a temporal
Messiah, and the last interrogatory they propose unto him is,
'Lord, wilt thou at this time restore the kingdom of Israel?'

After his assumption into heaven, they attended in Jerusalem
the coming of the Holy Ghost, which seized on them and gave
them the gift of tongues (as 'tis written) for a season, whereby
they preached to the Jews, Elamites, Parthians, Alexandrians,
etc. (whom Salmasius shows not to be absolute strangers to the
natives of those countries, but Jews planted there) as also to the
proselytes. These being surprised with the miracle of the cloven
tongues and gift of languages, as likewise being possessed with
the desire and hopes of a Messiah, and being further ascertained
by the apostle Peter that Jesus (whom Pilate had crucified) was
the Lord and Christ, were, to the number of 3000, immediately
baptized into his name. And such as were to depart, when they
came to their colonies did divulge the tidings and engage other
Jews and proselytes to the same belief, the apostles themselves
going about, and ordaining likewise others to preach the glad
tidings of a Messiah come, who (though dead) was risen again,
according to the obscure prediction of David, for the salvation
of Israel, and whose second appearance would complete the
happiness of all nations, as well Jews as Gentiles.

Having thus therefore given your Lordship an account of the
subversion of Judaism as well as of the foundation of Christianity, the origination of the millenaries is only the consequence
of the fall of the one and rise of the other. For it is apparent that
not only the Jews but also the Christians were millenaries and
did believe and expect the temporal reign of a Messiah, together
with the union of the Jews and Gentiles under one most happy
monarchy. Not one of the two first ages dissented from this
opinion, and they who oppose it never quote any for themselves

Salmasius: Claude de Sommaise (1588–1653), French scholar (and opponent
  of Milton).
millenaries: believers in a future 'millennium', or thousand-year period of
  blessedness following the second coming of the Messiah.

before Dionysius Alexandrinus, who lived at least 250 years after Christ. Of this opinion was Justin Martyr and (as he says) all other Christians that were exactly orthodox. Irenaeus sets it down exactly for a tradition, and relates the very words which Christ used when he taught this doctrine. So that if this tenet was not an universal tradition in the primitive times, I know not what article of our faith will be found to be such. This doctrine was taught by the consent of the most eminent fathers of the first centuries, without any opposition from their contemporaries, and was delivered by them, not as doctors, but witnesses, and not as their own opinion, but as the apostolic tradition. Moreover, it was with this pretence of Christ's being a-coming to reign with them here in glory that [they] stopped the mouths of the unbelieving Jews who, before, upon his death and suffering like other men, began to doubt very much of the power of the Messiahship, which made them distrust his reigning in glory amongst them here on earth, as it was foretold the Messiah should do. Wherefore this millenary invention of his coming again to reign in glory saved all.

And thus your Lordship sees, the wickedness of men's natures is such that all revolutions whatever, both in Church and State, as well as all mutations both in doctrine and matters of faith, be they never so pious and sacred, or never so beneficial and useful to mankind, both in their souls and bodies, yet they must still be seconded by some private temporal interest and have some human prop to support them, or else all will not do. My Lord, I am sensible I have a thousand pardons to ask your Lordship for this tedious impertinence, but to do so at this time were but to lengthen and consequently add to my crime. So I shall only beg the honour to subscribe my self at present,

(My Lord)

Your Lordship's most obedient

humble servant,

Blount.

Dionysius . . . Justin . . . Irenaeus: patristic writers.

15

To Rochester from Charles Blount   *February 8, 1679*

Ludgate Hill. February 8, 1679.

My Lord,

Nothing less than the honour of your commands could have inspired me with a confidence sufficient to trouble your lordship with this undigested heap of my father's thoughts concerning the soul's acting, as it were, in a state of matrimony with the body. But since it is your lordship's pleasure, as also to have them in his own very words, I have here set them down accordingly, and shall plead only your lordship's fiat for my pardon.

'The spirit does not remain the same in us, but is constantly renewed, like a flame (though by a swifter process, because it is a more spiritual entity). We are remade every day out of the things that pass through us. We die and are reborn every day, and we are not the same today as we were yesterday, and we are unaware of our character changing until we finally perceive that it has done so.

'Nothing can pass into us except by our food. All food, from the point of view of nourishment, is similar and weak. The body grows up bodily with nourishment, the spirit spiritually. However, the proportion of each kind of growth is not related either to food and drink or to spiritual material unless they are properly digested by us. Otherwise, the things we consume do not nourish us, but either oppress the system if they are too

Source: Blount's *Works*, ed. cit., pp. 154–7.

Date: as heading, February 8, 1679.

my father: Sir Henry Blount (1602–82), described by Gildon as 'the Socrates of his age' (*DNB*).

undigested heap of my father's thoughts: this heap (the reference is to Ovid's description of the beginnings of the world as 'rudis indigestaque moles' in *Metamorphoses*, i.7) is in difficult, badly-printed seventeenth-century Latin. The original text is printed in Appendix III. I am very grateful to the embarrassingly large number of people (particularly Margaret Watson and Mary Kean) I had to consult over the translation.

fiat: command.

strong or destroy it if they are incompatible, to much the same extent in our spirit as in our body. And so precautions must be taken for things to go well. First, there should be a judicious and moderate selection of what we are to digest, and then skilful preparation is needed, so that it is of the right strength for us. Our main contribution is regular but moderate exercise, through which our natural temperature can thrive.

'It seems likely that, according to the strength of their spirits or bodies, some are better at transforming nourishment into spirit for themselves, others at turning it into body. For this reason, in feasting and drinking some become more stupid than others, and some are more prone to sickness and surfeits than others. Excess in drinking generally affects the wits more than excess in eating, because drink is more spiritual, while the body is more oppressed by things that are eaten, because they weigh more.

'The wise spirit is a dry light; the healthy body a due mingling of elements which is dry and penetrable. It is therefore necessary to be dry but not blocked up, and this is achieved by a way of life adjusted to the atmosphere, distinguishing acutely between what is warm and cold, wet and dry. The workings of the universe do not lie in these qualities: there is something far diviner and intrinsically greater in matter, the pivot of reality on which it is turned, and which can be perceived only through experience, and feeling its effect. God is in matter. He is everything and he does everything. For every body and spirit are part of him, the infinite one. A creature is made of their union, and indeed is destroyed if it is broken. However, since all matter is in perpetual motion from one grouping together to another, the matter and spirit of the world are on the one hand eternal but on the other always taking new forms. So, too, we creatures are fleeting manifestations of the eternal God, whom the fates only show on earth like figures in a tapestry, denied any existence beyond it.

'We are God's work, our parents being his instruments; and

our actions are his works, for we in turn are instruments. We act according to our own choice, but this choice is entertained and controlled through suitably directed groupings and ideas.

'The material parts of the world become spirit, and the spiritual, body, through condensation and rarefaction. Thus, everything is continually driven to and fro. "The light of Jove, the shadows of Pluto; the light of Pluto, the shadows of Jove", as Hippocrates has it. When a microcosm leaves the world, the microcosm lives; when the world leaves a microcosm, the microcosm dies.'

These, my lord, are only such twilight conjectures as our human reason (whereof we so vainly boast) can furnish us with. This τὸ θεῖον, or *divinum aliquid*, as Hippocrates terms it, is that which does all things. But our capacity not being able to discern it, makes us fasten either upon elementary qualities, as Hippocrates and Galen do, or upon geometrical proportions, as our modern Descartes doth. So that, indeed, all philosophy excepting scepticism is little more than dotage. Pardon, I beseech you, this boldness from,

My lord,
        Your lordship's most faithful, humble servant,
        Blount.

Rochester to Elizabeth Barry   *1678-9*

Madam,
I am far from delighting in the grief I have given you by taking

Hippocrates: Greek physician and philosopher of the fifth centry, B.C.
τὸ θεῖον: the divinity.
divinum aliquid: the divine something.
Galen: Roman physician and philosopher of the second century, A.D.

Source: FL ii, p. 22.
Date: 1678-9 (see below).

away the child; and you, who made it so absolutely necessary for me to do so, must take that excuse from me for all the ill nature of it. On the other side, pray be assured I love Betty so well that you need not apprehend any neglect from those I employ, and I hope very shortly to restore her to you a finer girl than ever. In the meantime you would do well to think of the advice I gave you, for how little show soever my prudence makes in my own affairs, in yours it will prove very successful if you please to follow it. And since discretion is the thing alone you are like to want, pray study to get it.

To Rochester from Savile in Paris   *April 6, 1679*

Paris. Aprill. 16th 79.

By one Mr Hill (a Servant of Mr. Montaigue's) I have sent y^r L^p the first present I have made into England since my beeing heer, and it is that circumstance I would have your L^p consider, and not what it is I send you. There is a pott of Aigre de Cedre, and two bottles of Syrope de Capilaire, both great coolers, and I

taking away the child: the details are not known, but see p. 30.

Source: Bath MS, Portland Papers, ii, f. 233.

Date: April 6, 1679, English style.

Paris: Savile was appointed Envoy Extraordinary on January 30, 1679, to fill the gap left by the disgraced Montagu (see *CSPD*, and p. 200).

Mr. Montaigue: Ralph Montagu, see p. 200.

Aigre de Cedre: not, *pace* Wilson (p. 109), cedar gum, but an acid drink of lemon (see *OED, Cedre*). Lemon juice is recommended as a 'cooler' in John Quincy's *A Compleat English Dispensatory*, 1718, p. 209.

Syrope de Capilaire: an infusion of maidenhair fern and liquorice root. Quincy (op. cit., p. 371f.) thought little of syrups generally as medicines, and says that *Syrupus Capillorum Veneris* 'might be all taken in a Dose, and therefore cannot have any efficacy to be depended upon, in the Quantity it is usually order'd' (ibid., p. 375). But, as Wilson points out, the earlier physician Nicholas Culpeper (1616–54) recommended it for a wide variety of ailments including, significantly in Rochester's case, renal stone (Culpeper, *The English Physitian Enlarged*, 1653, p. 149).

suppose I need not tell you the way of using it is halfe a spoonfull in a great glasse and spring water powred upon it; the truth is I left you in soe good health that I doubted you would returne to your usuall course of life and in that case this may bee sometimes necessary to refresh you; there is further, in order to another vice y^r L^p is given to, a bottle of poudre de cypre to keep the ladyes heades sweet, and a bottle of myrtle water to keep theire tailes streight; with these conveniences and good health I shall not bee one of those friends who would advise you to keep your temperance or your virtue longer, they are both excellent in the way to health, but base companions of it; you see my Lord I can not yet give into the true and decent gravity of a Minister, but I hope I shall mend against I see y^r L^p at Bologne, the certainty of wch voyage dos yet continue though it is putt a little further off, because of a grave Spanish Embassadour who is yet at Brussells and comes [in] the paie of that Country; but you shall be certainly informed of every alteration in that kind that may bee of use to you for yr comeing upon that errand which I hope is allready secured for you, for I have sett my heart soe much upon meeting you there that I shall runn madd if anybody else should come in your place.

coolers: a cooler was any kind of palliative prescribed to ease the symptoms of a fever, or 'to check the inordinate Celerity of the Blood, which arises from a Debauch with spirituous Liquors' (Quincy, op. cit., p. 207). Quincy recommends lemon juice 'to take off *Nausea's* from the *Stomach*' and for the digestion generally. Almost any kind of fruit and salad plant counted as a cooler; so, interestingly, did cannabis seed, though it was 'very rarely met with in use' (ibid., p. 209).

---

poudre de cypre: cyperus is a marsh plant with an aromatic root, powdered for use on wigs (*OED, Cypress,* 2b).
myrtle water: a kind of scent.
a grave Spanish Embassadour: the Marquese de Los Balbaces, Spanish envoy in the negotiations concerning the marriage of Marie Louise (daughter of Philippe, Duke of Orleans and of Charles II's sister Henrietta) to Charles II of Spain. (*Savile Correspondence,* pp. 81, 83–4.)
that errand: the details are not known.

Our friend Mr S⁺ Johns with all his steeds is still at S⁺ Denis in order to the fatning his horses for sayle, so that it may bee hoped by that time they are disposed of, hee will not upon the whole matter bee above fifty pounds a looser by the expedition. His parts are taken notice of by those who attempt to bee his chapmen, and I have been asked allready if, besides not speaking the language, hee bee not un peu fol. I shall not presume to give yr Lᵖ any account of any other of your friends heer. The two Caledonian Countesses who are most in your favour doe I suppose give you an account of themselves; for yr Lᵖˢ comfort and their honours, I cannot heare that either of them have any inclinations besides yourselfe; if either they or any other alurement can at leasure draw your Lordship hither I cannot but thinke a long vacation as well past att Paris as at Woodstock, but as you have both time to consider of it and other circumstances to guide you I leave that consideration wholly to you, wᵗʰ att least this assurance that there lives not that man who shall bee welcome to the most faithfull, affectionate, and humblest of all yr Lᵖˢ servants.

Hen. Savile.

Mr Sᵗ Johns: perhaps, as Wilson suggests (p. 110), Rochester's cousin Henry (later Viscount) St. John; but the name was common, and Savile had a servant in Paris called Thomas St. John (see *CSPD*, February 27, 1681).

Sᵗ Denis: suburb of Paris.

chapmen: either dealers or, quite commonly in this period, purchasers. The point seems to be that people had difficulty in buying what St. John was trying to sell, because he did not speak their language.

un peu fol: a little mad.

the two Caledonian Countesses: one of them was Katherine, Countess of Kinnoull—see Savile's next letter (p. 222). Widowed in 1677, she moved to France with her children the following year.

  Her pass is dated December 31, 1678, three weeks after similar authorization to go abroad had been granted to 'The Comtesse Hamilton' (*CSPD*, December 8, 1678), who may well be the other woman Savile mentions. I take it that the *comtesse* in question was Elizabeth Hamilton, Comtesse de Grammont ('la belle Hamilton'), sister of the author of the *Memoirs of the Count of Gramont*. She was at the centre of Court life in both England and France, and a 'Caledonian' by birth: her father was Sir George Hamilton, son of the Earl of Abercorn.

Rochester in London to his wife   ?

You are very kind to wish mee in the Country perhaps that is
best for mee, & I wish I had rather bin in this towne a month
agoe than att this time & certainly w^{hn} I am in any tollerable
health I shall wayte upon you

For the Countess of Rochester.

Rochester in London to his wife   *?Spring, 1679*

Deare Wife
I have noe news for you but that London growes very tiresome
and I long to see you, but things are now reduc'd to that
extremity on all sides that a man dares nott turne his back for
feare of being hang'd, an ill accident to bee avoyded by all
prudent persons & therefore by
                        Y^r humble servant
                        Rochester

To Rochester from Savile in Paris   *June 20, 1679*

                                    Paris. June 30. 79
When I came first to this towne I found myselfe soe little capable

Source: MS. Harl. 7003, f. 222.

Source: MS. Harl. 7003, f. 230.
Date: ?Spring, 1679. (See below.)
extremity on all sides: perhaps the Popish Plot—see Rochester's letter to
    Savile begun May 30, 1679, p. 223.

Source: Bath MS., Portland Papers, ii, f. 234.
Date: June 20, 1679, English style.

of beeing happy without some commerce with yr L^p that I thought to draw you into a correspondance by sending you a small present of powder for your periwigg, and coolers for your head if you should bee like that gospell dogg that returned to his Vomitt; but this plott did not take, for either Mr Hill (Mr Montaigu's servant) did not deliver you my present, or yr L^p did not thinke it worth thankes, and I have now beene four monthes as much forgott by yr L^p as if I had not my whole life had a most particular kindnesse and service for you, by this, I may reasonably presume that either you are not well, or I am not well with you; either of these I assure yr L^p would afflict mee extreamly, and considering how well I thaught myself with yr L^p when I came away, if there bee a change, it is one that will trouble mee more then all the great changes that have hapned in England since I left it. After all I will hope that there is noe more in this matter than a little idle remissnesse to our absent friends to which God knowes the frailty of our poor natures dos too much expose us all, but for a mortall sinner in this kind commend mee to that stinking whelpe Sheppherd to whom I recommended a Lady's concerne three monthes since without ever having heard more of him, or her either, but that goeing in pilgrimage to Loretto shee with two other worthy persons of the same sex & nation, were robbed, stript of their mens

powder for your periwigg, etc.: see Savile's letter of April 6 and Rochester's belated reply of May 30–June 25.

that gospell dogg: see Proverbs 26: 11 and 2 Peter 2: 22.

Montaigu: Ralph Montagu, see p. 200.

all the great changes . . . in England: Wilson summarizes admirably (p. 110): 'a new Parliament elected, dominated by Whigs (March 6), Danby resigned and sent to the Tower (April 14), the Privy Council reconstituted with Shaftesbury as president (April 20), open opposition to Lauderdale in Parliament (May 8), Parliament prorogued in order to prevent the passage of an Exclusion Bill (May 26).'

Sheppherd: Sir Fleetwood Shepherd, see p. 109.

a Lady's concerne: I can find no other account of all this. 'The Lady they are goeing to visit' is a reference to the Virgin Mary, 'the lady of Loretto'.

cloathes, & beeing discovered to bee shee-pilgrims were layd in jayle where I suppose they now doe either rott or [fuck] to get out again, which will bee but an ill piece of courtship to the Lady they are goeing to visite. But not to entertain you with ladyes you doe not know, the inclosed was sent mee yesterday by one you doe know, I have not seen her, nor heard of her till shee had need of my conveyance for this letter to yr L^p. I doubt shee is a great object of charity, I am sure shee had had mine if shee had sent for it for I allwayes thaught her one of the most unfortunate and most meritorious of all the numerous traine of clean and unclean that have gone into Will. Chiffinch his Arke or my Ld Manchester's chamber. I have allwayes taken soe much pleasure in conversing with yr L^p that without any mercy upon you I should scribble on if I were not called on for my packett which must bee shutt, but I cannot forbeare telling you in a very good earnest I thinke my Lady Kennoul the devoutest creature living; as for her cosen the other Countesse I can give you noe account of her, nor doe I know how shee beares the depart of the Prince de Morbeque who is returned into Flanders. I heartily wishe yr L^p some of the good wine I dayly drinke, it is such as Mr Harvey himselfe would approve of, but I confesse the small beer is very badd, and a mann cannot gett a pipe of good tobacco for love nor money; Adieu my deare Lord I am most unfeignedly yours &c.

[*fuck*]: the word has been cut out of the MS.
the inclosed: the enclosure is lost.
one you doe know: again, the subject remains a mystery.
Will. Chiffinch: see p. 187.
Ld Manchester: see p. 137.
my packett: State parcel of letters and other documents.
the Lady Kennoul: see Savile's previous letter, p. 219.
the Prince de Morbeque: Eugene Montmorency, Marquis of Morbecque and Prince of Robecq. (A. de Boislisle, ed., *Mémoires de Saint-Simon*, Paris, 1879–1918, xxiv, pp. 71–2.)
Mr Harvey: probably John Harvey, Treasurer and Receiver General to the Queen. He died in 1680. See p. 172.

Rochester in London and Oxfordshire to   *May 30–June 25, 1679*
Savile in Paris

[As the letter indicates, May 1679 had been a particularly turbulent month at Court. In the midst of the anxiety caused by the Popish Plot, ever-increasing parliamentary suspicion of the King enabled Sir William Temple to persuade him to reconstitute the Privy Council, so as to make it a potentially effective organ of policy and mediator between parliament and the crown. The most immediate problem facing the 'new Council', formed on April 20, was to find a way of appeasing popular suspicion of the Catholic Duke of York, younger brother and heir of Charles, who had no legitimate son. Among the schemes gaining momentum was that of the Whig leader Shaftesbury, president of the new Council, to exclude York from the succession, replacing him with Charles's popular illegitimate son, the Protestant Duke of Monmouth. To this end a Bill of Exclusion was introduced into the Commons on May 15 and carried by a substantial majority on a second reading on May 22. Although Charles had promised to be guided by the Privy Council in all matters of policy, he gave it no warning of his next move, which was to prorogue parliament on May 27; an action causing fury in both houses, 'and such rage of my Lord Shaftesbury, that he said upon it aloud in the house, that he would have the heads of those who were the advisers of this prorogation' (quoted by G. Davies in 'Council and Cabinet, 1679–88', *English Historical Review*, xxxvii, 1922, 47–66).

[At the same time as this constitutional crisis, increasing Presbyterian restlessness in Scotland came to a head with military action south of the border, and a number of serious incidents. On May 3 the Archbishop of St. Andrews had been

Source: FL i, p. 16.
Date: as letter, May 30 to June 25, 1679.

dragged from his carriage and murdered, and three weeks later demonstrators near Glasgow celebrated the anniversary of the Restoration (May 29) by publicly burning all the Acts of government. Royal forces raised against the rebels were put under the command of the Duke of Monmouth. (Ogg, ii, pp. 389-420, 559-619; Davies, loc. cit.)]

Begun Whitehall, May 30th 1679.

Dear Savile,

'Tis neither pride or neglect (for I am not of the new Council, and I love you sincerely), but idleness on one side, and not knowing what to say on the other, has hindered me from writing to you after so kind a letter and the present you sent me, for which I return you at last my humble thanks. Changes in this place are so frequent that F—— himself can now no longer give an account why this was done today or what will ensue tomorrow, and accidents are so extravagant that my Lord W——, intending to lie, has with a prophetic spirit once told truth. Every man in this Court thinks he stands fair for Minister. Some give it to Shaftesbury, others to Halifax, but Mr Waller

new Council: see above.

F——: William Fanshaw, Master of Requests to Charles II; see p. 161, etc.

Lord W——: probably Charles Paulet, Marquess of Winchester, who was a privy councillor in 1679. Burnet says 'he was a very knowing and a very crafty politic man, and was an artful flatterer, when that was necessary to compass his ends.' (Burnet, History of His Own Time, iv, p. 403, quoted by Wilson, p. 111.)

stands fair for Minister: to succeed the Earl of Danby, who had resigned as Lord Treasurer on March 26. The post was subsequently in effect split up between the Lords Commissioners of the Treasury.

Shaftesbury: see above.

Halifax: Henry Savile's elder brother George, Viscount (later Marquess of) Halifax.

Mr Waller: the old poet Edmund Waller (1606-87), Member of Parliament for Hastings since 1661, and a popular figure at Court.

says S—— does all. I am sure my Lord A—— does little, which
your excellence will easily believe. And now the war in Scotland
takes up all the discourse of politic persons. His Grace of
Lauderdale values himself upon the rebellion and tells the King
it is very auspicious and advantageous to the drift of the present
Councils. The rest of the Scots, and especially D. H.——, are
very inquisitive after news from Scotland and really make a
handsome figure in this conjecture at London. What the D. of
Monmouth will effect is now the general expectation, who took
post unexpectedly, left all that had offered their service in this
expedition in the lurch, and being attended only by Sir Thomas
Armstrong and Mr C—— will, without question, have the full

S——: Savile's friend, Robert Spencer, Earl of Sunderland (see p. 22).
He was a member of the inner cabinet of the new Council and had been
made Secretary of State in February, 1679 (*DNB*). Dryden dedicated
Troilus and Cressida to him this year in opportunistically fulsome terms.

Lord A——: Wilson suggests the unpopular Lord Chamberlain, Henry
Bennett, Earl of Arlington, though neither laziness nor ineffectuality
figures among the many charges levelled at him in this period, and
Gramont refers to his 'grande avidité pour le travail' (*DNB*). Perhaps
Rochester is referring to Arthur Annesley, Earl of Anglesey, the cautious,
moderate Lord Privy Seal.

Lauderdale: Savile's enemy John Maitland, Duke of Lauderdale, powerful
Scots politician and intimate of Charles II (see p. 182). His friendship with
the Duke of York, and his arbitrary and destructive policies in Scotland,
led the English parliament to demand his removal from the King's
Councils in May, 1679, but he was saved by the prorogation on the 27th.
(Ogg, op. cit.).

values himself upon: takes pride in.

D. H. ——: William Douglas, Duke of Hamilton, leader of the opposition to
Lauderdale in Scotland. See p. 188.

Monmouth: see above. On June 22 Monmouth led the Royalists against the
Scottish Covenanters at Bothwell Bridge on the Clyde, and defeated them.

Sir Thomas Armstrong: Royalist soldier, associate of Shaftesbury and close
friend of Monmouth, executed in 1684 for his part in the Rye House
Plot. (*DNB*.)

Mr C——: Wilson (p. 112) says 'One is tempted to suggest John Churchill'
but discounts him because he was involved in a duel in London the day
after the Battle of Bothwell Bridge. (He was anyway the constant companion of the Duke of York between March and September, 1679.)
Another candidate suggested by Wilson is a certain Captain Crofts, whose

glory as well of the prudential as the military part of this action entire to himself. The most profound politicians have weighty brows and careful aspects at present, upon a report crept abroad that Mr Langhorn, to save his life, offers a discovery of priests' and Jesuits' lands to the value of fourscore-and-ten thousand pounds a year, which being accepted, it is feared, partisans and undertakers will be found out to advance a considerable sum of money upon this fund, to the utter interruption of parliament's—and the destruction of many hopeful—designs. This, I must call God to witness, was never hinted to me in the least by Mr P——, to whom I beg you will give me your hearty recommendations. Thus much to afford you a taste of my serious abilities and to let you know I have a great goggle-eye to business. And now I cannot deny you a share in the high satisfaction I have received at the account which flourishes here of your high Protestancy at Paris. Charenton was never so honoured as since your residence and ministry in France, to that degree that it is not doubted if the

name appears from time to time in connection with Monmouth's. But Monmouth was also attended by a Mr Crew (see for example George Roberts, *The Life, Progresses, and Rebellion of James, Duke of Monmouth*, 1844, i, p. 136), who may well be the man mentioned here.

Mr Langhorn: Richard Langhorne was convicted on June 14, 1679, of complicity in the Popish Plot. He was executed on July 14 (*DNB*).

undertakers: Members of Parliament who had undertaken to influence voting in favour of the monarch, especially over supply.

Mr P——: Hayward (p. 393) suggests Miles Prance, who perjured himself to gain convictions against three men accused on his evidence of the murder of Sir Edmund Berry Godfrey (see above). Wilson is dismayed by this—'I cannot believe that Rochester would number that ignoble creature among his acquaintance' (p. 112)—but the reference is presumably a joke.

your high Protestancy at Paris, etc.: as Ambassador, Savile became a conscientious Protestant in France. On June 5, 1679, he wrote to Halifax 'I hear from England I shall be forced to keep a chaplain, which I never less needed, having never fail'd Charenton one Sunday since I came into France.' (*Savile Correspondence*, pp. 94–5.) Charenton was the French Protestant church a few miles SE of Paris. During the years preceding the revocation of the Edict of Nantes, Savile sent home valuable reports of the French government's treatment of Protestants, and pressed with some success for the English reception of them as immigrants (*DNB*).

parliament be sitting at your return, or otherwise the Mayor and Common Council, will petition the King you may be dignified with the title of that place by way of earldom or dukedom, as His Majesty shall think most proper to give or you accept.

Mr S—— is a man of that tenderness of heart and approved humanity that he will doubtless be highly afflicted when he hears of the unfortunate pilgrims, though he appears very obdurate to the complaints of his own best concubine and your fair kinswoman M——, who now starves. The packet enclosed in your last I read with all the sense of compassion it merits, and if I can prove so unexpectedly happy to succeed in my endeavours for that fair unfortunate, she shall have a speedy account. I thank God there is yet a Harry Savile in England, with whom I drank your health last week at Sir William Coventry's and who in features, proportion and pledging gives me so lively an idea of yourself that I am resolved to retire into Oxfordshire and enjoy him till Shiloh come, or you from France.

Rochester.

Ended the 25th of June, 1679.

Common Council: city council (*OED, Council, sb.,* 15b).
Mr S——: Fleetwood Shepherd. See Savile's letter of June 20.
the unfortunate pilgrims: see previous letter.
M——: unidentified.
a Harry Savile in England: Henry Savile's nephew Henry, Lord Eland (1660–88), eldest son of the Marquis of Halifax, who had recently returned from visits to his uncle in Paris. (*Savile Correspondence,* passim; H. C. Foxcroft, *The Life and Letters of . . . Halifax,* 1898, i, p. 162.)
Sir William Coventry's: Coventry, who was Savile's great-uncle, had recently retired from politics to his country home at Minster Lovell in Oxfordshire, not far from Woodstock (*DNB*).
till Shiloh come: Genesis, 49 : 10. Shiloh was thought to be a name for the Messiah (see for example, R. Young, *Analytical Concordance to the Bible,* 1879, *Shiloh*); but modern translations differ widely in rendering this passage.

1679–80
Wise About Follies

Rochester in London to his wife at Adderbury   *?1679*

'Tis not an easy thing to bee intirely happy, But to bee kind is very easy and that is the greatest measure of happiness; I say nott this to putt you in mind of being kind to mee, you have practis'd that soe long that I have a joyfull confidence you will never forgett itt, but to show that I myself have a sence of what the methods of my Life seeme soe utterly to contradict, I must not bee too wise about my owne follyes, or els this Letter had bin a booke dedicated to you & publish'd to the world, itt will bee more pertinent to tell you that very shortly the King goes to Newmarkett & then I shall waite on you att Adderbury, in the mean time thinke of any thing you would have mee doe, & I shall thanke you for the occasion of pleasing you:

present my service to Mᵐ H:

Mʳ Morgan I have sent in this errant Because he playes the roghe here in towne soe extreamly, that hee is not to bee endur'd, pray if hee behave himself soe att Adderbury send mee word, & lett

Source: MS. Harl. 7003, f. 212.
Date: ?1679 (the penitent tone, and Elizabeth's kindness having gone on 'soe long').
measure: quantity, part.
to Newmarkett: to the races. He was there in late September/early October, 1678, and late September, 1679. (*CSPD.*)
Mʳʳ H.: ?Gertrude Hawley, wife of Elizabeth's step-brother Francis.

him stay till I send for him; pray Lett Ned come up to Towne I have a little buisness wth him and he shall bee Back in a weeke.

These for the Countess of Rochester.

Rochester to his son   ?

Charles I take itt very kindly that you write to mee (though seldome) & wish heartily you would behave y^r selfe soe as that I myght show how much I love you wth out being asham'd; Obedience to y^r grandmother & those who instruct you in good things, is the way to make you happy here & for-ever, avoyde Idleness, scorne Lying, & god will Bless you, for wch I pray
                                                                 Rochester

Rochester in London to Savile in Paris   *November 1, 1679*

Harry,
I am in a great strait what to write to you. The style of business I am not versed in, and you may have forgot the familiar one we used heretofore. What alterations ministry makes in men is not

Mr Morgan . . . Ned: servants.

Source: MS. Harl. 7003, f. 251.
Date: uncertain, but perhaps 1678–9, since Charles is now able to write letters, (cf. p. 143).

Source: FL i, p. 9.
Date: as letter, November 1, 1679.
16

to be imagined, though I can trust with confidence all those you are liable to, so well I know you and so perfectly I love you. We are in such a settled happiness and such merry security in this place that if it were not for sickness I could pass my time very well between my own ill-nature, which inclines me very little to pity the misfortunes of malicious mistaken fools, and the policies of the times, which expose new rarities of that kind every day. The news I have to send, and the sort alone which could be so to you, are things 'Gyaris et carcere digna' which I dare not trust to this pretty fool the bearer, whom I heartily recommend to your favour and protection and whose qualities will recommend him more. And truly if it might suit with your character at your times of leisure to [make] Mr Baptist's acquaintance, the happy consequence would be singing, and in which your excellence might have a share not unworthy the greatest ambassadors nor to be despised even by a cardinal-legate. The greatest and gravest of this Court of both sexes have tasted his beauties, and I'll assure you Rome gains upon us here in this point mainly, and there is no part of the Plot carried with so much secresy and vigour as this. Proselytes, of consequence, are daily made and my Lord S——'s imprisonment is no check to any. An account of Mr George Porter's retirement upon news

Gyaris et carcere digna: 'worthy of prison or the penal island of Gyara', a quotation (modified to fit the grammar of Rochester's sentence) from Juvenal, *Satires*, i, 73.

this pretty fool the bearer: Jean Baptiste de Belle-Fasse, Rochester's valet and presumably his lover. See also pp. 26, 243.

Rome gains upon us here: i.e. in its homosexuality. Cf. Rochester's reference to 'The Jesuits' fraternity' and its 'use of buggery' in *A Ramble in St. James's Park*, ll. 145–6.

the Plot: the Popish Plot.

my Lord S——: William Howard, Viscount Stafford, one of the 'five popish lords' accused of involvement in the Plot. He was executed on December 29, 1680 (*DNB*).

George Porter: see p. 172. The 'account' and its contents are unidentified.

that Mr Grimes, with one gentleman more, had invaded England, Mr S——'s apology for making songs on the Duke of M——, with his oration-consolatory on my Lady D——'s death, and a politic dissertation between my Lady P——s and Captain Dangerfield, with many other worthy treatises of the like nature, are things worthy your perusal, but I durst not send 'em to you without leave, not knowing what consequence it might draw upon your circumstances and character. But if they will admit a correspondence of that kind, in which alone I dare presume to think myself capable, I shall be very industrious in that way or any other to keep you from forgetting

> Your most affectionate, obliged, humble servant,
>
> Rochester.

Whitehall, November 1, [16]79.

Mr Grimes: As Wilson points out (p. 114), Grimes was a common spelling for Graham, and one possible Graham in this context is Col. James Graham, Keeper of the Privy Purse to the Duke and Duchess of York. He may have 'invaded England' in company with the Duke on one of his visits from exile in Brussels on September 2 and October 14, 1679. (*DNB*; *CSPD*; F. C. Turner, *James II*, 1948, p. 168.)

Mr S——: perhaps Fleetwood Shepherd, though the songs have not been identified.

the Duke of M——: Monmouth.

my Lady D——: Buckhurst's wife Mary, Countess of Dorset, who died in child-bed on September 12, 1679. (*GEC*, Dorset.)

a politic dissertation: presumably *Mr. Tho. Dangerfeild's Second Narrative wherein is Contained a Faithful Charge Against the Lady Powis. . . . Relating to the Murther of Sir Edmundbury Godfrey, and the Late Plot made by the Papists, to be Cast upon the Protestants,* printed in 1680, and not as suggested by Wilson (p. 114) the *First Narrative,* which does not refer to Lady Powis.

Lady P——s: Elizabeth, Lady Powis, was the wife of one of the 'five popish lords' imprisoned in October, 1679 (see above). She herself was imprisoned in the Tower on November 4 on the information of Thomas Dangerfield for her supposed share in the 'Meal-tub Plot' (*DNB*).

Captain Dangerfield: Thomas Dangerfield (1650?–85), one of the perjured witnesses in the Plot, and the author of a number of political broadsides including the one mentioned above (*DNB*).

Rochester in London to Savile in Paris   *November 21, 1679*

Dear Savile,

The lousiness of affairs in this place is such (forgive the unmannerly phrase! Expressions must descend to the nature of
things expressed) 'tis not fit to entertain a private gentleman,
much less one a public character, with the retail of them. The
general heads under which this whole island may be considered
are spies, beggars and rebels. The transpositions and mixtures of
these make an agreeable variety: busy fools and cautious knaves
are bred out of them and set off wonderfully, though of this
latter sort we have fewer now than ever, hypocrisy being the
only vice in decay amongst us. Few men here dissemble their
being rascals and no woman disowns being a whore. Mr O——
was tried two days ago for buggery and cleared. The next day he
brought his action to the King's Bench against his accuser,
being attended by the Earl of Shaftesbury and other peers to the
number of seven, for the honour of the Protestant cause. I have
sent you herewith a libel in which my own share is not the least.
The King having perused it is no ways dissatisfied with his. The
author is apparently Mr ——, his patron my ——, having a

Source: FL i, p. 47.
Date: November 21, 1679. See note on *Mr O*——, below.
Mr O——: Titus Oates was indicted for 'an attempt to commit . . . the
  horrid and abominable crime of sodomy, on November 19, 1679. A week
  later he brought a successful action for perjury and defamation against his
  accusers, John Lane, Thomas Knox and a servant of Perigrine Osborne.
  (*CSPD*, November and December, 1679, passim; John Pollock, *The
  Popish Plot, a Study in the History of the Reign of Charles II*, 1903, p. 339.)
a libel: Mulgrave and Dryden's *An Essay Upon Satire*, a general lampoon on
  the Court and its writers, beginning with an attack on 'saunt'ring Charles'
  and culminating in 40 lines on Rochester. (See Yale *POAS*, i, pp. 401f.)
  The poem was part of a protracted literary squabble, which seems to have
  led to the beating-up Dryden suffered in Rose Alley, Covent Garden, on
  December 18, 1679. See also p. 120.
apparently: manifestly.
Mr ——: First Collected Edition (1714), *Mr. D*—, i.e. Dryden. The poem
  was at the time assumed to be entirely Dryden's work.

panegyric in the midst, upon which happened a handsome
quarrel between his L——, and Mrs B—— at the Duchess of
P——['s]. She called him the hero of the libel and complimented
him upon having made more cuckolds than any man alive, to
which he answered she very well knew one he never made nor
never cared to be employed in making. 'Rogue!' and 'Bitch!'

his patron my ——: First Collected Edition (1714), my *L—M—*, i.e. John
   Sheffield, Earl of Mulgrave, whom Dryden turned to in 1676 when
   Rochester, previously a patron of his, had withdrawn his support in
   favour of John Crowne. Mulgrave's supposed sexual attractiveness,
   generosity and contentment are praised in ll. 194–209 of the *Essay Upon
   Satire*.

----

a handsome quarrel: the incident is described in a letter from Colonel Edward
   Cooke to the Duke of Ormonde:

   22 November, 1679.
   If I may be permitted to play at small game I shall repeat a particular
   that I was informed part this week at the Duchess of Portsmouth's,
   where just before the King came in a most scurrilous, libellous copy
   of verse was read, severe upon almost all the courtiers save my Lord
   Mulgrave, whose sole accusation was that he was a cuckold-maker.
   This brought him under suspicion to be (if not guilty of the making,
   yet) guilty of being privy to the making of them, who just coming
   in with the King, Mrs Buckley saluted him (in raillery) by the name of
   cuckold-maker, who taking it in earnest replied she knew one
   cuckold he never made, which she took for so great an affront that it
   seems her husband was entitled to the revenge. But the King, it
   seems, came to the knowledge of it, and interfered his authority to
   antidote bloodshed.

   (*HMC*, p. 36, *Ormonde*, v, p. 242; quoted in Maurice Irvine, 'Identification
   of Characters in Mulgrave's "Essay Upon Satyr",' *S.P.*, xxxiv, 1937, pp.
   533–51.)
his L——: his Lordship (Mulgrave).
Mrs B——: Lady Sophia Bulkely, wife of Henry Bulkely, Master of the
   Household to Charles II and a member of the Court circle.
the Duchess of P——: Portsmouth, see above.

ensued, till the King, taking his grandfather's character upon
him, became the peace-maker. I will not trouble you any longer,
but beg you still to love

Your faithful humble servant,

Rochester.

To Rochester from Blount   *February 7, 1680*

Ludgate Hill. Feb. 7th, 1679/80.

My Lord,
I had the honour yesterday to receive from the hands of an
humble servant your most incomparable version of that passage
of Seneca's, where he begins with 'Post mortem nihil est,
ipsaque mors nihil', etc., and must confess, with your Lordship's
pardon, that I cannot but esteem the translation to be, in some
measure, a confutation of the original, since what less than a
divine and immortal mind could have produced what you have
there written? Indeed, the hand that wrote it may become
lumber, but sure the spirit that dictated it can never be so. No,
my Lord, your mighty genius is a most sufficient argument of
its own immortality, and more prevalent with me than all the
harangues of the parsons or sophistry of the schoolmen.

No subject whatever has more entangled and ruffled the

his grandfather: James I, whose motto was *Beati pacifici.*

Source: Blount's *Works*, ed. cit. (p. 209), pp. 117–27.
Date: as heading, February 7, 1680. The letter was published under the
    heading 'To the Right Honourable the most Ingenious Strephon. . . .
    Concerning the Immortality of the Soul.'
your most incomparable version, etc.: Rochester's translation of Seneca's *Troades,*
    ll. 397–408, beginning 'After death nothing is, and nothing, death'
    (*Complete Poems,* p. 150).
lumber: a reference to l.7 of Rochester's version, 'Dead, we become the
    lumber of the world.'

thoughts of the wisest men than this concerning our future state. It has been controverted in all ages by men of the greatest learning and parts. We must also confess that your author Seneca has not wanted advocates for the assertion of his opinion, nay, even such who would pretend to justify it out of the very scriptures themselves: ex. gr., as when Solomon says (Eccles. 12:7) 'Then shall the dust return to dust as it was and the spirit to God that gave it'; and Eccles. 3:20, 21, when he declares 'All go to the same place, all are of dust and all turn to dust again. Who knoweth the spirit of man that goeth upward, and the spirit of the beast that goeth downward to the earth'; again Eccles. 3:19, when he tells us 'That which befalleth the sons of men befalleth beasts, even one thing befalleth them both. As the one dieth, so doth the other; yea, they have all one breath, so that a man hath no preeminence above a beast.' Likewise to such who are desirous to know what their friends are in the other world, or (to speak more properly) their dead friends know, Solomon answers their inconsiderate *utinam* (Eccles. 9:5) with these words, 'The living know they shall die, but the dead know not anything'. Moreover, others for the purpose cite that passage of Luke 20:38 where it is said 'He is not a God of the dead but of the living.' All which texts (through the weakness of understanding) have by some men been misapplied as concurrent with the *anima mundi* of Pythagoras, which has been since in great measure revived by Averroes and Avicenna, although in one

his opinion: that there is no life after death.

ex. gr.: e.g.

Solomon: he was thought to have written the Book of Ecclesiastes.

utinam: 'if only. . . .'

anima mundi: spirit of the world.

Pythagoras: is associated with the idea of the transmigration of souls. Neopythagoreanism, the revival of his thought in the first century B.C., eventually merged with neo-platonism. (*OCD*).

Averroes: twelfth-century Arabian commentator on Aristotle, influenced by neo-platonism.

Avicenna: eleventh-century Arabian philosopher.

point they differed among themselves. For that Averroes
believed, after death our souls returned and mixed with the
common souls of the world, whereas Avicenna thought it a
distinct portion of the *anima mundi*, which after our deaths
remained entire and separate, till it met with some other body
capable of receiving it, and then being clothed therewith, it
operated *ad modum recipientis*. Monsieur Bernier likewise gives us,
agreeable to Averroes, an account of much the same opinion
held at this time by some of the Indians of Indostan, whose faith
he illustrates after this manner: 'They believe' (says he) 'the soul
in man's body to be like a bottle filled with sea water, which
being close stopped and cast into the sea, tides up and down till
by some accident or other the unfaithful cork or decrepit bottle
becomes disordered, so as the water evacuates and disgorges
itself again into the common ocean from whence it was at first
taken', which agrees very well with what (as Philostratus tells
us, lib. 8. chap. 31) Apollonius after his death revealed to a
young man concerning the immortality of the soul, in these
words as rendered from the Greek:

> Est anima immortalis, et incorrupta manebit,
> Non tua res, verumque providet omnia divae;
> Quae velut acer equus, corrupto corpore vinclis
> Prosilit, et tenui miscetur flamine caeli:
> Qui grave servitium est, atque intolerabile visum . . .

> The soul's immortal, and once being free,
> Belongs to Providence, and not to thee:
> She, like a horse let loose, doth take her flight
> Out of the carcass, and her self unite

ad modum recipientis: in the manner of the recipient.
Bernier: François Bernier, whose *Travels in the Mogul Empire* first appeared in
   English in 1671.
Philostratus: Flavius Philostratus, born about A.D. 170, author of a Greek
   life of Apollonius of Tyona, a mystic of the previous century.

With the pure body of the liquid sky;
As weary of her former slavery . . .

But he, among the heathens, who spake plainest and fullest of
this matter was Pliny in his *Natural History*, lib. 7. ch. 55, where
he writes to this purpose:

'After the interment of our bodies, there is great diversity of
opinions concerning the future state of our wandering souls or
ghosts. But the most general is this: that in what condition they
were before they were born men, in the same they shall remain
when dead. Forasmuch as neither body nor soul hath any more
sense after our dying day than they had before the day of our
nativity. However, such is the folly and vanity of men that it
extendeth even to future ages; nay, and in the very time of death
even flattereth itself with fine imaginations and dreams of I
know not what after this life. For some crown the soul with
immortality, others pretend a transfiguration thereof, and others
suppose that the ghosts sequestered from the body have sense,
whereupon they render them honour and worship, making a
god of him that is not so much as a man, as if the manner of men's
breathing differed from that of other living creatures, or as if
there were not to be found in the world many more things that
live much longer than man. And yet no man judgeth in them the
like immortality.

'But show me, if you can, what is the substance and body of
the soul (as it were) by itself? What kind of matter is it apart
from the body? Where lieth the cogitation that she hath? How
is her seeing? How is her hearing performed? What toucheth
she? Nay, what one thing doth she? How is she employed? Or
if there be none of all this in her, what good can there be without
the same? Again, I would fain know where she resides after her

Pliny: Pliny the Elder (A.D. 23/24–79), author of the *Naturalis Historia*. The
paragraphs which follow are a translation of the whole of Book VII,
chapter 55.

departure from the body? And what an infinite multitude of
souls, like shadows, would there be in so many ages as well past
as to come? Now surely these are but fantastical, foolish and
childish toys devised by men that would fain live always.
The like foolery is there in preserving the bodies. Nor was the
vanity of Democritus less, who promised resurrection of the
body and yet himself could never rise again. But what a folly of
follies is it to think that death should be the way to a second life.
What repose, what rest could ever the sons of men have if their
souls did remain in heaven above with sense, whilst their
shadows tarried beneath among the infernal spirits? Certainly
these sweet inducements and pleasing persuasions, this foolish
credulity and easiness of belief, destroy the benefit of the best
gift of nature, death, likewise doubleth the pains of a man that is
to die, if he does but consider what is to become of him hereafter. How much more easy and greater security were it for each
man to ground his reasons and resolutions upon an assurance
that he should be in no worse a condition than he was before
he was born!'

Now these, my Lord, with what others I have mentioned in
my *Anima Mundi*, are the chief opinions of the moralists among
the ancient heathens. In answer to which, some of our moderns
argue that if the soul be not immortal, the whole universe
would at this time be deceived, since all our laws do now suppose
it so. But to this it has been replied that if the whole be nothing
but the parts (as must be allowed), then since there is no man who
is not deceived, as Plato says, it is so far from an offence that it is
absolutely necessary to grant either that the whole world is
deceived or at least the greater part of it. For supposing that
there be but three laws, viz. that of Moses, that of Christ and
that of Mahomet, either all are false, and so the whole world is
deceived, or only two of them, and so the greater part is deceived.
But we must know, as Plato and Aristotle well observe, that a
politician is a physician of minds, and that his aim is rather to

my *Anima Mundi*: published in 1679 (see p. 206).

make men good, than knowing wherefore according to the diversity of men he must render himself agreeable to the diversity of humours for the attainment of his end. Now there are some men so ingenuous and good-natured that they are induced to virtue by the mere excellency thereof, and withdraw themselves from vice, purely for the sake of its own deformity; and these are men the best disposed, though rarely to be met with. Others, who are worse inclined, notwithstanding the beauty of virtue and turpitude of vice, do still practise virtuous things and refrain from those that are vicious, merely out of rewards, praises, honours, punishments and dispraises, whom we may enrol in the second rank. Again others, for hope of some good as well as for fear of corporal punishment, are made virtuous. Wherefore politicians, that they may attain such virtue, allure them with the hopes of riches, dignity and command. At the same time, to prevent their committing vice, they terrify them with some punishment either in purse, honour or body. But others, out of a savageness and ferocity of nature, are moved with none of these things, as daily experience sheweth. Wherefore for such, they have proposed to the virtuous rewards in another life, and to the vicious punishments which do most of all terrify, since the greater part of man, if they do good, do it rather out of fear of eternal loss than hope of eternal gain, forasmuch as we have a more sensible idea of suffering and losses than of Elysium and the good entertainment there.

Now, because this last expedient may be profitable to all men of what condition soever, lawgivers, considering the proneness of men to evil, and themselves aiming at the public good, established the immortality of the soul, perhaps at first not so much out of a regard to truth as to honesty, hoping thereby to induce men to virtue. Nor are politicians to be so much blamed herein more than physicians, who many times, for the benefit of their patients, are compelled to feign and pretend diverse things, since, in like manner, politicians devise fables only to regulate the people, notwithstanding in these fables, as Averroes saith (*Prolog. in 3. Phys.*) 'There is properly neither truth nor falsehood.' Thus nurses bring their children to those things which they know are good for them after the like manner, whereas if the man or the child were either found in body or mind neither would the physician or the nurse stand in need of such contrivances. Likewise, if all men were in that first rank abovementioned, though we should admit the mortality of the soul, they would yet (perhaps) be virtuous and honest. But such are rare to be found and therefore it is necessary to use other expedients. Neither is there any absurdity therein, since almost all human nature is immersed in matter, and partaketh but little of the intellect, whence man is more distant from intelligences than a sick man from him that is sound or a fool from a wise man. So that it is no wonder if a politician makes use of such ways or means for the public establishment of good manners.

And therefore, my Lord, besides the authority of the Holy Scriptures, as also the innumerable other arguments which may be deduced as well from philosophy as reason to prove the immortality of the soul, together with its rewards and punishments (though I determine not their duration), yet there is no argument of greater weight with me than the absolute necessity and convenience that it should be so, as well to complete the justice of God as to perfect the happiness of man, not only in this world, but in that which is to come. And for this very reason, when I hear Seneca the philosopher and others preaching up the doctrine of the soul's immortality with a 'quid mihi curae erit transfuga?' tacked to the end of it, nothing under heaven to me seems more unaccountable or contradictory. For,

Averroes: see above, p. 235.
quid mihi curae erit transfuga?: not a quotation from Seneca, and I have not been able to trace its author. Blount may have meant *transfusio*, in which case the question means 'What concern will transmigration [of my soul] be to me?' Seneca does discuss the possibility of immortality, particularly in his three moral essays entitled *De Consolatione*.

as to suppose a hum-drum deity chewing his own nature, a droning God sit hugging of himself and hoarding up his providence from his creatures, is an atheism no less irrational than to deny the very essence of a divine being. So, in my opinion, to believe an immortality of the soul without its due rewards and punishments is altogether as irrational and useless as to believe the soul itself to be mortal. By such a faith we rob the soul of its best title to immortality, for what need is there of an executor where there are no debts to pay nor any estate to inherit? But Pomponatius, and especially Cardan in his *Theonoston*, will furnish your Lordship with great variety upon this subject, although I am sure you will meet with so noble an entertainment nowhere as in your own thoughts.

My Lord,
Your Lordship's most obedient,
humble servant,
Blount.

Rochester to his wife at Adderbury   *?1680*

soe greate a disproportion t'wixt our desires & what it has

droning: inactive, like a male honey-bee.
Pomponatius: Pietro Pomponazzi (1464–1525), Italian author of the *De immortalitate animae* ('Concerning the immortality of the soul'), 1516.
Cardan in his Theonoston: Girolamo Cardano's *Opus novum*, Basle, 1582, was republished in Rome in 1617 under the title *Hieronymi Cardani Theonoston*.

Source: MS. Harl. 7003, f. 191.
Date: ?1680. The melancholy philosophical tone of the fragment seems to relate it to his letter of April 5, 1680 to Savile, p. 243.
it: ?Fate. It is clear from what follows that the missing page has been concerned with immortality. Perhaps the first part of the sentence said something like 'If we believe in a benevolent deity, we must believe that it will grant us satisfaction in the next world, if only to make up for our disappointment that in this one there is so great a disproportion . . .', etc.

ordained to content them; but you will say this is pride & madness, for theire are those soe intirely satisfyed wth theire shares in this world, that theire wishes nor theire thoughts have not a farther prospect of felicity & glory, I'le tell you were that mans soule plac't in a body fitt for it, hee were a dogg, that could count any thing a benifitt obtain'd wth flattery, feare, & service,

Cow:
Is there a man yee gods whome I doe hate
Dependance & Attendance bee his fate
Lett him bee busy still & in a crowde
And very much a slave & very proude

Remember mee to my dearest Aunt & my good Unkle; I would [not] have you lose my letter it is not fitt for every body to finde. Rochester.

Y^r wine was bought last weeke but neglected to bee sent.

These For the Countess of Rochester
at Adderbury neare Banbury.
Oxfordshire

Is there a man, etc.: a quotation, as D. M. Vieth points out (*TLS*, October 12, 1951, p. 645), from Cowley's translation of a Martial epigram beginning 'Well then, Sir, you shall know how far extend', appended to his essay *Of Liberty*. The passage runs:

Can any Man in guilded rooms attend,
And his dear houres in humble visits spend;
When in the fresh and beauteous Fields he may
With various healthful pleasures fill the day?
If there be Man (ye Gods) I ought to Hate
Dependance and Attendance be his Fate.
Still let him Busie be, and in a crowd,
And very much a Slave, and very Proud:
Thus he perhaps Pow'rful and Rich may grow;
No matter, O ye Gods! that I'le allow.
But let him Peace and Freedom never see . . .

Cow: Cowley (see above).
[not]: word obliterated in MS.

Rochester at Bishops Stortford to Savile   *April 5, 1680*

Dear Savile,

In my return from Newmarket I met your packet, and truly was not more surprised at the indirectness of Mr P's proceeding than overjoyed at the kindness and care of yours. Misery makes all men less or more dishonest and I am not astonished to see villainy industrious for bread, especially living in a place where it is often so *de gaieté de coeur*. I believe the fellow thought of this device to get some money, or else he is put upon it by somebody who has given it him already. But I give him leave to prove what he can against me. However, I will search into the matter and give you a further account within a post or two. In the meantime you have made my heart glad in giving me such a proof of your friendship, and I am now sensible that it is natural for you to be kind to me, and can never more despair of it.

   I am your faithful, obliged, humble servant,

       Rochester.

Bishop Stafford, April 5, [16]80.

Source: FL i, p. 14.

Date: as letter, April 5, 1680.

Newmarket: the King and Court were brought back hurriedly from the races on March 31 by news of an Irish plot. (Arthur Bryant, *King Charles II*, revised edn, 1955, p. 242.)

packet: of mail.

Mr P's proceeding: evidently a blackmail attempt against Rochester which Savile had done his best to suppress. Mr P. has not been identified, but the previous November Rochester had sent his servant 'Mr Baptist' to Savile in Paris, with various broad hints about his attractions (see p. 230). It seems possible that 'Mr P.' is a misprint for 'Mr B.', and that Jean-Baptiste had betrayed him, see p. 26.

de gaieté de coeur: [done] out of sheer high spirits.

Bishop Stafford: the normal contemporary form of Bishops Stortford, 30 miles north of London and a common stopping-place on the Newmarket road. Rochester was on his way to his wife's estates at Enmore (see Robert Parsons, *A Sermon Preached at the Funeral of . . . John Earl of Rochester*, Oxford, 1680, p. 22).

Rochester at Woodstock to Gilbert Burnet   *June 25, 1680*

Woodstock Park: June 25°: 80°:
Oxfordsh'

My most hon'd D' Burnett

my Spiritts & body decays soe equally Together; that I shall
write you a Lett' as Weak as I am In person I beginn To value
Churchmen aboue all men in the World: & you aboue all the
Churchmen I know in itt If God bee yett pleasd' to Spare mee
Longer in this World I hope in your Conversationn to bee
exalted to that degree of Piety, that the World may See how
much I abhorr what I Soe long loued, & how much I Glory in
repentance in Gods Service. bestow your prayers upon mee that
God would spare mee, (if itt bee his Good Will) to shew a true
repentance, & amendment of life for the Time to come, or els if
the Lord Pleaseth to put an end to my Worldly being now, that
hee would mercifully except of my death bed repentance, &
performe that promise hee hath binn pleased to make, that att
what time soever a sinner doth repent hee would receiue him;
putt up these pray's most Deare D' to all=mighty God for your
most obedient & languishing Servant.

Rochester

Source: Harvard MS. pf. Eng. 1063. The letter is in Rochester's mother's
hand, though the signature is his own.

Date: as heading June 25, 1680.

Gilbert Burnet: see Introduction, p. 35.

except of: accept.

att what time soever, etc.: an interesting example of the hold the Prayer Book
liturgy had on Rochester's memory. This is a quotation from Ezekiel
18:27, not as it appears in the 1611 Bible but as it had been read every day
in the first sentence before Morning Prayer in the 1604 liturgy, descended
from the time of Edward VI but revised in 1662. The sentence was
altered beyond recognition in the 1662 Prayer Book, so was remembered
here from before that time. The 1604 version is 'At what time soever a
sinner doth repent him of his sin . . . I will put all his wickedness out of
my remembrance, saith the Lord.'

Rochester at Woodstock to Dr Thomas Pierce in Oxford   July, 1680

John Wilmot, Earl of Rochester: Letter to Dr. Tho. Pierce of Magdalen College, Oxon.

My indisposition renders my intellectuals almost as feeble as my person, but considering the candour and extreme charity your natural mildness has always shewed me, I am assured at one and both of a favourable construction of my present lines, which can but faintly express the sorrowful character of a humble and afflicted mind, and also those great comforts your inexhaustible goodness, learning and piety, plenteously affords to the drooping spirits of poor sinners, so that I may truly say, holy man! To you I owe what consolation I enjoy in urging God's mercies against despair, and holding me up under the weight of those high and mountainous sins my wicked and ungovernable life has heaped upon me. If God shall be pleased to spare me a little longer here I have unalterably resolved to become a new man, as to wash out the stains of my lewd courses with my tears and weep over the profane and unhallowed abominations of my former doings; that the world may see how I loathe sin and abhor the very remembrance of those tainted and unclean ways I once delighted in—these being, as the apostle tells us, the things

Source: Bodleian Library, MS. Ballard 10, f. 28. (A copy, in a seventeenth-century hand.)
Date: as letter, July, 1680.
Dr Thomas Pierce: (1622–91), a controversial and popular theologian and preacher, tutor to the young Robert Spencer, Earl of Sunderland, chaplain to Charles II from 1660 and President of Magdalen College, Oxford from 1661 until he was forced to resign in 1672 after constant battles with the fellows. A calvinist in his youth, he had later become a prominent, outspoken critic of both calvinism and the Roman Catholic Church. One of his duties as chaplain was to be in attendance at the Private Oratory at court, where he was consulted by anyone who wanted religious advice: Rochester may have found him helpful, and he was one of the many clergy who visited him in his last illness—see Introduction, p. 35. (*DNB*; Evelyn, *Diary*, February 6, 1678.)
intellectuals: mind.

17

whereof I am now ashamed. Or if it be His great pleasure, now, to put a period to my days, that He will accept of my last gasp, that the smoke of my death-bed offering may not be unsavoury to His nostrils and drive me like Cain from before His presence. Pray for me, dear Doctor, and all you that forget not God, pray for me fervently. Take heaven by force, and let me enter with you as it were in disguise, for I dare not appear before the dread majesty of that Holy One I have so often offended. Warn all my friends and companions to a true and sincere repentance today, while it is called today, before the evil day comes and they be no more. Let them know that sin is like the angel's book in the Revelations, it is sweet in the mouth but bitter in the belly. Let them know that God will not be mocked, that He is a Holy God and will be served in holiness and purity that requires the whole man and the early man. Bid them make haste, for the night cometh when no man can work. Oh that they were wise, that they would consider this and not, with me, with wretched me, delay it until their latter end! Pray, dear sir, continually pray for your poor friend,

Rochester.

Ranger's Lodge in Woodstock Park.
July 1680.

like Cain: see Genesis 4:16.
the angel's book, etc.: see Revelation 10:9. The sentences that follow are a
tissue of biblical quotations.

Appendixes

I

To the Kings Most Excellent Ma^{stie}
The Humble Peti̅con of y^e Earle of Rochester.

Sheweth

That noe misfortune on earth could see soe sensible to y^r Peti̅oner as y^e losse of y^e Maties favour.

That Inadvertency, Ignorance in ye Law, and Passion were ye occasions of his offence.

That had hee reflected on ye fatall consequence of incurring y^r Ma^{sties} displeasure, he would rather have chosen death ten thousand times then have done it.

That y^r Peti̅oner in all Humility & sence of his fault casts himself at y^r Maties feet, beseeching you to pardon his first error, & not suffer one offence to bee his Ruine.

> And hee most humbly prayes, that y^r
> Matie would bee pleased to restore him
> once more to y^r favour, & that he may kisse
> your hand;
> And he shall ever pray &c

Source: P.R.O. MS. SP 29, f. 122.

II

'Five letters of Anne, Countess Dowager of Rochester, wrote when 80 years old, to her sister-in-law, Lady St. John, giving an account of her son's behaviour during his sickness, copied from the originals in the hands of Mrs Meredith, granddaughter to Lady St. John.'

Letter I

Sweet sister,

It has pleased God to lay his afflictive hand upon my poor son in visiting of him with a sore sickness, and whether for life or death we cannot guess, but he is reduced to great weakness in the outward man. But in the midst of punishment He has remembered mercy and strengthened him in the inward man, to the comfort of me his poor mother. For never all the former sicknesses he has had did in the least measure work so much upon him to the knowledge and acknowledgement of God, and to repentance of his former life and the sense how he has gone astray, as this doth. I am not able to write you a long letter. I can only say this, that though he lies under as much misery almost as human man can bear, yet he bears his sufferings with so much patience and resignation to God's will that I confess I take more comfort in him under this visitation than ever I did in all

Source: British Library. MS. Addl. 6269, f. 33.

his life before. And though the Lord has been pleased not to work this work upon him till the last hour, yet I have great reason to believe he will find mercy through the merits and satisfaction of Christ, on whom he throws himself for the favour of God. Oh sister, I am sure, had you heard the heavenly prayers he has made since this sickness, the extraordinary things he has said to the wonder of all that has heard him, you would wonder, and think that God alone must teach him, for no man could put into him such things as he says. He has, I must tell you too, converted his wife to be a Protestant again. Pray, pray for his perseverance, dear sister, and pardon me that I can say no more but to rest,

Madam,

Your affectionate servant,

Anne Rochester.

I did not receive the letter Mr Foot says you sent by the post. To the Lady St. John's at her house in Battersea.

Letter II

My dear sister,

Mr Blancourt did not deliver me your letter till this Monday morning, and just now I am going to Adderbury, where I have not been these five weeks, but intend to return to my son again in a day. The account I can give you of him is much as my last. He continues weak, but is sometimes better than he is others. The greatest comfort he enjoys is his sleep, and that he does much. He has a kind of hectic fever upon him, as the doctors call it, which is not at all times, for sometimes his temper is good outwardly, but the doctor says he is hot inwardly; yet I cannot think it, because he is seldom dry. He drinks ass's milk and it

Source: British Library MS. Addl. 6269, f. 33v.

digests well with him, and some other spoon-meats, but he takes no broths made with meat, for fear of heat. He spits mightily within these two days, which some say is good for him, but I find all evacuations weaken him. I confess I cannot discern amendment in him yet, but as long as life is we have hopes. I thank God his sense continues very well and, when his strength will give him leave, expresses himself with great devotion both upon the account of his former ill life, with great humility he lays himself low before the throne of grace, begging favour and pardon from God upon the account of the merits of Christ alone, acknowledging himself the greatest of sinners. Truly, sister, I think I may say without partiality that he has never been heard say, when he speaks of religion, an unsensible word, nor of anything else. But one night, of which I writ you word, he was disordered in his head, but then he said no hurt, only some little ribble rabble which had no hurt in it. But it was observed by his wife and I particularly, that whenever he spoke of God that night, he spoke very well and with great sense, which we wondered at. Since that night, he has never had a minute of disorder in his head: that was a[l]most a fortnight ago. This last night, if you had heard him pray, I am sure you would not have took his words for the words of a madman, but such as come from a better spirit than the mind of mere man. But let the wicked of the world say what they please of him, the reproaches of them are an honour to him and I take comfort that the devil rages against my son: it shows his power over him is subdued in him, and that he has no share in him. Many messages and compliments his old acquaintance send him, but he is so far from receiving of them that still his answer is, 'Let me see none of them, and I would to God I had never conversed with some of them.' One of his physicians, thinking to please him, told him, the K[ing] drank his health the other day. He looked earnestly upon him and said never a word, but turned his face from him. I thank God, his thoughts are wholly taken off from the world and I hope, whether he lives or dies, will ever be so.

But they are fine people at Windsor, God forgive them! Sure there never was so great a malice performed as to entitle my poor son to a lampoon at this time, when, for aught they know, he lies upon his death-bed. My comfort is, he will partake of that joy unspeakable and full of glory in the highest heavens that you wish him, I hope. Last night the very expression you have made in your good wishes for his soul, he made to God in the conclusion of his prayer last night, that he might enjoy that unspeakable bliss of a place in heaven, though he were but a door-keeper, to sing praises to the Lord with the heavenly host. I do believe, if any has reported that he should speak ridiculous, it has been the popish physician, who one day listened at the door whilst my son was discoursing with a divine. But my son spoke so low that he could hear but half words, and so he might take it for nonsense, because he had a mind so to do. But I thank God, my son lays hold on the merits of his Saviour Jesus Christ for all his comfort from God, in whose arms, I trust he will be received whene'er he goes out of this world; which is the great comfort she has who is, Madam,

Your affectionate sister and servant,
Anne Rochester.

My daughter Ro[chester] and my son remember their service to you and my brother, to whom I present my affections.

For the Lady St. John's, at Sir Walter St. John's house at Battersea, these.

Letter III

June the 19.

I must, dear sister, give you an account of the first hopes of comfort I have [had] of my son Rochester, who, though he is very weak, yet these two days has produced strange alterations in him. He sleeps very well, is but little feverish, his great tortures of pain almost abated, gathers some strength, though but little yet. But God is infinitely merciful upon all accounts, both to his soul and body. 'Tis my great hopes he will persevere in the way God has put him in for his soul's happiness.

I cannot omit one passage lately. Mr Fanshaw, his great friend, has been here to see him, and as he was standing by my son's bedside he looked earnestly upon him and said, 'Fanshaw, think of a God, let me advise you, and repent you of your former life, and amend your ways. Believe what I say to you: there is a God, and a powerful God, and he is a terrible God to unrepenting sinners. The time draws near that he will come to judgement with great terror to the wicked, therefore delay not your repentance. His displeasure will thunder against you if you do; believe me, do not defer the time. You and I have been long acquainted, done ill together. (I love the man, and speak to him out of conscience for the good of his soul.)' Fanshaw stood and said never a word to him, but stole away out of the room. When my son saw him go, 'Is a gone?' says he, 'poor wretch, I fear his heart is hardened.' After that, Fanshaw said to some in the house that my son should be kept out of melancholy fancies. This was told my son again, upon which says he, 'I know why he said that, it was because I gave him my advice. But I could say no less to him than I did, let him take it as he pleases.'

Dear sister, my hope is great, and God is good on whom I depend for good both for his soul and body. I believe I have tired you with my discourse. I have nothing more at present but to assure [you] I am, Madam,

Your faithful friend and servant,
A. Ro.

You must not let Fanshaw know what I have told you. Before I sealed this I received yours, and two waters for my son

Source: British Library MS. Addl. 6269, f. 35.

Ro[chester]. He and his lady give you thanks and present their service to you. I thank God my son continues at all times very devout, ever since God struck him with a sense of his sins. He is very tender and fearful, but it does not carry him to despair. He is sensible the satisfaction of Christ is his comfort, and relies wholly upon Christ's merits for his salvation. This day has not been so good a day with him as yesterday. He has had some faint fits.

Letter IV

June the 26th.

I am sure, dear sister, 'tis your desire to hear some time how my poor weak son does. He gives us little hopes of his life, his weakness increasing so much. But as his outward man decays, I thank God his inward increases and strengthens. For he is very pious and devout, and willing to resign himself into the arms of his saviour, when God pleases to take him. I hear Mr Fanshaw reports my son is mad, but I thank God he is far from that. I confess for a night and part of a day for want of rest his head was a little disordered, but it was long since Mr Fanshaw saw him. When he reproved him for his sinful life, he was as well in his head as ever he was in his life, and so he is now, I thank God. I am sure if you heard him pray you would think God has inspired him with true wisdom indeed, and that neither folly nor madness comes near him. I wish that wretch Fanshaw had so great a sense of sin as my poor child has, that so he might be brought to repentance before it is too late; but he is an ungrateful man to such a friend. Dear sister, pray for us, and believe me to be, Madam,

Your faithful friend and servant,

A. Rochester.

Source: British Library MS. Addl. 6269, f. 36.

My son and my daughter present their service to you and we all thank you for your waters.

Letter V

July the 2.

I did, dear Madam, receive yours dated the 28th of June, full of kindness, and full of Christianity in your good wishes and kindness to my poor sick son, who I thank God is yet alive; but whether it will please God to restore him again out of this bed of sickness, none but Himself knows. He is full of mercy and good upon all accounts, and my prayers are that whether my poor son lives or dies, the Lord may be glorified in all. His conversion is mercy enough for us, though we enjoy him not in this world; the comfortable hopes that he will be a saint in heaven is beyond my expression. I cannot tell you that there is much sign of a recovery of my son, though his fever has left him. Little heats he has still, which we imagine proceeds from his ulcer. But that as I like worst in him is, he gathers no strength at all, but his flesh wastes much, and we fear a consumption, though his lungs are very good. He sleeps much. His head for the most part is very well. He was this day taken up and set up in a chair for an hour, and was not very faint when he went to bed. He does not care to talk much but when he does, speaks for the most part well. His expressions are so suddenly spoken that many of them are lost, and cannot be taken; yet I believe some of what he has said will be remembered. I told my son that I heard Mr Fanshaw said that he hoped he would recover and leave those principles he now professed. He answered, 'Wretch, I wish I had conversed all my life-time with link-boys rather than with him and that crew, such I mean as Fanshaw is. Indeed I would not live to return to what I was for all the world.' I desire the continuance of your prayers, and all the good people who has

Source: British Library MS. Addl. 6269, f. 36v.

been kind in remembering my son in their prayers. I told him that you prayed for him heartily. He said 'Pray thank my good aunt, and remember my service to her and my uncle.' My daughter remembers her service to you. Dear sister, whatever becomes of me through my afflictions, I am sincerely, Madam,

Your faithful friend and affectionate servant,

A. Rochester.

For the Lady St. John at Battersea.

Leave this to be sent with safety at Mr Dryden's in King's Street, at the sign of the pestle and mortar, Westminster, London.

III

Latin text of Blount's letter (p. 214).

Spiritus in nobis non manet in identitate, sed recens ingeritur per renovationem continuam, sicut flamma, sed velociore transitu, quia res est spiritualior. Nos quotidie facti sumus ex iis quae transeunt in nos: morimur et renascimur quotidie, neque iidem hodie et heri sumus, et personam quam transeuntem non sentimus, tandem pertransisse agnoscimus.

Nulla est rerum transitio in nos, nisi per viam alimenti; omne alimentum respectu alimentandi est consimile et debilius: alimentantis corpus succrescit nobis in corpus, spiritus in spiritum. Non tamen proportio utriusque fit nobis at proportionem cibi et potus, aut aeriis nisi a nobis bene superantur; aliter etenim non alunt ingesta, sed opprimunt si fortiora sunt, corrumpunt si dissimilia, idque plus minusve pro gradu in utroque. Ideoque quo melius res procedat multa fieri oportet: primum prudens electio et moderatio eorum, quae ingerenda sunt; et deinceps debita praeparatio per artem, ut nobis similiora et debiliora fiant: ex parte nostri praecipuum est exercitium frequens sed modicum quo calor naturalis vigeat.

Credibile est homines prout in iis pollet: spiritus corpusve, alios melius in se convertere alimentantium spiritum, alios corpus: ideoque inter gulones et potores nonnulli minus stupidi redduntur quam alii, et nonnulli minus morboso et oppleto corpore evadunt quam alii; plaerumque tamen ingenio plus obest excessus in potu, quam in cibo; quia potus spirituosior est, corpus vero magis opprimitur esculentis quoniam ea in magis corporea plus gravant.

Anima sapiens lumen siccum; corpus sanum temperies sicca et pervia: ideoque siccare sed deobstruere convenit: idque fit victi exercitio et aere idoneis sed parum sagaciter plaeraque solum ut calida, frigida, humida vel sicca notamus: in illis qualitatibus non est rerum energia: longe divinius magisque intrinsecum quiddam est in rebus, quo rei cardo vertitur quodque solum experientia et effectu agnoscitur: est deus in rebus; estque omnia, et omnia agit: illius namque infiniti corpus est omne et spiritus: ex eorum unione oritur creatura; quae etiam disperditur dissolutione istius unionis: cum autem omnia perpetuo sunt in motu de una coniectura in aliam, mundi autem corpus et spiritus aeterna sed novas continuo coniuncturas ineunt; ideoque nos creaturae sumus aeterni dei apparitiones momentaneae, quas tantum terris ostendunt fata, nec ultra esse sinunt, veluti effigies in auleis.

Dei opus sumus nos parentibus instrumentis; actionesque nostrae dei sunt opera instrumentis nobis, sed per electionem nostram agentibus: ista vero electio per aptas coniuncturas et ideas adeo immissas invitatur et regitur.

Per condensationem et rarefactionem partes mundi corporeae fiunt spiritus, et spirituales fiunt corpora: sicque aeterne retro aguntur omnia: lumen Iovi, tenebrae Plutoni; lumen Plutoni, tenebrae Iovi: ut Hippocrates habet; cum microcosmus a mundo trahit, vivit microcosmus: cum mundus a microcosmo trahit, deficit microcosmus.

IV

A further note on the text

Except in two cases, all the letters taken from manuscript sources exist in their authors' holograph and belong to ancient collections of contemporary and near-contemporary materials—chiefly the Harleian Collection in the British Library and the Portland Collection at Longleat House. Both the exceptions are letters attributed to the dying Rochester. One, the letter to Burnet dated June 25, 1680, is in his mother's hand but carries his own signature. The other, to Dr Thomas Pierce, is in an unidentified late seventeenth-century hand. While this letter cannot be attributed to Rochester with absolute certainty, the plea 'Take heaven by force, and let me enter with you as it were in disguise' seems too idiosyncratic to have been invented. Even so, both these letters need to be considered in the light of the general questions raised in the Introduction about the stage-management, as it can seem, of Rochester's final months.

The letters from printed texts fall into two main groups: those few from the eighteenth-century magazine *The Museum*, whose authenticity is argued in *MLR*, 71 (1976), pp. 19–25; and the much more numerous and important letters to a lady, clearly Elizabeth Barry (see p. 28f.), and to Savile, in the two volumes of *Familiar Letters*, first published in 1697.

The claims of the Savile letters in this collection are simplest to establish and, it may be argued, lend further authenticity to the letters in *FLi*. Several of Savile's letters in *FLii* still exist in holograph. Comparison of the manuscripts shows the printed text to be very reliable (despite certain tidyings-up of spelling, punctuation and syntax). With the exception of one missing letter (p. 158), the 1699 text contains fewer errors, including misprints, and is therefore adopted as the copy-text.

There are other reasons for feeling confident that the Rochesterian items in *Familiar Letters* are genuine. In the first place, Elizabeth Barry was alive when they came out, and indeed presumably supplied them to the publisher, Briscoe, along with those of her admirer Otway, which he also prints. Briscoe's prefaces to the two volumes, included among other relevant materials below, naturally assert their authenticity and invite the sceptical to come and check the originals, which he still has 'by him'. But the substance of his claims lies not so much here, or in his soliciting other letters which he promises to have 'faithfully Transcrib'd for the Press', as in the fact that the letters themselves are often circumstantial and oblique to the point of obscurity. Had they been invented—as those of Alexander Smith are (see p. 38)—they would have been comprehensible, and would doubtless also have included Barry's own contributions (which in real life Rochester presumably threw away or destroyed). No one can read through these letters, with their private allusions, their ellipses, their sheer absence of explication or exposition, without sensing that—however 'artificial' their style and elusive their content—they are the genuine, though mostly unreconstructable, shards of a substantial relationship.

From the Dedicatory Epistle to Familiar Letters *Volume i*

TO DR. RATCLIFF, OF BOW-STREET

[*Text is in italics: this transcript reverses the typography.*]

I have presumed, tho' I knew at the same time how heinously I trespass'd against you in doing so, to Inscribe your Name to the following Collection of Letters. As you were no Stranger to that

Excellent Person, whose Pieces Compose, by far, the most valuable part of it, so I was satisfied that everything, from so celebrated a Hand, wou'd be acceptable and welcome to you; and in that Confidence, made bold to give you the Trouble of this Address. My Lord *Rochester* has left so established a Reputation behind him, that he needs no officious Pen to set out his Worth, especially to you, who were acquainted so perfectly well with all his Eminent Qualities, that made him the Delight and Envy of both Sexes, and the Ornament of our Island. In every thing of his Lordship's writing there's something so happily exprest, the Graces are so numerous, yet so unaffected, that I don't wonder why all the Original Touches of so incomparable a Master, have been enquired after, with so publick and general a Concern. Most of his other Compositions, especially those in Verse, have long ago blest the Publick, and were received with Universal Delight and Admiration, which gives me Encouragement to believe, that his Letters will find the like Reception. Tho' most of them were written upon private Occasions, to an Honourable Person who was happy in his Lordship's Acquaintance, with no intention to be ever made publick; yet that constant good Sence, which is all along visible in them, the Justice of the Observations, and the peculiar Beauties of the Stile, are Reasons sufficient, why they should no longer be conceal'd in private Hands. And indeed at this time, when the private Plate of the Nation comes abroad to relieve the present Exigencies, it seems but just, that since the Dearth of Wit is as great as that of Money, such a Treasure of good Sence and Language shou'd no longer be buried in Oblivion. With this difference, however, That whereas our Plate, before it can circulate in our Markets, must receive the Royal Stamp, must be Melted down, and take another Form, these Unvaluable Remains want no Alterations to recommend them; they need only be taken from the Rich Mines where they grew; for their own Intrinsick Value secures them, and his Lordship's Name is sufficient to make them Current. . . .

I need not, and I am sure I cannot make you a better Panegyrick than to acquaint the World, that you were happy in my Lord *Rochester*'s Friendship, that he took pleasure in your Conversation, of which even his Enemies must allow him to have been the best Judge, and that in the Politest Reign we can boast of in *England*. The Approbation of so impartial a Judge, who was, in his Time, a Scourge to all Blockheads, by what Names or Titles soever dignified, or distinguish'd, is above all the Incense that a much better Hand than mine can presume to offer: Shou'd I put out all the Dedication Sails, as 'tis the way of most Authors, I cou'd soon erect you into a great Hero, and Deliverer. . . . But after all, the highest thing I will pretend to say of you here is, That you were esteem'd, and valu'd, and Lov'd by my Lord *Rochester*. . . .

From the Bookseller's Preface to Familiar Letters *Volume i*

[*Typography as in the original*]

Having, by the Assistance of a Worthy Friend, procured the following Letters, that were written by the late Incomparable Earl of *Rochester* (the Originals of all which I preserve by me, to satisfie those Gentlemen, who may have the Curiosity to see them under his *Lordship*'s Hand) I was encouraged to trouble others of my Friends, that had any Letters in their Custody, to make this Collection, which I now publish.

Indeed the Letters that were written by the abovemention'd Honourable Person, have something so happy in the Manner and Stile, that I need not loose my Time to convince the World they are genuine. . . .

Our Neighbouring Nations, whom I don't believe we come short of in any respect, have printed several Volumes of Letters, which meet with publick Approbation, I am satisfied that if the Gentlemen of *England* wou'd be as free, and Communicative to part with theirs, we might show as great a Number, and as good a Choice as they have done. It has been used as an Objection against publishing things of this Nature, that if they are written as they ought to be, they shou'd never be made publick. But I hope this Collection will disarm that Objection; for tho' the Reader may not understand every particular Passage, yet there are other things in them that will make him sufficient Amends.

I have only a word more to add: Upon the Noise of this Collection, several Gentlemen have been so kind, as to send me in Materials to compose a Second. Besides a pretty good number of my Lord *Rochester*'s, I have some of the late Duke of *Buckingham*, some of Sir *George Etherege*, not to mention what I am promis'd from several Eminent Modern Hands. I am in so good a Forwardness already, that I don't question to have it soon compleated; and therefore those Gentlemen that have any Curious Letters by them, and are willing to oblige the Publick, by letting them come abroad, are desired to send them to me, who will take care to have them faithfully Transcrib'd for the Press.

Sam. Briscoe.

From the Bookseller's Preface to Familiar Letters *Volume ii*

[*Italics and ordinary type reversed*]

The Extraordinary Success of the First Volume of my Lord *Rochester*'s Letters, and the great Encouragement of several Persons of Quality, (who had seen the Original Papers) to go on with the Undertaking, have engaged me to present You with this Second Volume, (in Compliance with the frequent Importunities of Gentlemen for the Speedy Edition of it) before an Excellent Collection of Fifty more of my Lord's, and a considerable Number of the Duke of *Buckingham*'s and Sir *George Etheridge*'s came to my Hands; and which are now transcribing for the Press, being sufficient to make a Volume by themselves; and therefore I shall mingle none with them, unless any Gentleman or Lady, who have any of these Incomparable Authors by them, will send 'em to gratifie the Publick, which has with so much Pleasure received those already Published. This Volume I design to get ready in *Trinity* Term.

If any one should doubt the Reality and Authentickness of these Letters in either of these Volumes, I have yet the Originals by me, and shall willingly shew 'em to any Gentleman or Lady that desires it; which must convince all that know my Lord's Hand. ...

S. BRISCOE.

Editors' Preface, The Museum: or, the Literary and Historical Register, *xxxi, 23 May 1747*

[*Typography as in the original*]

That there is a kind of Veneration, which may be stiled Natural, for whatever belongs to great Men, appears from hence, that in all Ages and in all Countries this Humor has prevailed, and the most trifling Things have been thought precious on the Score of their belonging to, or having been left by some Person of high Distinction. We may add to this, that the Value of these Relicks is very little, if at all, enhanced by their Materials. The rusty Sword of *Scanderbe*[*r*]*g* would be looked upon (except by a Goldsmith) as infinitely a better Thing than a modern gold Hilt ever so finely finish'd; and hence it is, that we see such large Sums given for Things of very little intrinsic Value, and sometimes too of very doubtful Authority.

It is from these Considerations, and many more of a like Nature that might be mention'd, that it is hoped the Publick will receive Pleasure from the Publication of these few genuine Remains of a Nobleman, esteemed the greatest Wit in an Age the most fertile of Wits this Island has ever had to boast. We cannot indeed say, that they relate either to striking or important Subjects, for they are addressed to the Countess his Wife, (to whom if not ever constant, he was always civil), and to his Son, while a Child of eight Years old at *Eaton*. We cannot therefore expect any thing of that Flame and Passion, which would have appear'd in his Epistles to Mrs. *Barry*, who is known to have been his Favourite, and to have owed to his Instructions a very large Share of that Fame, which she acquired upon the Stage. Neither are we to look for the grave, sententious Discourses of one who was or had a Mind to pass for a Philosopher, that being neither his Lordship's Character; nor would it have been a Stile proper to have been comprehended by one of so tender an Age, as the Child to whom these Epistles are address'd.

But we may look for good Sense, good Humour, and a good Manner of Writing to a Wife and Child, without being disappointed. They have in this Respect all the Beauties that can be wished for; they are easy, and correct; those to his Lady full of Humour; those to his Son, of paternal Tenderness and good Sense. They shew us, that he was not able to set Pen to Paper, on the slightest or most trivial Occasion, without leaving those Marks of Genius, which distinguish a true Wit, and which one who affects it can never reach. The Letter to his Lady, ill spelt and full of hard Words, is no doubt a very natural Burlesque on that kind of Stile, which then was and still is in use among a certain Sort of People; the Verses also have probably the same Character, and in the last Letter there are Allusions, which we live at too great a Distance of Time to hope for any Lights, that may enable us fully to understand. But what then? the same Thing happens in the familiar Letters of all the Ancients, and yet they are not thought trivial, or below our Notice. We enter as far as we can into the Family Circumstances of such Epistles; and yet we have nothing more to do with them than with these. The only rational Cause that can be assign'd for the Pleasure we receive in reading them, is the Delight that constantly results from looking into human Nature, and examining the Recesses of the Mind. This we may gratify here as well as there: and therefore those who have a true Taste, cannot fail of approving the Pains taken to convey these glittering Fragments, long buried in the Dust of a Closet, with due Respect to Posterity.

Index